KT-448-737

Soils and Landforms

Soils and Landforms

An Integration of Geomorphology and Pedology

A. J. GERRARD

Department of Geography, University of Birmingham

London
GEORGE ALLEN & UNWIN
Boston Sydney

George Allen & Unwin (Publishers) Ltd,
40 Museum Street, London WC1A 1LU, UK

George Allen & Unwin (Publishers) Ltd,
Park Lane, Hemel Hempstead, Herts HP2 4TE, UK

Allen & Unwin Inc.,
9 Winchester Terrace, Winchester, Mass 01890, USA

George Allen & Unwin Australia Pty Ltd,
8 Napier Street, North Sydney, NSW 2060, Australia

First published in 1981

British Library Cataloguing in Publication Data

Gerrard, John
Soils and landforms.
1. Soil Science
I. Title
551.4 GB401.5
ISBN 0-04-551048-2
ISBN 0-04-551049-0 Pbk

Library of Congress in Publication Data

Gerrard, A. J. (A. John)
Soils and landforms.
Bibliography: P.
Includes Index.
1. Landforms. 2. Soil Formation. I. Title.
GB406.G5 551.4 81-10812
ISBN 0-04-551048-2 AACR2
ISBN 0-04-551049-0 (PBK.)

Set in 10 on 12 point Times by Preface Ltd, Salisbury, Wilts.
and printed in Great Britain
by Mackays of Chatham

For Judith, Helen and Andrew

Preface

Geomorphology and pedology are two of the more important disciplines in the Earth sciences. The former deals with the arrangement and differentiation of landforms and the processes that have been or are shaping them. Pedology is concerned with the processes involved in soil formation. For many years the two disciplines went their separate ways. Soils and landforms were treated separately with only a token awareness of the influence of one on the other and vice versa.

Geomorphology was concerned essentially with producing time-dependent models of landscape evolution such as W. M. Davis's *Geographical cycle of landscape evolution.* The form of the land was the major focus with little mention of process and scant attention to the soil and regolith materials. There were, of course, exceptions. Gilbert, in the late 19th century, was emphasising the equilibrium between landforms, soils and slope processes. In Europe, W. Penck, while concentrating on a grand scheme of landform evolution, did attempt to relate the progression of soil formation towards maturity with slope processes.

The change in emphasis in geomorphology in the 1960s and 1970s led to a greater concentration on surface processes and the short-term changes occurring in the landscape. Investigations of drainage basins and storm hydrographs demonstrated the influence exerted on these phenomena by the surface covering of soil and vegetation. It was recognised that many soil processes were also geomorphological processes and the distinction between geomorphology and pedology was being blurred at the edges of the disciplines.

At the same time pedology was making increasing use of geomorphological techniques and methodology. Topography was always recognised as being an important factor in soil formation but it was given a conceptual 'boost' by the formalisation of the concept of the catena by Milne in the 1930s and 1940s. In the 1950s and 1960s workers, such as Ruhe, Walker, Butler and many others, were advancing the integration of the two subjects. Modern research is increasingly demonstrating the close dependence of soils and landforms, and a new discipline, 'soil geomorphology', or pedogeomorphology as proposed by Conacher and Dalrymple (1977), seems to be emerging, incorporating traditional approaches to soils as well as modern soil engineering. This trend has been emphasised by the creation of new journals such as *Geoderma* and *Catena*.

These developments were forecast by Robinson (1949) in his introduction to *Soils, their origin, constitution and classification*, with the words 'the domain of pedology may come to engross a considerable amount of dynamic geology'. It is this close interaction between soils, landforms and geomorphological processes that is the approach adopted in this book.

There are many ways in which the integration between geomorphology and pedology is expressed. Geomorphological and pedological processes interact on hillslopes especially where the movement of soil and water is considered. Geomorphological processes may create distinctive landforms, such as erosion surfaces, which have a great influence on soil types and distribution. Usually, however, it is the creation of landform type and superficial materials in harness which is of greatest significance. The characteristic suite of landforms and materials created by glacial and fluvioglacial deposition is a classic example. Patterns of landforms are matched, almost on one-to-one correspondence, by soil patterns. Fluvial and marine processes also produce a characteristic assemblage of landforms which is paralleled by the soil types.

Pedology and geomorphology are vitally important, in an interpretive sense, in association with other disciplines, in deciphering the phases of development within the Quaternary period. A multi-disciplinary approach is essential if the complicated history of this period is to be unravelled.

The applied aspect of the two subjects has also to be stressed. Geomorphology is rapidly becoming an applied subject as the book by Cooke and Doornkamp, *Geomorphology in environmental management*, has shown. Soil can be regarded as a resource in its own right. Thus, an integrating approach between soils and landforms is vital in many aspects of land management.

It is the aim of this book to illustrate these various themes. The number of possible topics is large and the literature is voluminous and the treatment must, of necessity, be selective. It is an elaboration of a theme and it is hoped that it will stimulate the work of others and will enhance the integration of the discipline of geomorphology and pedology.

A. J. Gerrard
December 1980

Acknowledgements

Thanks are due to the following authors, publishers and learned bodies for permission to reproduce figures and tables:

R. R. Arnett (Table 5.4); Figure 9.1 reproduced from *Glaciers and landscape* (D. E. Sugden & B. J. John) by kind permission of the authors and Edward Arnold Ltd; Figure 10.5 reproduced from *Process in geomorphology* (C. Embleton & J. Thornes) by kind permission of Edward Arnold Ltd; E. Bettenay (Fig. 8.6); D. Brunsden (Fig. 10.5); B. E. Butler (Fig. 10.6); Figure 3.1 reproduced from *Hillslope form and process* (M. A. Carson & M. J. Kirkby), Figure 4.4 reproduced from *Tropical soils and soil survey* (A. Young), Figure 10.6 reproduced from *Landform studies from Australia and New Guinea* (J. Jennings & J. A. Mabbutt, eds) and Table 4.1 reproduced from *The soil resources of tropical Africa* (R. P. Moss) all by kind permission of Cambridge University Press; C. J. Chartres (Tables 7.5, 7.6); R. J. Chorley (Fig. 1.2); Commonwealth Scientific and Industrial Research Organisation (Fig. 8.6); A. J. Conacher (Table 5.4); D. T. Currey (Fig. 7.1); Elsevier Scientific Publishing Co. (Fig. 7.1); Elsevier Scientific Publishing Co. (*Geoderma*) (Fig. 1.5, Tables 7.5, 7.6); C. B. England (Table 2.3); A. E. Foscolos (Table 10.2); Geographical Society of New South Wales (Table 5.4); Geological Society of America (Fig. 2.3); K. Gilman (Fig. 2.9); R. D. Green (Figs 8.2, 8.3, 8.4, Table 8.1); J. R. Hails (Fig. 7.1); J. D. Hewlett (Fig. 2.8); H. N. Holtan (Table 2.3); Houghton Mifflin Co. (Fig. 7.4); R. J. Huggett (Fig. 1.5); D. L. Hughes (Table 10.2); Figure 4.8 reproduced from *The geography of soil* (B. Bunting) by kind permission of Hutchinson General Books Ltd; Figures 5.2, 5.3 and Table 5.2 reproduced from *Slopes: form and process* by kind permission of the Institute of British Geographers; International Association of Hydrological Sciences (Fig. 2.6); International Society of Soil Science (Fig. 1.3, Table 5.3); Iowa State University Press (Fig. 9.2); B. A. Kennedy (Fig. 1.2); R. T. Legget (Fig. 9.4); D. M. Leslie (Fig. 10.8); Longman Group Ltd (Fig. 4.9); W. M. McArthur (Fig. 8.6); Figures 4.1 and 8.5 reprinted by permission from *Nature* vol. 138, p. 549 and vol. 196, p. 836, copyright © 1936 and 1962 Macmillan Journals Ltd; W. C. Mahaney Figs 10.2, 10.3, Table 10.2); B. Matthews (Fig. 9.3); R. B. Morrison (Figs 10.2, 10.3); R. P. Moss (Table 4.1); M. Newson (Fig. 2.9); the Editor, *New Zealand Journal of Geology and Geophysics* (Fig. 10.8); North Holland Publishing Co. (*Journal of Hydrology*) (Table 2.3); W. L. Nutter (Fig. 28); N. V. Vitgeverij W. van Hoeve (Table 2.1); Oxford University Press (Figs 4.2, 4.3, 4.5, 4.6, 6.2, 7.3, 10.7, Tables 7.1, 7.2, 7.3, 7.4, 10.3); Oxford University Press (New York) (Fig. 10.4); Figure 9.4 reproduced from *Glacial till* (R. T. Legget, ed.) by kind permission of the Honorary Editor, Royal Society of Canada; R. V. Ruhe (Table 6.1); N. W. Rutter (Table 10.2); Soil Survey of England and Wales (Figs 8.2, 8.3, 8.4, 9.3, Table 8.1); Springer Verlag (Fig. 8.1); United States Department of Agriculture (Table 2.1); Figures 2.4 and 2.5 reproduced from United States Geological Survey Professional Papers 347 (J. T. Hack & J. G. Goodlett 1960) and

662A (W. Emmett 1970); University of Chicago Press (Fig. 9.5); Tables 3.2 and 3.3 reproduced from *Earth Surface Processes*, vol. 1, copyright © 1976 John Wiley & Sons Ltd, reprinted by permission of John Wiley & Sons Ltd; Figure 3.3, Tables 3.4 and 3.5 reproduced from *Earth Surface Processes*, vol. 3, copyright © 1978 John Wiley & Sons Ltd; reprinted by permission of John Wiley & Sons Ltd; Figure 2.7 and Table 2.2 reproduced from *Hillslope hydrology* (M. J. Kirkby, ed.), copyright © 1978 John Wiley & Sons Ltd; Table 6.1 reproduced from *Soil Science* vol. 82, no. 6, p. 453, copyright © 1956 The Williams & Wilkins Co., Baltimore; the Editor, *Zeitschrift für Geomorphologie* (Figs 1.4, 5.1, 6.1).

Contents

List of tables

List of tables

1 Models of soil genesis and geomorphology

Soils can be regarded as a natural body formed by the accumulation of organic and inorganic materials at the Earth's surface. Soil formation is the result of the interaction of various processes, both geomorphological and pedological, and therefore, the soil body must be treated as a dynamic medium. Ruellan (1971) has made the distinction between those workers who attach great importance to the geomorphological processes of erosion and deposition (the allochthonists) and those who attribute the major characteristics of soils to pedological processes (the autochthonists). But, soils are the result of the interaction of both these sets of processes and the most realistic approach is to treat soils and landscapes as open systems and to utilise the concepts that have evolved with system analysis.

Soils as open systems

Soils behave as open systems in that they lose and receive materials and energy at their boundaries. This has implications both for the theoretical consideration of soil behaviour and for the choice of soil parameters to measure in the field in order to specify the system state. The analysis of soils as open systems directs attention to the basic concepts involved in such a framework. These concepts have been enumerated by Strahler and Strahler (1973) in the following terms:

(a) Systems possess boundaries, either real or arbitrary.
(b) Systems possess inputs and outputs of energy and matter crossing these system boundaries.
(c) Systems possess pathways of energy transport and transformation associated with matter within the system.
(d) Within systems matter may be transported from place to place or have its physical properties transformed by chemical reaction or change of state.
(e) Open systems tend to attain a dynamic equilibrium or steady state in which rate of input of energy and matter equals rate of output of energy and matter, while storage of energy and matter remains constant.
(f) When the input or output rates of an open system change, the system tends to achieve a new dynamic equilibrium. The period of change

leading to the establishment of the new equilibrium state is a transient state and the period of time involved will depend on the sensitivity of the system.

(g) The amount of storage of energy and matter increases (decreases) when the rate of energy and material flow through the system increases (decreases).

(h) The greater the storage capacity within the system for a given input, the lesser is the sensitivity of the system.

Not everyone would agree that dynamic equilibrium and steady state are exactly interchangeable terms, but, the framework is a good one for assessing the relationships between, and within soils, and between soils and other factors. Although early models of pedogenesis were not stated purely in systems terminology, many of the concepts outlined above were tacitly acknowledged. This is especially true of points one and two which, in a general way, were embodied in attempts to define soil formation in terms of state factors and state factor equations.

State factor equations

It is generally agreed that Dokuchaev in 1898 was the first to suggest a soil-forming factor equation. His equation was:

$$s = f(cl, o, p)t^0$$

where s = soil, cl = climate, o = organisms, p = parent materials and t^0 represented relative age (youthfulness, maturity, senility). The equation should be taken as a symbolic expression or a conceptual model and does not imply that it can be 'solved' in a mathematical sense. Although relief or topography is not one of the factors, Dokuchaev did acknowledge relief as important, but chiefly in the formation of 'abnormal' soils. Later workers, such as Hilgard (Jenny 1961b) and Shaw (1930), modified this synthesis and added relief to the soil-forming factors. This culminated in Jenny's (1941) state factor equation:

$$s = f(cl, o, r, p, t, \ldots)$$

where s denotes any soil property, cl is the environmental climate, o is animal organisms, r is relief, p is parent material and t is time since the start of soil formation. The important point to stress is that the factors are variables that define the state of the soil system. Jenny, in 1961, modified the equation to make it more applicable to modern thought concerning ecosystems. The revised equation is:

$$l, s, v, a = f(L_0, p_x, t)$$

where l is any property of the ecosystem in its totality, soil properties are denoted by s, vegetation by v and animal properties by a. L_0 represents the assemblage of properties at time zero, p_x the flux potentials and t is the age of the system. The configuration of the system, such as its slope, exposure and topography, is a subgroup of L_0, as are considerations of the mineral and organic matrix of the soil. Climate is a subgroup of the flux potential p_x.

Five broad groups of factors in accordance with the five state factors are suggested. These are:

$$l, s, v, a = \begin{cases} f(cl, o, r, p, t, \ldots) & \text{climofunction} \\ f(o, cl, r, p, t, \ldots) & \text{biofunction} \\ f(r, cl, o, p, t, \ldots) & \text{topofunction} \\ f(p, cl, o, r, t, \ldots) & \text{lithofunction} \\ f(t, cl, o, r, p, \ldots) & \text{chronofunction} \end{cases}$$

The dominant factor is placed first. A more convenient way of writing this, as suggested by Jenny (1961a), is:

$$l, s, v, a = f(r)_{cl, o, p, t} \quad \text{topofunction}$$

The great problem with this type of approach is that it is extremely difficult to handle in a modern quantitative fashion. Although expressed in a mathematical way, it is really a verbal model in the sense used by Dijkerman (1974). Yaalon (1975) has reviewed the attempts that have been made to solve these state factor equations. Lithofunctions present problems because of the difficulties in assigning numerical values to parent materials, however, the use of binary attributes might be profitable. Topofunctions are easier to manage and there have been many graphical and numerical attempts to relate soil properties to landscape elements, such as slope angle and position. Some of these are discussed in Chapter 5. One of the problems in fitting linear or curvilinear relationships to this type of data is that both slope angle and soil properties are strongly autocorrelated. This means that individual soil properties and gradient angles on single slopes are correlated with themselves and are not independent entities, which may invalidate many of the statistical findings.

There have been numerous qualitative studies of the effect of climate on soils and a number of general conclusions have emerged which may well be capable of quantification in the future. Most graphical solutions to date have been concerned with chronofunctions, but there is also a rapidly growing number of studies which have attempted to quantify the rate of change of particular soil properties. The major fact to emerge from these studies is that not only does the rate of change vary from one soil property to another but so does the form of the mathematical function. This is important when considering vexing questions such as soil maturity and whether dynamic equilibrium, as a concept, can even be applied to soils. Numerical solutions of true biotic functions are rare, but knowledge of the general role of vegetation is substantial. Thus progress in the quantification of state factors is being made, albeit slowly, and it seems that much greater insight can be gained by pursuing the systems analogy with respect to parts of the soil system rather than in its entirety.

Types of systems

Chorley and Kennedy (1971) distinguished between morphological and cascade systems. Morphological systems are the formal instantaneous physical properties which are integrated to form a recognisable operational part of reality. Cascade systems are composed of a chain of subsystems which are dynamically linked by flows of mass or energy. In soils, the equivalent may be Kubiena's (1938) distinction between the soil skeleton and plasma. The skeleton is composed of the relatively stable and not readily translocated mineral grains and resistant organic bodies larger than colloidal size. The plasma is that part of the soil capable of being moved, reorganised and concentrated within the soil. It is the active part and includes all material, mineral or organic, of colloidal size and the relatively soluble material which is not bound up in the skeleton (Brewer & Sleeman 1960). At a larger scale, hillslope hydrology integrates the morphological (slope, shape, length, angle, soil depth, etc.) with the cascade components (water and sediment movement). This integration of the morphological and cascade elements produces process-response systems which exist at all spatial scales.

The workings of soil systems can be treated at different levels of detail. At the 'black box' level, the whole system is regarded as a unit with no consideration of internal structure. An example of this approach would entail the measurement of precipitation as input and water emerging at the soil base as output with no consideration of pathways, stores or lags. At the 'grey box' level, a partial view of the system is adopted. At this level the soil body is recognised both as a potential regulator of water movement and as having a storage capacity. The most realistic and, therefore, complex treatment is the 'white box' procedure where an attempt is made to identify and analyse as many of the regulators, stores and flows as possible. Water movement in individual soil layers would be assumed at this level of analysis. All three levels of analysis with respect to the movement of water on slopes are represented in Chapter 2. A mathematical simulation for soil profile development on initially undifferentiated till by Kline (1973) is an example of a 'white box' approach. The soil column is viewed as a series of compartments through which there is continuous movement of materials. Material is exported from the system by vegetation uptake, erosion and drainage and is imported through atmospheric inputs, from vegetation and animal activity. The horizontally adjacent soil compartments in this model represent transfers along pathways rather than transfers in space, whilst vertical arrangements of compartments imply transfer of material in space. The output of this model would be a series of curves, one for each compartment, showing compartmental content of the materials as a function of time.

Energy status of soil systems

Three components can be recognised in the energy status of soil systems. There is a decay component in which the energy status gradually declines and eventually the system should be brought to a state of virtual exhaustion. Soils existing on the very level ancient erosion surfaces approach this condition. Lack of relief means potential energy is at a minimum and vertical movement of soil water is the only possibility. Thick soils and possibly thick weathered regolith also inhibit chemical action at the interface or weathering front between regolith and rock (see Ch. 6). These soils will still have a cyclic or rhythmic component in which energy, and perhaps material input, increases and decreases in a rhythmic manner such as diurnal and seasonal climatic cycles. There will also be a random component in which input of energy and matter occur irregularly, such as rainstorms. The soil systems evolve in response to all these components. Energy can flow through soil systems in a variety of ways and one of the problems is how to assess the energy status of a soil body. This has been attempted in an enterprising fashion by Runge (1973).

One of the major drawbacks in Jenny's synthesis is that the state factors are discrete, nonoverlapping units and offer little opportunity of obtaining the data necessary to determine the differential rates of change which are an essential feature of soil formation. Runge (1973) has argued that some vectors are more important than others in controlling soil development. The energy source, in the model developed by him, is the gravitational or potential energy that is available to the soil system when water runs off the soil surface or percolates through the soil profile. Soil development, at a particular site, is dependent on the relative amount of water running off, and therefore not contributing to soil development, versus the amount infiltrating and therefore available to influence soil formation. This is why the geomorphology of the area is so important because if the change in soil development between soil profiles is being examined, it is essential to have the same soil material and equal stability within the landscape. Landscapes and soil profiles become a record of how the internal and external energy fluxes have been dissipated over time.

In the energy model, the analogy of systems and thermodynamics is used. The first law of thermodynamics states that the total amount of energy remains constant. The second law states that, with time, systems develop towards states of maximum entropy. Entropy is an expression of the degree to which energy has become unable to perform work. The state of lowest available energy and maximum disorder occurs when entropy is at a maximum and to decrease entropy and increase order energy has to be imported from another source. Runge (1973) argues that loess soil parent material is at maximum disorder or has no profile development, alternatively, a well developed soil profile with horizon differentiation is considerably more ordered. This leads to the idea that water flow through the soil profile is the principal source for increasing order and decreasing the entropy of the soil body.

The essence of the model developed by Runge (1973) and Smeck and Runge (1971a,b) is that soil development is a factor of organic matter production, the amount of water available for leaching and time. Phosphorus was used as a surrogate for organic matter production because, under natural conditions, it is only supplied by the soil parent material. Phosphorus is also considered to be essentially immobile in soils but, during the time spans involved in soil formation, redistribution does occur. As pH drops, the relatively soluble forms of phosphorus decrease and more occluded forms increase. Therefore, the relative amounts of the different phosphorus forms may serve as a measure of soil development.

Soil–landscape systems

Dijkerman (1974) has stressed that scientific explanation is a satisfactory answer to a why or how question. The first question seeks a genetic explanation to questions such as how did the system originate and develop. An explanation to a question of this nature must be in terms of the sequence of events that produced the situation being explained. The second question seeks a functional explanation to questions such as how does the system function. It asks for an assessment of the status and role of the many forces and factors acting on the system. In answering these questions with respect to soils it is necessary to consider the significance of topography and position. The geomorphological history of an area is fundamental for an answer to the first question and an assessment of the interactions of geomorphological and pedological processes is important for a satisfactory answer to the second question. Soils do not exist in isolation but are organised within the landscape. This is embodied in the concept of pedons and polypedons (Simonson 1968). A pedon consists of a small volume of soil starting at the surface and extending downwards to include the full set of horizons. It must be large enough to include a full set of horizons and to permit observation of the boundaries between them. Larger units composed of a number of similar contiguous pedons are called polypedons. The relationships between these are depicted in Figure 1.1.

The interaction between soils and topography or pedology and geomor-

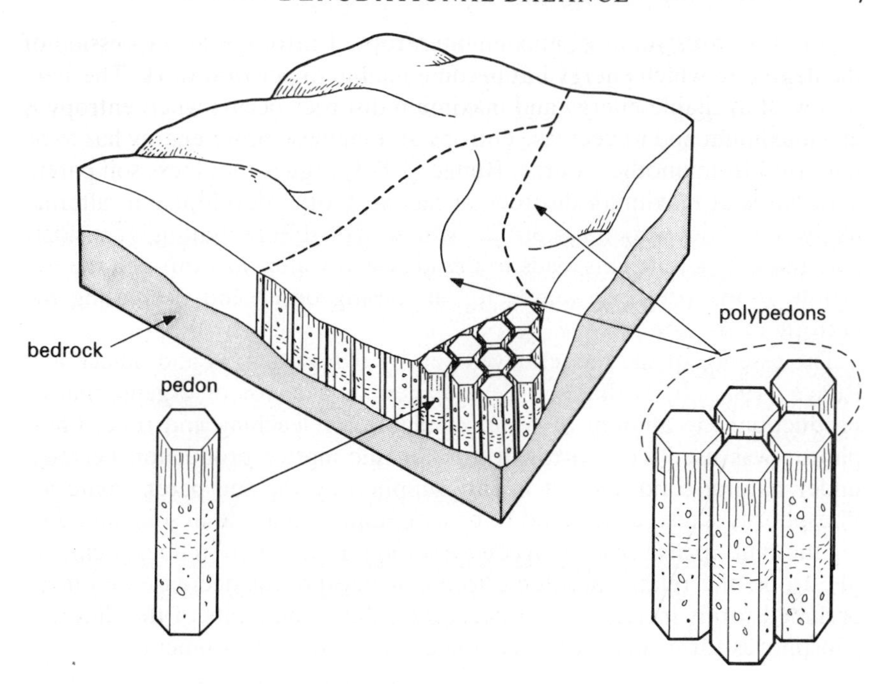

Figure 1.1 Relationships between pedons and polypedons.

phology can be treated at several levels. In the state factor model the interactions can be construed as being a function of the topographic and lithofunction being acted upon by climatic and biotic factors at some point in time. This approach does little to assess the detailed operations of the processes; it is a black box approach. More realistically, soils and landform systems must take account of the flux of materials and energy through the systems and this depends not only on topography or slope angle but relative position. This involves consideration of balance between input and output, i.e. equilibrium.

Denudational balance

The thickness of soil and regolith at any point will depend on the relative rates of soil removal and soil formation. At some sites removal will be minimal and deep soils and regolith will develop, whilst at other, more erosionally active sites, soils will be kept thin and permanently youthful. These aspects have been embodied in the distinction between accumulative and non-accumulative soils (Nikiforoff 1949). In geomorphology, the situation has been conceptualised by Jahn (1968) in terms of denudational balance. The three components that Jahn used were the accumulation of material by *in situ* production of waste and by inflow of material from upslope, and the removal of material by slopewash, surface deflation and mass movements. The arrangement of these factors yields the following three alternatives:

$$A = S + M \qquad A < S + M \qquad A > S + M$$

where A = the accumulation of slope material, S = the processes of slopewash and surface deflation and M = mass movement. Soil thickness will, thus, remain constant or increase and decrease according to the efficacy of the respective processes. If transport processes are more rapid than weathering, only a thin soil cover will exist because material is removed as fast as it becomes loose. The development of such a site is then said to be weathering-limited. If weathering rates are more rapid than transport processes, a thick soil cover develops and the site is said to be transport-limited. Hillslope and soil development, in weathering-limited situations, depends on the variations in weathering rate and the rate of transport is reduced to the rate at which fresh material weathers. On transport-limited sites, soil and slope development depends on the transporting capacity of the processes and the rate of weathering is reduced to an equilibrium value less than its potential maximum by the increase in soil thickness. In thin soils, very little water is retained and weathering rates are low. In very thick soils, water moves so slowly towards the weathering front that the rate of weathering is again below the potential maximum. Thus, weathering and soil formation are at a maximum at intermediate soil thicknesses. In practice, the rate of soil formation will fluctuate around a mean value as the relative efficiency of transporting processes varies. Carson and Kirkby (1972) have argued that these different controls lead to different slopes and sequences of slope development. Weathering-limited slopes, possessing thin soils, have prominent straight sections with important threshold angles and develop by parallel retreat. Transport-limited slopes, possessing thick soils, are essentially convex–concave and become progressively less steep with time. This is a very specific example of the interaction between soils and long-term landscape development.

Two-dimensional soil–landscape systems

One of the simplest ways of analysing soils in the landscape is to assume they are two-dimensional bodies existing at some point on a topographic transect. The topographic transect is usually, but not necessarily, a valley-side slope profile. It is embodied in the concept of the catena and numerous examples of this approach can be cited, some of which are analysed subsequently. The model adopted in fitting topofunctions to soils is that summarised by Yaalon (1971). In terms of the processes involved it may be necessary to subdivide this 'line' system into separate working subsystems.

Just as the inner workings of the system can be assessed at different levels of complexity so can the input, throughput and output. This can be illustrated by the movement of water through the upper soil horizons on an individual slope. In the simplest case, it can be assumed that all water enters the soil system at the top of the slope and leaves it at the slope base (Fig. 1.2a). This situation is extremely rare but may be convenient for the sake of simple analysis. Slightly more realistic is the situation where inputs and outputs are still *en bloc* but the soil system has been subdivided and transfers between these subelements considered (Fig. 1.2b). Using the soil water movement analogy, this is equivalent to subdividing soils on the basis of slope position and form, e.g. crest, mainslope and footslope. The third case (Fig. 1.2c) allows input to occur throughout the length of the slope but the slope is not subdivided. A more complex case is where inputs and throughputs are seen to be composed of discrete, though related, components on different slope zones (Fig. 1.2d). The most realistic approach is where inputs, throughputs and outputs are all composed of discrete units (Fig. 1.2e). In the analogy being used, this allows percolation to lower soil horizons as well as throughflow, deep percolation and groundwater flow. Although formulated differently this is essentially the conceptual embodiment of the catena (see Ch. 4).

The geochemical landscapes and geochemical soil sequences of

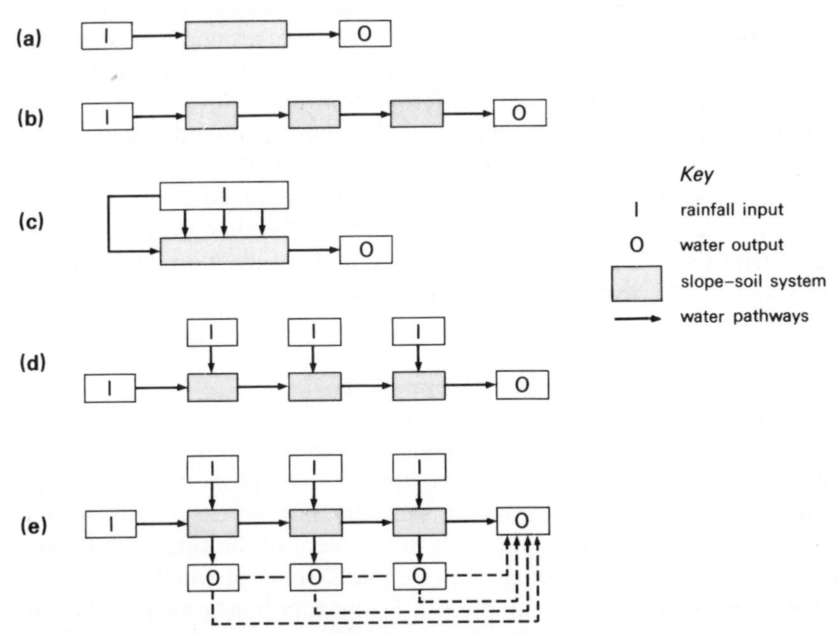

Figure 1.2 Different ways of organising input, throughput and output in systems (from Chorley & Kennedy 1971).

Glazovskaya (1968) involve similar concepts. Landscapes and soils that are adjacent, but at different elevations, are united by the lateral migration of chemical elements into a single geochemical landscape. Two examples, one from the Central Tien Shan in Central Asia and the other from Norway, illustrate the principles involved. In the Central Tien Shan, granite surfaces outcrop at the tops of slopes with the lower slopes composed of reworked weathered granite debris (Fig. 1.3a). Zone 1 is an eluvial landscape of

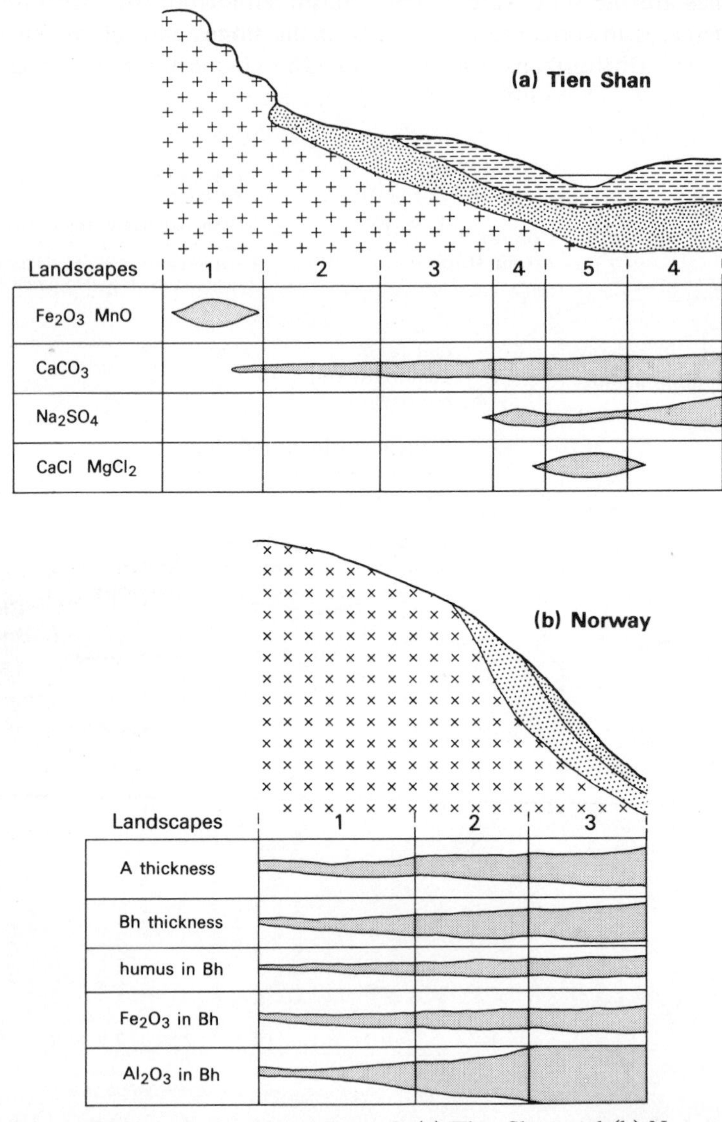

Figure 1.3 Geochemical soil sequences of: (a) Tien Shan and (b) Norway (from Glazovskaya 1968).

granite rocks with desert varnish, while zone 2 is a transeluvial landscape of denudation surfaces with slightly carbonaceous polygonal soils. Zone 3 is mostly an accumulative landscape of morainic hillslopes with highly carbonaceous takyr-like desert soils. Zones 4 and 5 are less well-drained with meadow salinised soils giving way to landlocked basins with wet solonchaks. The more readily soluble salts such as calcium and magnesium chlorides reach the lowest levels. Sodium sulphates are partly retained on the lower slopes. Although the soils in the Norwegian sequence are different the principles are the same (Fig. 1.3b). Due to solifluction the depth of the soils increases towards the lower parts of the slopes and the thickness of both A and Bh horizons also increases. The chemical status changes as

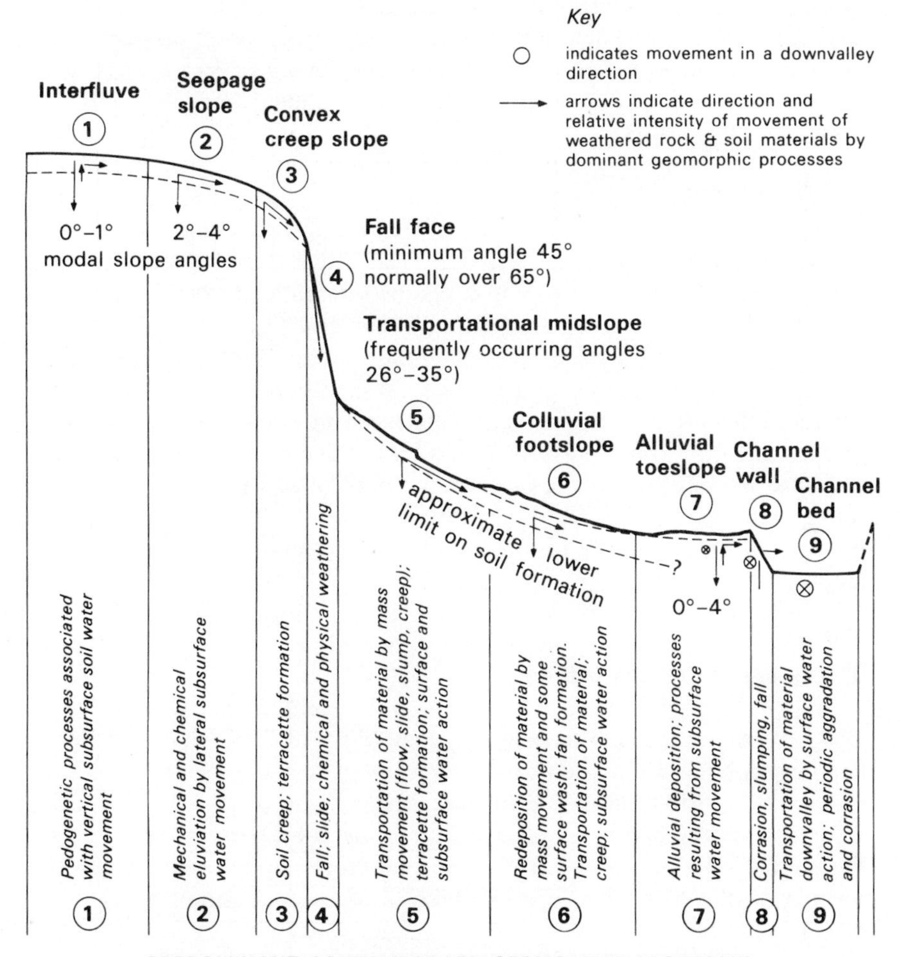

Figure 1.4 Hypothetical nine-unit landsurface model (from Dalrymple *et al.* 1968).

there is an intersoil migration of aluminium fulvates with subsequent accumulation in the lower part of the slope. There is a close link between this analysis and the energy models of Smeck and Runge (1971a,b) described earlier.

The nine-unit landsurface model of Dalrymple *et al.* (1968) is essentially a two-dimensional approach although it can be extended to encompass entire drainage basins. It is a model based both on form and contemporary geomorphological and pedogenetic processes. It attempts to subdivide slope profiles and yet at the same time to integrate the components by considering material and water flow. The model is depicted in Figure 1.4. On units 1 and 2, pedogenetic processes and vertical water movement dominate. The convex creep slope (unit 3) is characterised by both pedogenetic and geomorphological processes. Units 4 and 5, free face and transportational midslope, are controlled by the processes of weathering and mass movement. The colluvial footslope (unit 6) contains both geomorphological and pedogenetic processes. The alluvial footslope (unit 7) is controlled by subsurface water movement and periodic incursions by the river in flood. Units 8 and 9 are fluvially controlled. Since the model was presented in 1968 it has been refined, culminating in a seminal publication in 1977.

The various units or components are separate process–response systems in the sense used earlier. In some cases the integrative factor is the mobilisation, translocation and redeposition of materials by overland flow. On other units, the subsurface movement of water is the more important. Thus, unit 2 is defined as an area where the response to mechanical and chemical eluviation by downslope subsurface soil water movements distinguishes this from other parts of the landscape and unit 5 is defined by the response to transportation of a large amount of soil material relative to other units (Conacher & Dalrymple 1978). These process–response pedogeomorphic units can be mapped both in detail and over extensive landsurfaces.

Three-dimensional soil–landscape systems

The necessity of viewing the soil as a component of the broader landscape has always been recognised but the means of formulating this has been difficult. Consistent surface geometric soil patterns at a variety of scales which are approximately coincident with topographic patterns demonstrate the spatial relations between soils and landforms. The major geometric forms that these relationships can take have been classified by Fridland (1974) and are:

(a) Dendritic, linear-dendritic and streaming forms, connected with various forms of erosional relief such as river valleys.

(b) Rounded, spotted (including ring-like) forms, connected with various depressional forms (sink holes, former lakes) and hilly morainic relief.
(c) Linear and wavy-linear forms connected with different linear forms of an accumulative origin.
(d) Streak-phacoid forms characteristic of modern and ancient floodplains and deltas.
(e) Fan-shaped forms characteristic of alluvial fans and deluvial trains.

These patterns are the result of the interactions of many processes and it is only with the advent of high speed computers that the three-dimensional situation can be handled. The best example of this is the attempt by Huggett (1973, 1975) to simulate the flux of plasmic material in an idealised valley basin.

The valley basin was chosen as the basic organisational unit for both the geomorphological and pedological materials. The model is really an extension of the nine-unit landsurface model in that it argues that definable flowlines of material can be organised into soil–landscape system units. In a valley system, flowlines diverge and converge; convex contour patterns lead to divergent flow and concave patterns to convergent flow. Extension of this into the third dimension allows the theoretical direction taken by infiltrating water to be examined. Zaslavaky and Rogowski (1969) found that convex slopes led to divergent infiltration and concave slopes to convergent infiltration. Thus, divergent throughflow of water on spurs is enhanced by divergent vertical flow.

The computer-simulated pattern of change in the concentration of a plasmic constituent in an idealised valley is shown in Figures 1.5a and b. Figure 1.5a shows the pattern of concentration values one depth increment below the soil surface, after 2 and 4 time steps. The accumulation of material in the hollows is evident. Figure 1.5b depicts the changes in concentration at the same position in the soil body along two side spurs and along the hollow thalweg. Material has moved down all the slopes but spur 1 has lost material over most of its length whereas spur 2 has lost material in its upper concave section and gained material in its lower concave section. The thalweg line has gained material at all points except the valley head. Different constituents will move through the system at different rates. Huggett (1975) has suggested that one time step might represent one day for mobile salts such as chlorides and sulphates but as much as a millenium for a fairly immobile element such as aluminium.

An iterative procedure, such as this, provides valuable information concerning the rate and spatial characteristics of plasma movement that can be compared with more static field studies. The approach also has the ability to allow the system states, boundary conditions, etc. to be altered and is an extremely valuable contribution to understanding the relationships between soils and landforms.

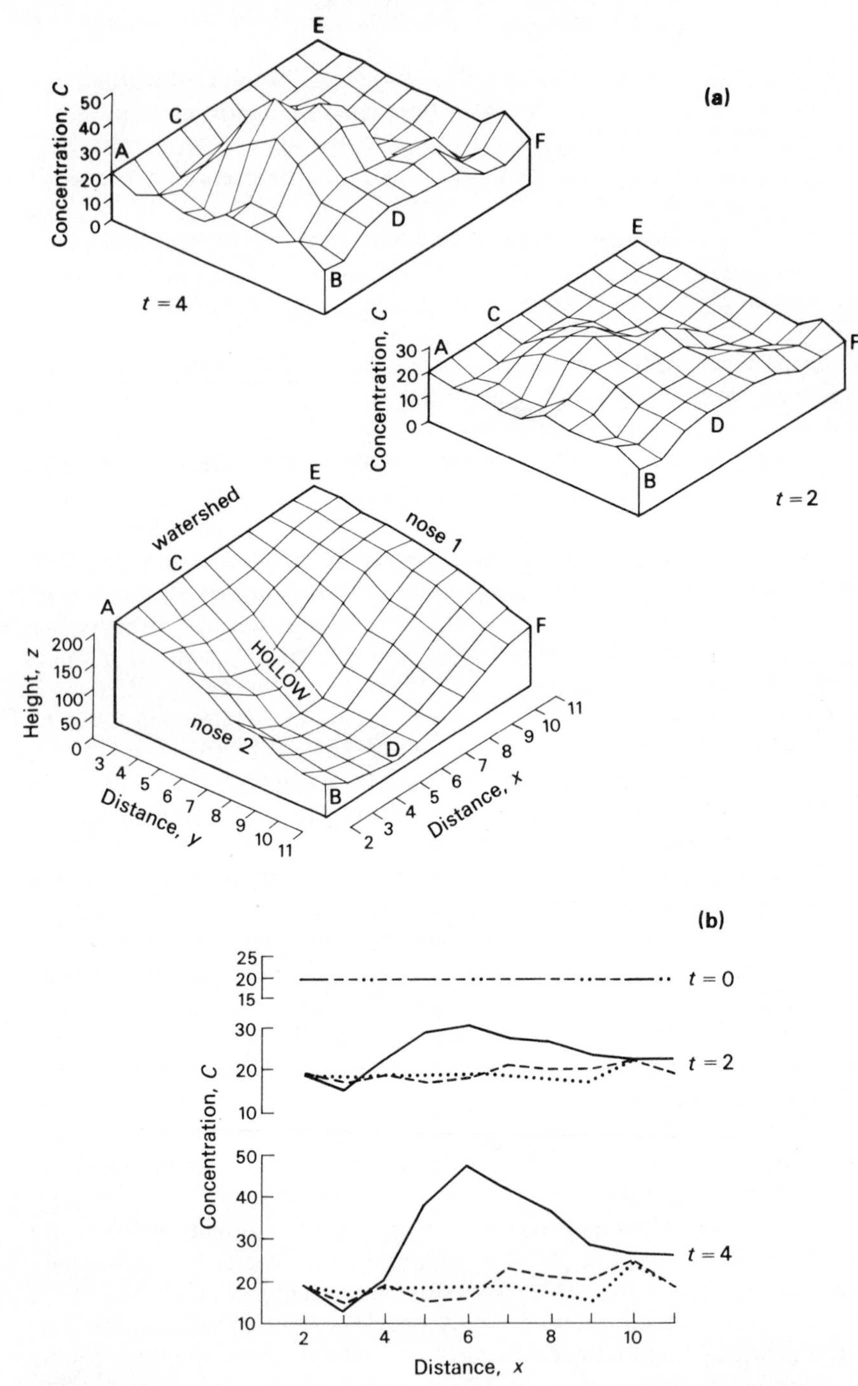

Figure 1.5 Computer simulated flux of plasmic material in an idealised basin (from Huggett 1975).

Conclusions

The purpose of this chapter has been to review briefly the development of ideas concerning the relationships between soil, landscape and geomorphology and also to provide the methodological framework for the rest of the book. Many of the examples given a cursory treatment are elaborated in subsequent chapters, such as the movement of water and soil examined in the next two chapters. The philosophy behind the choice of examples is that the movement, or flux of material, can be organised into functional units or soil–landscape systems and that both pedogenetic and geomorphological processes are involved. It is further suggested that the basic soil system units can be clearly defined and that there is a complex, but intelligible, web of relationships between the soil system and landform system elements. A systems approach to the study of these relationships is appealing in its logic and rigorous methodology and in the way it directs a stage by stage advance to particular problems. It directs attention to the delimitation of entities or parts and the choice of relationships which are of interest.

2 The movement of water on slopes

The movement of water on slopes is governed by a complex set of interrelated factors. Some of these factors, such as rainfall duration and intensity, are external to the soil–landscape system. But the major controlling factors are intrinsic to the system and are determined by soil and vegetation properties, topographic characteristics such as slope form and angle, and positional attributes such as relative height and distance from the slope base. The distribution of water on slopes has a fundamental control on the nature of the soils, and water movement integrates soils existing on different parts of the slope. This is fundamental to the catena concept as stressed in Chapter 4. A knowledge of the speed and timing of water movement is also critical in watershed management schemes.

There are many possible approaches to the study of water movement. Careful field observations will enable the passage of water through the soil and over the slope to be assessed. This is usually combined with detailed sampling and analysis of the soil properties. A second approach, a variant of the first, involves the artificial application of water to natural slopes with

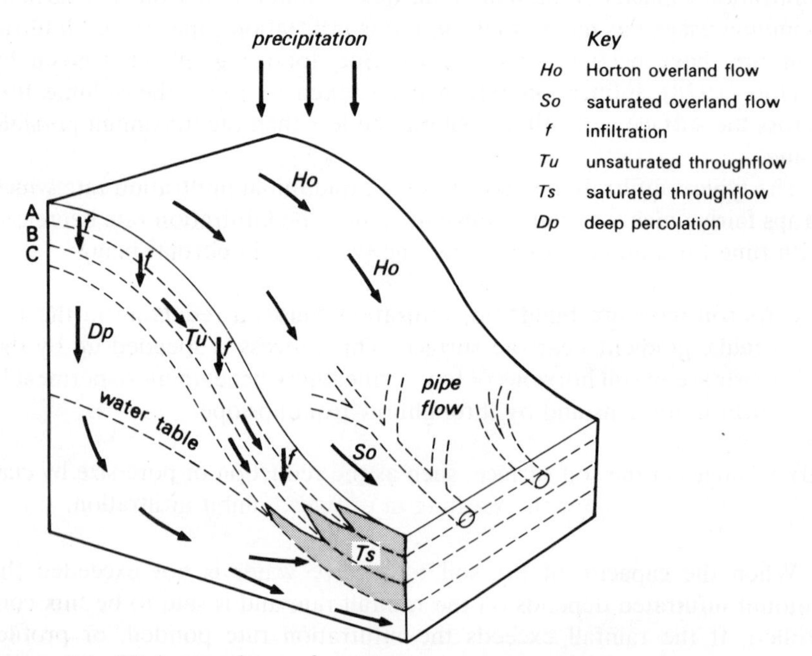

Figure 2.1 Various pathways for water movement on slopes.

the subsequent monitoring of water movement. Alternatively, soil troughs or soil profiles can be constructed in the laboratory and water movement noted under carefully controlled conditions. This allows a small number of relevant factors to be isolated and examined. A somewhat different but, nevertheless, fruitful approach is the mathematical modelling of the processes such as through the development of theoretical infiltration and throughflow equations. No one approach on its own is entirely satisfactory but taken together a valuable insight into the processes involved can be gained.

Water can move across and through soil in a variety of ways. The major pathways are illustrated in Figure 2.1. It is these pathways that are defined and their characteristics examined in this chapter. It is not possible to examine all the processes involved in great detail and all that is attempted is to highlight the factors that are fundamental to an understanding of soil distribution and behaviour. More detailed accounts are available in the excellent book on hillslope hydrology edited by Kirkby (1978). The related issue of the movement of soil by water on slopes is left to the next chapter.

Infiltration

Infiltration may be simply defined as the process of water entering the soil. In this respect it should not be confused with the hydraulic conductivity of the soil which is only one of several factors affecting the rate of infiltration. Infiltration capacity is the maximum flux of water across the soil surface. Common usage has meant that the terms infiltration capacity and infiltration rate have become synonymous. But, following the lead given by Knapp (1978), infiltration rate will be taken to mean the volume flux across the surface and will, in general, be less than the maximum possible value.

The typical infiltration curve shows a rapid initial infiltration rate which drops fairly quickly to some constant value. The infiltration rate decreases with time for a number of reasons, the two most important being:

(a) As soil moisture builds up, saturation causes a reduction in the hydraulic gradient near the surface. This process is speeded up by the existence of soil horizons of low permeability beneath more permeable surface horizons and by throughflow from upslope.

(b) Changes in the soil surface, such as the reduction of pore size by clay mineral swelling or the washing in of fines, inhibit infiltration.

When the capacity of the soil to receive water is not exceeded the amount infiltrated depends on the rainfall rate and is said to be flux controlled. If the rainfall exceeds the infiltration rate ponded, or profile-controlled, infiltration results. Rubin (1966) has identified three modes of

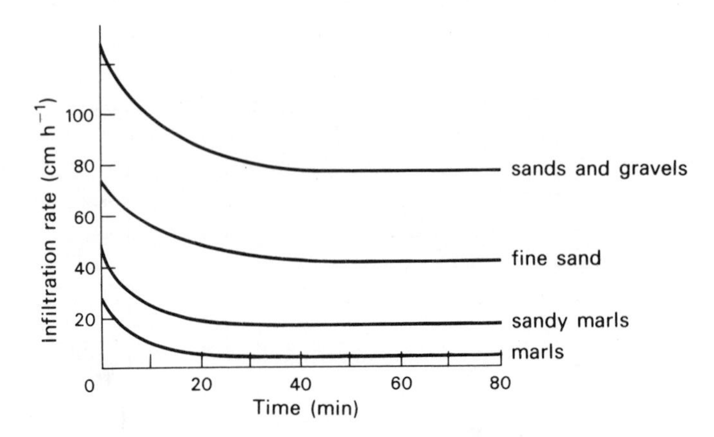

Figure 2.2 Typical infiltration curves for ponded infiltration on different materials.

rain infiltration on the basis of relative rainfall intensity; these are non-ponding, pre-ponding and ponded forms of infiltration. Non-ponding infiltration occurs when the rainfall is less than the infiltration capacity. As rainfall intensity increases, the limiting moisture content of the surface soil increases and eventually, when capacity is exceeded, a pre-ponding and, finally, a ponding mode occurs.

The shape of the infiltration capacity curve is influenced by a number of factors. External factors such as rainfall intensity and duration and drop size are clearly important, but, perhaps the most important are soil characteristics such as texture, structure, depth, nature and proportion of clay minerals, vegetation and land-use. Figure 2.2 gives an indication of the effects of soil texture on the infiltration process. A much more complete review of the literature has been provided by Dunne (1978). The investigations by Free *et al*. (1940) on some 54 soil types at 68 sites have highlighted some of the characteristics of the infiltration process. Galvanised-steel tubes 20 cm in diameter were inserted into the soil and a head of water of about 6 mm was maintained. The water content of the soil was determined initially at three depths and then the rates of infiltration determined. A second run of infiltration determinations was carried out 24 hours later with the soil still wet from the first run. Some of the results of these experiments are shown in Table 2.1. The data demonstrate the fall-off of infiltration rate with time and the second run emphasises the importance of antecedent soil moisture content. The major influence exerted by soil texture is also apparent.

The passage of water through soils is greatly influenced by the size and arrangement of particles and voids. The larger mineral particles form the skeleton of the soil with finer-textured materials, such as clay minerals, iron oxides and organic products, acting as coatings on and bridges between the skeleton. The combination of these elements produces the

Table 2.1 Infiltration rates on different soil types of the United States (after Free, Browning and Musgrave 1940, Mohr and Van Baren (1954)).

		Rate of infiltration in mm per hr					*% soil moisture at start at depth of*		
Soil type		*first quarter*	*second quarter*	*3rd and 4th quarters*	*2nd hour*	*3rd hour*	*9 cm*	*28 cm*	*51 cm*
Honeoye graveley	I	478	306	224	170	146	15	15	14
silt loam	II	230	177	163	145	121	32	24	22
Austin clay	I	208	85	69	63	61	17	18	18
	II	134	48	45	45	45	20	22	21
Fayette silt loam	I	139	28	13	7	6	10	10	11
	II	18	7	6	6	6	30	23	16
Buell clay loam	I	150	45	22	12	10	15	16	19
	II	30	6	4	4	3	24	22	21
Crown light clay	I	106	30	14	4	2	16	12	8
	II	0	0	0	0	0	34	24	16
Westmorland clayey	I	2	1	0.5	0	0.5	30	32	32
silt loam	II	0	0	0	0	0	29	30	31

macrofeatures which give structure to the soil. Each unit in the soil structure is called a ped and water is transmitted between peds as well as between particles. A well-developed crumb structure has numerous well-connected voids which allow water movement in all directions. Blocky structures have many voids but regular packing keeps void sizes small and water movement is again possible in all directions. Prismatic structures possess large peds with well-defined voids having a dominant downward orientation and water movement is mainly in a vertical direction. Platey structures have large peds with ill-defined voids possessing a dominant lateral water movement. As water percolates through the soil it displaces water previously retained by the soil. At low rainfall intensities much of this movement takes place through the finer pores and it is only when the soil is saturated, or close to saturation, that appreciable amounts of water move through the larger pores such as root holes. Horton and Hawkins (1965) have showed, by experiment, that most of the water that enters larger pores is drawn by capillary forces into the smaller surrounding pores.

Infiltration equations and the mechanics of infiltration

A number of different formulae for the infiltration process have been proposed. The aim of all such formulae is to express the rate of infiltration as a function of time and to account for the decrease from the initial high values to the asymptotic approach to an ultimate constant value. Several admirable summaries of these formulae exist (e.g. Childs 1969, Knapp 1978) and only the barest summary is presented here.

(a) Infiltration law of Green and Ampt

In 1911 Green and Ampt proposed a model for infiltration under ponded water conditions. They regarded water moving through soil as an advancing water front at which the pressure, H_f, is negative because suction is a constant characteristic of the soil. The equation is expressed as:

$$i = k_{sat}(H_0 + l - H_f)/l$$

where

i = infiltration rate
k_{sat} = saturated hydraulic conductivity
H_0 = depth of ponded water
l = vertical depth of saturated zone
H_f = capillary pressure at wetting front

When the formula was first proposed several factors were difficult to measure but more recently Swartzendruber and Huberty (1958) and Mein and Larson (1973) have computed values for the parameters. Green and Ampt envisaged a sharp reduction of moisture content at the water front whereas recent work has suggested that there is a transition zone rather than an abrupt zone (Morel-Seytoux & Khanji 1974).

(b) *Infiltration law of Kostiakov*

In 1932, Kostiakov introduced an empirical formula of the form:

$$(f) = f_0 t^{-\theta}$$

where

(f) = instantaneous infiltration rate at time t
f_0 = minimum infiltration capacity at $t = 0$
θ = constant

This implies that (f) must become zero after a sufficient time and this is contrary to experience and to theory based on physical principles.

(c) *Infiltration law of Horton*

A very similar formula to that of Kostiakov was suggested by Horton (1933, 1945) although another similar one was proposed earlier by Gardner and Widtsoe (1921). The formula proposed by Horton was:

$$(f) = f_c + (f_0 - f_c)e^{-ct}$$

where

(f) = instantaneous infiltration rate at time t
f_c = minimum infiltration capacity at $t \rightarrow \infty$
f_0 = minimum infiltration capacity at $t = 0$
c = constant for the soil

This equation was developed as part of a wider conceptual model of overland flow and surface erosion and assumes unimpeded movement of water into the soil. However, it gives poor results for short-term infiltration rates.

(d) *Infiltration law of Philip*

Baver (1937) pointed out that water moves into and within the soil under the influence of gravitational and capillary forces, the latter being due to molecular forces between the soil particles and water giving very slow water movement from thicker to thinner capillary films. Laboratory models developed by Bodman and Coleman (1943) showed that infiltration can be divided into three parts:

(a) A transmission zone occupying the upper part of the wetted soil. Once established it absorbs no more moisture but simply conducts water from the surface.
(b) A wetting zone below the transmission zone with a moisture gradient which increases with depth.
(c) A wetting front which occurs as a highly irregular surface with a very high potential gradient.

These discoveries were incorporated in the classic work of Philip (1957–58), culminating in the following equation (Philip 1957c):

$$i = A + \tfrac{1}{2}Bt^{-1/2}$$

where

i = infiltration rate
A = a constant close to the hydraulic conductivity value at the surface for $t = 0$
B = a sorptivity value obtained from the rate of penetration of the wetting front

The first factor, A, is generally thought to represent conductivity flow under gravity by unimpeded laminar flow through a continuous network of large pores. The second term, B, is a diffusion term representing the filling up of the smaller pores by slow diffusion from one pore space to the next.

The Horton equation seems to underestimate infiltration rates at $t = 0$ and approaches the minimum infiltration capacity at $t = \infty$ more abruptly than observed infiltration curves. The Philip equation overestimates initial infiltration rates but is a remarkably good fit otherwise. As soon as the infiltration capacity of the soil is exceeded surface ponding occurs and water may begin to move downslope as surface flow. The first major attempt to explain overland flow was that of Horton (1945).

Horton overland flow

The essence of Horton's model is depicted in Figure 2.3. It predicts that prolonged rain falling on the slopes of a drainage basin possessing relatively uniform infiltration capacity will, if the rain intensity is greater than the infiltration capacity, produce overland flow over all the basin approximately simultaneously. It is assumed that all depression storage must be filled before surface runoff occurs. Horton (1935) estimated that on mod-

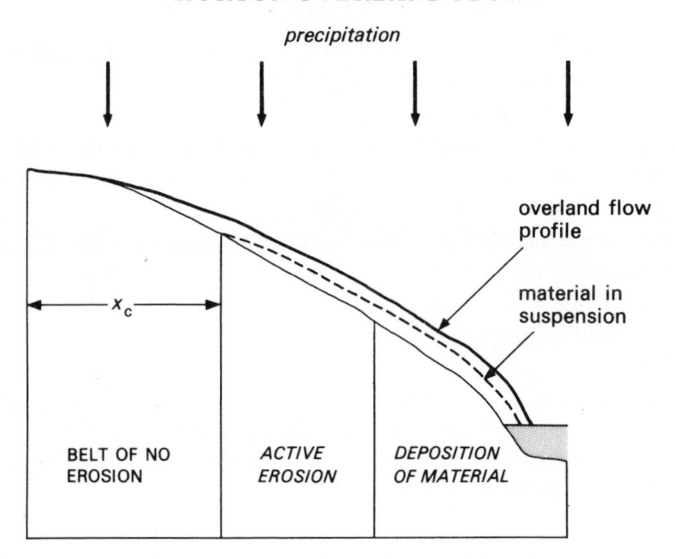

Figure 2.3 The form of hillslope overland flow according to the model of Horton (after Horton 1945).

erate slopes surface depressions can hold the equivalent of 0.25–0.50 in (6.35–12.70 mm) of water but Chow (1964) later estimated that bare smooth surfaces stored between 0.20 in (5.1 mm) and 0.10 in (2.5 mm) of water for sand and clay respectively. Horton considered this surface runoff to be the sole contribution to the storm runoff hydrograph peak and to be solely responsible for surface fluvial erosion. At a critical distance downslope from the divide the depth of overland flow would become sufficient to generate a shear stress competent to entrain the surface soil particles and erosion would occur in the form of rills. These rills might eventually form new channels. The sequence of events involved in this process has been listed by Cook (1946) as follows:

(a) A thin water layer forms on the surface and downslope surface flow is initiated.
(b) The flowing water accumulates in surface depressions.
(c) When full these depressions begin to overflow.
(d) Overland flow enters microchannels which coalesce to form rivulets which discharge into small gullies. This continues until discharge into major channels occurs.
(e) Along each microchannel, lateral inflow from the land surface takes place.

Slope form influences the operation of these processes in a fundamental way. Hack and Goodlett (1960) classified slopes within a drainage basin and noted different relationships with surface runoff (Fig. 2.4). Runoff on

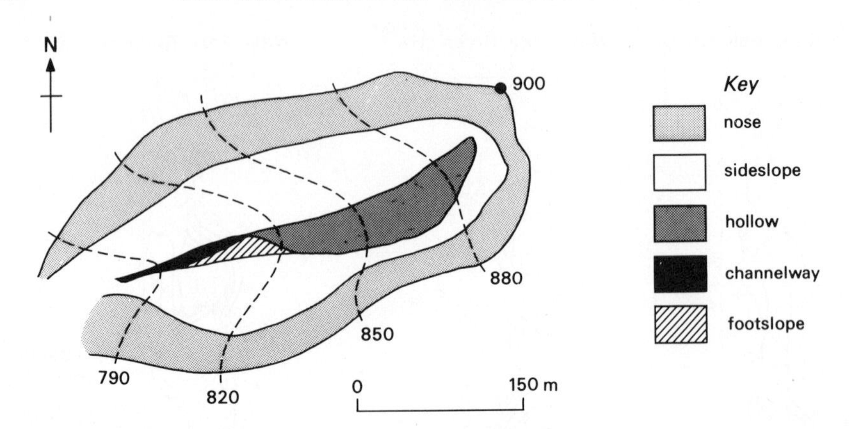

Figure 2.4 Classification of slope areas in the Crawford Mountains, central Appalachians (after Hack & Goodlett 1960).

the nose slopes or spurs was proportional to a function of the radius of curvature of the contours. On the sideslopes, runoff was proportional to a linear function of slope length and in the hollows was proportional to a power function of slope length. In the channelway, runoff was proportional to a power function of channel length whilst the footslope was transitional between sideslope and channelway.

Overland flow can be simulated relatively easily in the field. A classic series of experiments have been conducted in North America by Emmett (1978). Each field site was sprinkled with artificial rain at an intensity of approximately 200 mm/h (8 in/h) which generated runoff of about 100 mm/h (4 in/h). Flow rarely occurred as a uniform sheet of water and the majority of the water travelled downslope in several lateral concentrations of flow. But these concentrations were not considered to be rill flow, and it is generally accepted that they possess the characteristics of sheet flow. Each site exhibited a unique flow pattern dependent on the physical characteristics of the slope. Runoff from some of the sites was also characterised by surface detention in a series of puddles formed by barrier dams of organic debris. Surface runoff occurred partly by a succession of failures of these barriers. Three of the sites are shown in Figure 2.5 where the lines show only the major concentrations of flow and not all of the flow. Pole Creek site 1 was relatively free of topographic irregularities and surface runoff was essentially downslope with the flow pattern in the lower half of the plot according well with the curvature of the contours. The ground slope at New Fork River site 1 was flat enough for small microrelief features to be obvious on the topographic map. These features were readily discernible in the resulting flow patterns. The gradient at the lower end of the plot was such that water was ponded in the lower 0.6 m of the slope. Sediment was also deposited indicating the effectiveness of this type of overland flow in eroding and transporting sediments. These sediments

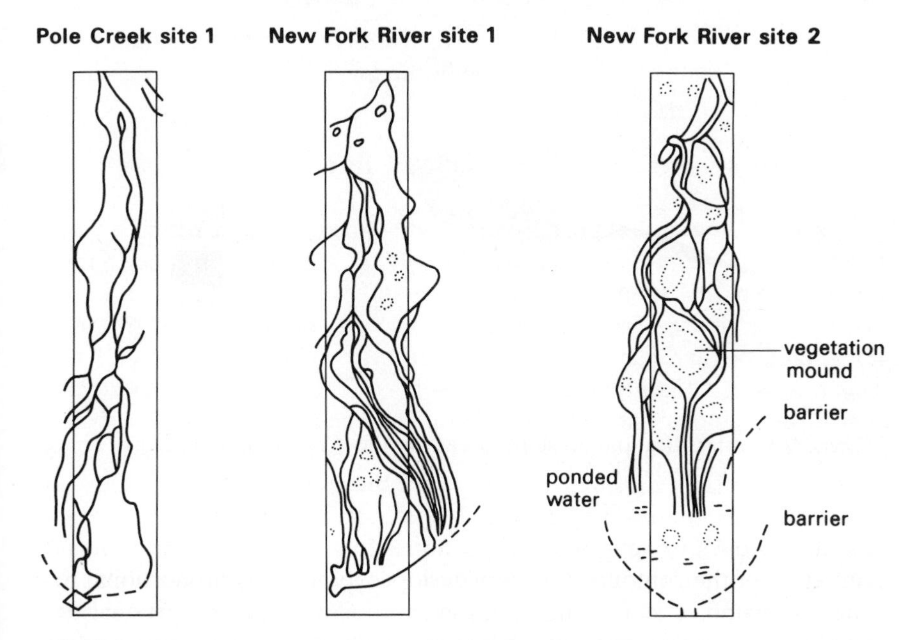

Figure 2.5 Overland flow patterns for three experimental sites (from Emmett 1970).

were derived as sheetwash since no rilling was observed. New Fork site 2 was the gentlest of the slopes analysed. Considerable microrelief existed on these slopes and flow was directed around the topographic highs. Water was also ponded in the lower portions with the deposition of sediment.

These experiments show that given the right rainfall conditions and surface characteristics overland flow as suggested by Horton can be very important. But, Chorley (1978) has suggested it was fortunate that some of the most influential work being carried out not long after Horton's 1945 paper was on small, unvegetated drainage basins, with short slopes, little soil cover and low infiltration capacities (e.g. Schumm 1956a & b). However, in 1947, Kirkham was already suggesting that during intense precipitation water infiltrated downwards into the soil near the top of the hill, horizontally outwards over the middle of the slope and vertically upwards near the hillslope base due to the downward seepage over the higher parts of the slope. Surface water movement would then tend to occur on the lower slopes. Since then it has been shown that, where there is appreciable soil and vegetation cover, little Horton overland flow will occur. Tischendorf (1969) observed 55 storm events in the south-eastern Piedmont in 1967 and 1968 and observed no overland flow; results which were substantiated by Rawitz *et al*. (1970) in Pennsylvania. Horton overland flow will occur relatively instantaneously over a basin only if the basin is small and has homogeneous soil, soil moisture, interception, depression storage and infiltration conditions. Much more important is the diffuse downslope movement of water through the soil layers.

Throughflow and saturated overland flow

It is now recognised that the downslope movement of water within the soil layers is more important than overland flow, especially in most humid regions where the supply of humus and the effects of microfauna create an open soil structure. This movement has been variously termed throughflow, interflow and lateral flow. The term throughflow will be used here. This means that the properties of the soil assume a rather greater significance, thus, Hoover and Hursh (1943) concluded that soil characteristics were more important in controlling runoff than basin morphometry. The physical properties and depth of the soil are the most important controls on the production of subsurface flow. Vertical flow within the soil usually dominates in coarse-textured soils. If the soils are fine-textured silts and clays, resistance to vertical flow occurs and downslope subsurface throughflow is initiated. The structure of the soil is also critical. Fissures, cracks and channels are of lesser importance in coarse-textured soils but, in fine-textured soils, they largely replace textural voids as the main avenues for flow. Their significance is enhanced if the cracks and channels penetrate different soil layers and textural discontinuities.

Throughflow is considerably enhanced by differing permeabilities at depth. These hydraulic discontinuities are usually caused by specific soil horizons, illuvial hardpans, zones of partially weathered bedrock or, perhaps, layers of unweathered rock. Ruxton and Berry (1961) have stressed the hydrological significance of the basal surface of weathering on granitic rocks in Hong Kong. In many parts of the western uplands of the British Isles the major impeding horizon is the iron pan found in many podzols. Typical of these areas is Dartmoor where the iron pan layer, although discontinuous, has a considerable effect on moisture distribution and is an initiator of throughflow. Even when there are no obvious discontinuities in the soil, subtle differences in the proportions of solid matter and water occur which may be sufficient to initiate the movement of water downslope.

The detailed action of throughflow has been investigated in a number of ways. One of these involves field monitoring of slopes under conditions of natural or artificial rainfall. Whipkey (1969) measured flow within the soil resulting from a simulated storm of 5.1 cm/h lasting two hours on a 16° (29%) slope. His results are summarised in Figure 2.6. The small surface flow of Hortonian type resulted from a low initial infiltration capacity of the dry surface soil which, however, rapidly increased with wetting. A less permeable zone existed in the soil at about 90 cm and the lag before throughflow begins is the time taken for water to infiltrate to this layer.

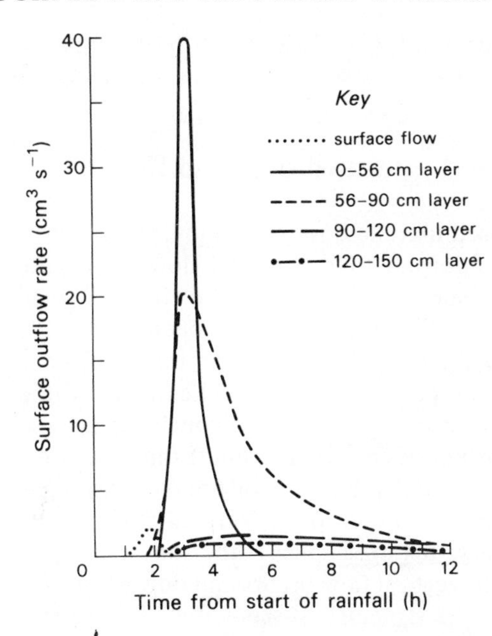

Figure 2.6 An example of discharge hydrographs of flow within the soil (after Whipkey 1965).

This type of study has been extended to encompass entire drainage basins and the three most important of these have been summarised by Chorley (1978). They are the Whitehall Watershed, a 60 acre forested catchment in the southern Piedmont of the USA (Tischendorf 1969), Sleepers River experimental watershed in Vermont (Dunne and Black 1970) and East Twin Brook, a 0.21 km^2 basin in Somerset (Weyman 1970). In the Whitehall Watershed only 19 out of 55 observed storm events produced peaked direct runoff not attributable to direct channel precipitation. Soil moisture response took place in the top metre of soil near stream channels. Maximum throughflow peaks, in the East Twin Brook, occurred in the B horizon. Runoff processes were simulated in the Sleepers River catchment and the sequence of events during a 54 mm, 3.5 h rainstorm are shown in Figure 2.7. This emphasises that the movement of water across the slope surface is related to the growth of the saturated wedge at the slope base. Early in the storm the saturated area is close to the surface and throughflow or subsurface storm flow (SSSF) has just begun. Eventually the saturated area intersects the ground surface over the lower part of the slope and return flow (RF) is initiated. This type of overland flow is augmented by direct precipitation (DPS) onto the saturated area. As the storm continues the saturated wedge increases upslope and the amount of surface flow also increases. When the storm ceases there is a very sudden drop in the contribution of direct precipitation water to the

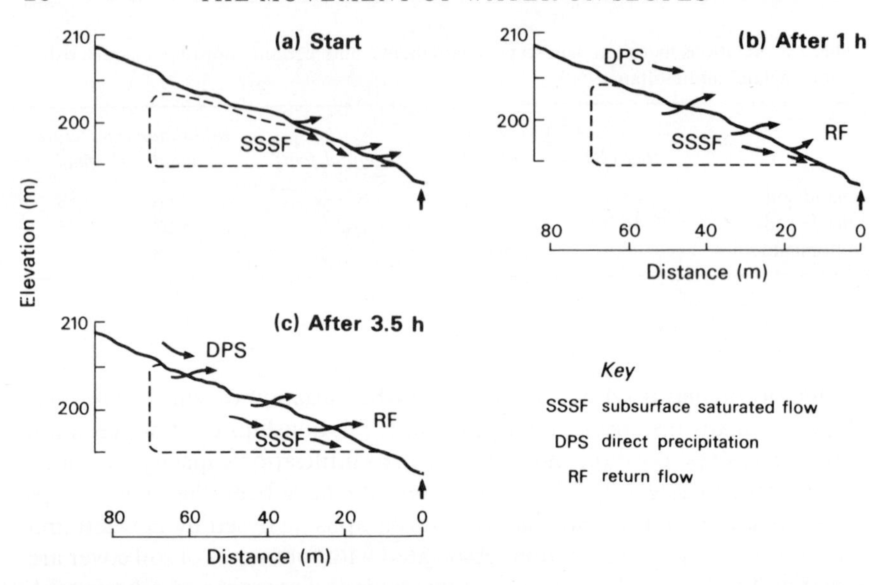

Figure 2.7 Runoff processes during a 54 mm, 3.5 h rainstorm in the Sleepers Watershed, Vermont (from Dunne 1978).

surface flow and the return flow also decreases very rapidly. But subsurface flow continues for a long time. Fluctuations in the area contributing to flow are related to topography, soils, antecedent moisture and rainfall characteristics so that different parts of slopes and drainage basins vary in the magnitude of the storm required to bring the water table to the surface (Table 2.2).

The spatial variation of soil moisture is, clearly, a significant factor in these processes. Kirkby and Chorley (1967) suggested that maximum water flow would occur in four areas: at the base of slopes, in hollows, in slope profile concavities and in areas of thin or less permeable soils. This is substantiated by the work of Anderson and Burt (1978) which vividly demonstrated the role of hollows as against spurs in providing hillslope discharge.

Table 2.2 Approximate recurrence intervals of storms producing runoff from different parts of a 3.9 ha basin in Vermont (from Dunne 1978).

Drainage basin component	*Recurrence interval of runoff producing events (yr)*
lower part of valley floor	10^{-2}
upper part of valley floor	10^{-1}
lower part of shallow, moist swale	10^{-1}
upper part of shallow, moist swale	1
lower, concave portion of well drained hillside	10^{1}–10^{2}
straight well drained hillside	10^{2}–10^{3}

Table 2.3 Relations between landscape components and certain moisture characteristics (from England and Holtan 1969).

	Watershed area (%)	*Average slope (%)*	*Storage potential (cm)*	*Infiltration rates (cm/h)* initial	*final*
upland soils	44.4	35.6	8.6	14.66	0.58
hillside soils	46.7	12.7	3.8	5.03	0.25
bottomland soils	8.9	61.0	14.2	28.88	0.58

One of the major influencing factors is the variation of soil thickness on slopes. In many instances simple systematic relationships exist between soil properties, slope position and factors such as infiltration capacity and moisture storage (Table 2.3). Rather more specific have been the relationships between soil thickness and channel hydrographs analysed by Hewlett and Nutter (1970). The hydrographs associated with four types of soil cover are illustrated in Figure 2.8. Type (a) represents the response of a basin with

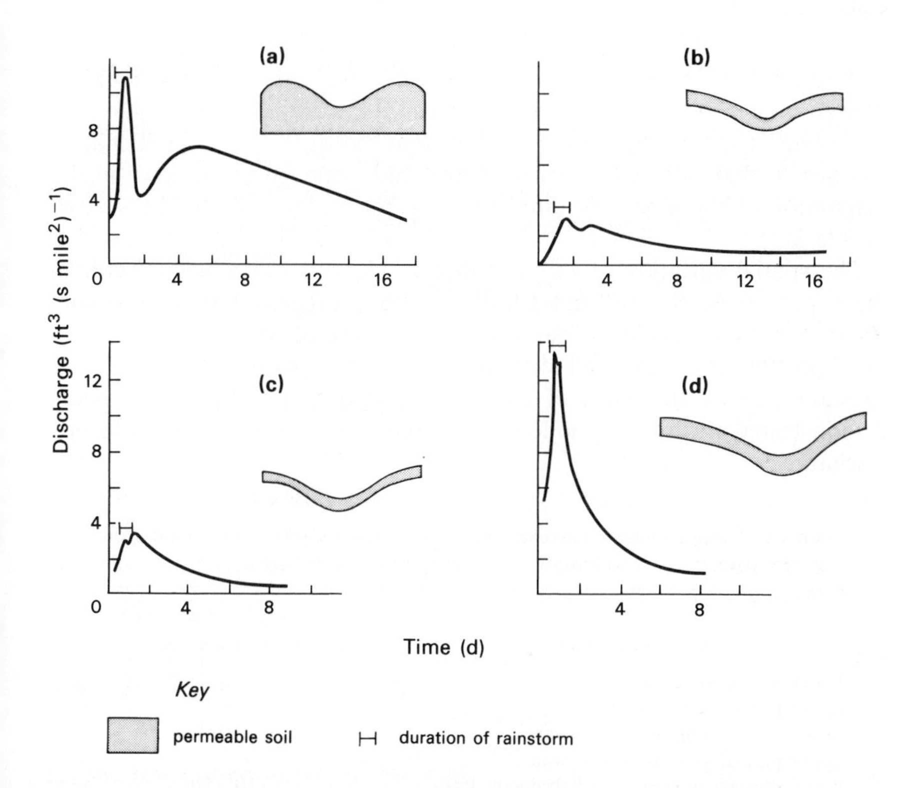

Figure 2.8 Hydrographs associated with different types of soil cover (after Hewlett & Nutter 1970, Chorley 1978).

deep volcanic ash soils from the Kimakia Basin, Kenya following a rainstorm of 61 mm in 24 h. Type (b) is the response of the Wagon Wheel Gap Basin, Colorado following a rainstorm of 80 mm in 24 h. This basin perhaps possesses deep soils on the divides but thin soils on the valley slopes. Type (c) represents a basin with shallow soils and is the Whitehall Watershed, Georgia. There is a zone of restricted permeability in these soils at 1–2 m depth and the hydrograph is in response to 27 mm of rain in 8 h. Type (d) possesses deep soils in the divides and valley bottoms but shallower soils on the main valley slopes and is the Coweeta 17 Basin in North Carolina. The 32 mm rainstorm in 6 h produced a well-marked initial peak caused by channel flow and non-Hortonian flow from the expanded source area, which would have been obliterated by the main rising limb if the rainfall had been of longer duration and lower intensity. The small proportion of rainfall involved in quickflow and the marked delay of the runoff until after cessation of rain show that the majority of stormflow is not derived from simple overland flow. Also, soil depth is usually considerably more variable and, even if trends can be identified, the distribution and movement of water on slopes is extremely complicated.

These results have considerable significance for both soil and landscape evolution. The spatial variation in overland flow governs the zones of potential soil movement and incipient gully formation. The differential concentration of moisture in the soil makes certain parts of the slope more susceptible to mass movements such as debris flows and rotational landslips. Therefore, knowledge of surface and subsurface flow characteristics is crucial to establishing the relationships between soils and slopes.

On the basis of these and similar studies in temperate areas certain generalisations can be made (Dunne 1978). These are:

(a) In most rainstorms Horton overland flow does not occur.

(b) The major processes contributing to stormflow are subsurface stormflow, return flow and direct precipitation onto saturated areas.

(c) The relative importance of these processes varies with soil and topography. Unfilled soil storage capacity varies from zero in channel depressions to small in shallow swales and large on steep well-drained hillslopes.

(d) During short-interval rainstorms most stormflow comes from direct precipitation onto saturated areas around the channels. These saturated areas also vary with the season.

(e) During large rainstorms, subsurface stormflow increases and can be observed in deep well-drained soils on steep slopes. The saturated areas expand greatly, especially in the hollows.

Concentrated throughflow or pipe flow

Piping has been recorded in many areas of the world and clearly provides a macropore network for the quick transmission of throughflow. Pipe networks are usually discontinuous and may discharge onto the same slope segment as the pipe inlets (Fig. 2.9). Jones (1971) has noted several areas in the British Isles where piping is important. One of these areas was upland Wales and detailed investigations of pipe networks in this region by the Institute of Hydrology have provided a great deal of information on the subject (Gilman & Newson 1980). Some of the pipes were up to 0.6 m wide and the mean cross-sectional area of pipes in part of the Wye catchment was found to be 67.5 cm^2. This work has shown that it is possible to predict where throughflow and pipe flow will occur by examining certain soil properties. Soil and site properties, such as drainage, depth to impermeable horizons, permeability and slope angle, were used to derive an index known as the 'winter rain acceptance potential' (WRAP). This

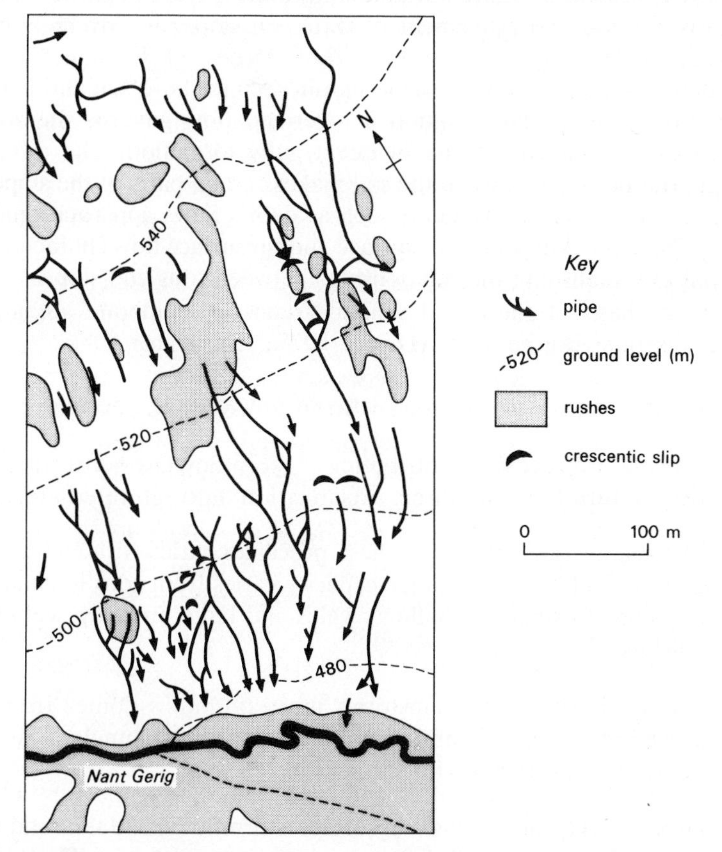

Figure 2.9 Pipe network in the lower Nant Gerig Valley, central Wales (from Gilman & Newson 1980).

index enables the soils most likely to permit throughflow and pipe flow to be identified. Soils most likely to produce pipes are either those with peaty surface horizons and impermeable layers at shallow depth or those where surface horizons are loamy and the slope steep.

Eluviation and desiccation are the processes thought most likely to produce pipes. Eluviation allows the fine fraction to be removed progressively through the soil matrix. This is indicated by the deposition of clay and silt where the pipes emerge. But, eluviation sufficient to lead to the creation of pipes only occurs in soils possessing an initial weakness caused by low bulk density, an unusual particle size distribution or a structure which has been altered by chemical effects. Also, the aggregation–dispersion status of the soil seems to be important. Other workers have argued that pre-existing voids are necessary for the development of pipes.

The literature on the creation of pipes by desiccation is extensive (e.g. Henkel *et al*. 1938, Heede 1971, Hughes 1972, Rathjens 1973). The precise manner of formation is still uncertain since desiccation cracking is a complicated process depending on a number of soil properties such as strength and shrinkage potential. This depends largely on the type and amount of clay minerals present. Thus, Parker (1964) considered the enlargement of desiccation cracks was the principal mechanism of piping in cohesive clay soils whilst eluviation was important in cohesionless materials. Piping appears to be particularly prevalent in semi-arid regions where the regolith contains clays such as montmorillonite which crack on drying. Desiccation cracking is also thought to be the initiating mechanism in upland Wales (Gilman & Newson 1980).

Pipes are important hydrologically because they reduce considerably the lag time of peak flood runoff in small catchments. Geomorphologically, pipes are responsible for the movement of silt and clay particles downslope in areas where surface processes are mainly ineffectual. Also, dissection of blanket peat may be initiated by subsurface erosion. In arid and semi-arid areas pipes quite frequently develop into gully systems.

A slightly different form of concentrated throughflow has been demonstrated by Bunting (1961). Many upland slopes possess seepage lines which are not apparent on the surface because they possess neither surface nor vegetational expression. Bunting discovered these seepage zones by a closely spaced grid of auger borings and termed them percolines. Major soil differences were discovered between the percolines and the intervening areas. The upper humic layers were always thicker in the percolines, as was the soil in general. The soils in Bunting's study were podzols and humic staining of the bleached sand layer was always quite marked in the percolines. This was taken to indicate a predominantly vertical component of seepage moisture movement. Percolines pass downslope into visible seepage lines and corrosion of bedrock in these hollows may be a major factor in the headward extension of first-order streams.

This chapter has been concerned simply with the movement of water on and across slopes. But observations and simulated experiments have shown that considerable quantities of soil material are also moved. This is especially true of concentrated flow where the dividing line between subsurface piping or seepage, and surface linear erosion or gullying is thin. The next chapter, therefore, examines the various ways in which soil can be moved and redistributed on slopes.

3 The movement of soil on slopes

Materials can be moved across slopes in a variety of ways. The main processes involved are rainsplash, surface wash, solution and mass movement. These processes are all influenced, to some extent, by factors of topography and soil. Wind action is the only other major process of soil removal and, although extremely important in many areas, is not examined in as much detail as the other processes because it is not influenced in the same way by factors of topography and slope angle. The relative importance and interaction of the processes are largely, but not entirely, governed by climate. Under tropical rainforest conditions the removal of material in solution is extremely important. In dry savanna areas, wash is important but as rainfall increases so does vegetation cover and wash rates are reduced to a minimum value near the savanna/rainforest boundary. Mass movement will be important on steep slopes everywhere but the more intense rainfalls in the tropics lead to greater degradation by mass movement. Soil creep processes are probably of greater relative importance in temperate areas where soil wash is minimal.

The interaction of the various processes in any specific site can be extremely complicated as Schumm (1956a & b, 1964) has shown in a series of papers. In the bare badland topography in which he was working, frost action broke up the soil surface during the winter months. At the start of the spring rains the soil aggregates were broken up by raindrop impact and washed into the frost cracks produced during the winter, partially closing them. This produced an impermeable crust which initiated a great amount of runoff and rill action. Frost action in the succeeding winter again obliterated the rill patterns by breaking up the surface. This situation emphasises the danger of employing gross climatic generalisations because during the winter months infiltration rates were high, runoff negligible and the processes were characteristic of humid temperate areas. During late summer, infiltration was reduced, runoff rates were high and the surface processes were more characteristic of those in semi-arid areas. Many of the severely eroded areas in Iceland exhibit the same characteristics. Frost action in winter prepares the surface for wind and water removal in the summer and autumn months. But raindrop impact temporarily halts these processes by producing a thin crust which eventually dries out and is blown away. The rills become infilled with wind blown material which is flushed out of the system during the next heavy rainstorm. The process of rill formation is aided by the collapse of near-surface pipes which are common in loessic material. A series of changes thus takes place throughout the year as local conditions vary and it is difficult to examine the processes in isolation. But, in order to simplify complex phenomena, the processes will be treated separately.

Surface water erosion

Universal soil loss equation

Early research into the variables affecting soil loss allowed Musgrave (1947) to derive the following equation:

$$E = IRS^{1.35}L^{0.35}P_{30}^{1.75}$$

where

E = soil loss (acre/in)
I = erodibility of the soil (in)
R = cover factor
S = slope (per cent)
L = length of slope (feet)
P_{30} = maximum 30-min rainfall amount, 2-yr frequency (in)

Since the development of this equation a considerable amount of research has been directed towards the establishment of a universal soil loss equation, the main aim of which was to define the main controlling factors. This resulted in the following:

$$A = RKLSCP$$

where

A = average annual soil loss
R = rainfall factor
K = soil erodibility factor
L = slope length factor
S = slope steepness factor
C = cropping and management factor
P = conservation practice

Many of these variables have now been standardised to enable the equation to be used in a variety of circumstances. Soil erodibility is a function of the intrinsic characteristics of the soil properties. Soil particles have first to be detached before they can be entrained and transported.

Both raindrop impact, or rainsplash, and flowing water will achieve this. The nature of the ultimate soil movement depends on the relationship between the erosivity of raindrops and running water and the erodibility of the soil material.

Soil erodibility

Variation in soil properties is one of the major influences on soil erosion. Soil erodibility, a term first used by Cook (1946), can be assessed by measuring soil loss under controlled conditions and by identifying soil properties as indices of erodibility. It is a largely 'hit or miss' process depending, as it does, on choosing certain soil properties and then arranging them in a variety of ratios to achieve the best statistical 'fit' with measured soil loss. Although certain theoretical assumptions are involved, one can never be certain that the correct soil properties have been used. Also, many of the relationships are site specific and not necessarily applicable in a wider context.

Most of the erodibility indices that have been developed are based on properties affecting soil dispersion, soil aggregation, aggregate stability and the transmission of water. Aggregate size distribution is important because aggregates below a certain size will be removed intact by water. Aggregate size also influences water transmission. Aggregate stability governs the ease with which large aggregates will be broken down to small aggregates and become susceptible to erosion. Disruptive forces occurring in aggregates on wetting are attributed to the swelling of oriented clay and to the compression of trapped air. A negative correlation between degree of clay orientation and aggregate stability was found in the soils of northern Luxembourg (Imeson & Jungerius 1976). The disruptive forces can be balanced by organic matter strengthening the bonds between clay and quartz particles. Conaway and Strickling (1962) tested 24 indices of aggregate stability and found that the percentage weights of water-stable aggregates greater than 0.5 mm and greater than 2 mm diameter were the most reliable measures. The more commonly used soil erodibility indices were tested for their relative efficiency on soils in the Peak District, Derbyshire, England, and Alberta, Canada by Bryan (1969, 1977). These indices, together with several measures of aggregation added by Bryan, are listed in Table 3.1; definitions of the indices are given in the glossary. The results demonstrated that none of the indices were simple to measure and reliable in operation but that indices involving estimates of aggregate stability were the most efficient.

Many of the assumptions behind the early indices can be questioned. Middleton's dispersion ratio is based on the assumption that only material which is in a dispersed condition can be eroded. But this makes no allowance for high velocity raindrops being able to disperse undispersed material and, while it may be accurate for soils with a high silt–clay content, it

Table 3.1 Most commonly used erodibility indices (from Bryan 1977).

dispersion ratio (Middleton 1930)
erosion ratio (Middleton 1930)
clay ratio (Bouyoucos 1935)
surface-aggregation ratio (Anderson 1954)
water-stable aggregates (WSA) : > 3 mm, > 2 mm, > 1 mm, > 0.5 mm
slaking loss
slaking loss/WSA : > 2 mm
moisture equivalent : > 2 mm
dry aggregates > 3 mm, 2–3 mm

will be inefficient for soils with a high sand content. The limitations of the erosion ratio stem from the use of the colloid content : moisture equivalent ratio as an index of water transmission. Colloid content and moisture equivalent are very closely related and it is difficult to know what the ratio measures. The use of either one on its own may well be more accurate. The clay ratio becomes meaningless when the clay content of the soil is very low; it also attaches great importance to clay as a binding agent and ignores the influence of organic matter. Similar criticisms can be levelled at the surface : aggregation ratio. Organic matter is omitted from the binding fraction and there is no evidence that silt possesses a binding function; the reverse might be true.

Results on the Canadian soils showed that wash loss substantially exceeded splash loss and that splash-entrained, wash-transported material was the dominant form of erosion. But wash loss did not show the same correlation with soil properties as splash loss. This suggests that a large amount of wash-loss material is entrained by wash. Surface microrelief disturbs the flow, eddies are generated and patterns of stress around large particles become complex. Entrainment is, therefore, more effective.

Rainsplash detachment and transport

The nature and effect of the rainsplash process depend on the relations between rainfall characteristics and the nature of the soil and groundsurface. The critical properties of rainfall are its duration and intensity, and raindrop mass, size and terminal velocity. These variables affect the kinetic energy and momentum of the rainfall. The median size of raindrops increases with rainfall intensity for low- and medium-intensity falls, but declines slightly for high-intensity rainfalls. There have been numerous attempts to relate factors such as kinetic energy to soilsplash and to devise the best index of rainfall intensity. Free (1960) established that the splash erosion of soil was proportional to the 1.46 power of kinetic energy. Bisal (1960) established that:

$$G = kDV^{1.4}$$

where

G = weight of soil splashed (in grams)
k = a constant for particular soil types
D = raindrop diameter (mm)
V = impact velocity (m/sec)

In 1945 Ellison produced the formula:

$$E = kV^{4.33}d^{1.07}I^{0.63}$$

where

k = a constant for the type of soil
V = velocity of raindrops
d = raindrop diameter
I = rainfall intensity

Since 1945 there have been many attempts to devise the best index of rainfall intensity. Foster (1950), after a comparison of nine such indices, found that the best was:

$$\text{index} = I_{15}I_{30}(bn)^{1/3}$$

where

I_{15} = maximum 15-min intensity
I_{30} = maximum 30-min intensity
b = function of the moisture content/infiltration relationship and storm intensity curve
n = number of peaks of intensity exceeding a given value

At the same time as these attempts were being made to devise indices of raindrop erosivity, other studies were concerned with understanding the nature of rainsplash detachment and transportation. Splash leads to the piling and burying of the topsoil causing changes in the physical condition of the soil. One of these changes is the creation of a surface crust (McIntyre 1958). Initially soil aggregates are broken down by slaking or direct raindrop impact. Fine particles are moved into the upper few centimetres of the soil and deposited in the pores. The use of high speed photographic techniques has shown that when the soil surface is covered with water, the water surface is kicked back and vertically into a crown by raindrop impact, which is initially closed at the top but which bursts on descent. An outward water wave followed by a return wave is created which causes soil distur-

Table 3.2 Relative erodibility of 4–5 mm aggregates from different slope positions under forest and farmland (from Imeson & Jungerius 1976).

Slope unit	*Aggregates surviving test (%)*	*Reduction in weight (%)*	*Organic material (%)*	*Material (g) splashed from cup after 50 drops*
Forest				
0–2°	90	22	7.8	0.13
2–5°	50	56	10.2	0.15
5–11°	90	35	6.1	0.014
11°	75	35	8.6	0.62
Arable				
0–2°	5	96	4.0	0.36
2–5°	0	100	3.7	0.55
5–11°	5	95	4.0	0.83

bance and temporarily destroys the soil crust. The full sequence can now be described: the initial wetting of the surface lowers the cohesion and there is a high soil splash rate; a surface crust then develops and the splash rate decreases; water accumulates on the surface which, by turbulent action, can remove part of the crust; the permeability of the soil is temporarily increased, percolation occurs and the soil splash rate increases again. Palmer (1963) has shown that splash loss increases with water layer depth up to a threshold equal to the diameter of the raindrops and thereafter decreases. But a stage will be reached when so much material has been washed into the soil surface that the removal of the surface seal will have little effect on the infiltration rate, surface water will be maintained and runoff occurs.

Interesting insights into the factors involved have been provided by Imeson and Jungerius (1976) in their study of the way in which aggregates of forest and arable soils differed in their composition and response to raindrop impact. Few arable soil aggregates survived the water drop test but most forest ones did (Table 3.2). Differences in the composition of the aggregates may explain the different response to raindrop impact (Table 3.3). The biological activity of the forest soils produces a large number of primary aggregates and much root tissue which probably increases the resistance of the soil. In contrast, the greater amount of oriented clay in arable soils is crucial because of the forces exerted during expansion on wetting. The greater organic matter content of the forest soils produces greater binding and the aggregates are more resistant. The study also showed that the aggregates found in the colluvium beneath the arable soils were too weak to have survived transport by splash, the implication being that slope wash was the process involved.

The direct measurement of soilsplash has been attempted by installing splash boards with collecting troughs (Ellison 1944), by embedding small funnels to catch splashed particles (Bolline 1976) and by using radioactive

Table 3.3 Composition of aggregates under forest and farmland (from Imeson & Jungerius 1976).

	Slope class (forest)				*Slope class (farmland)*		
	0–2°	*2–5°*	*5–11°*	*11°*	*0–2°*	*2–5°*	*5–11°*
planes	4	15	5	11	22	20	49
channels	29	158	25	91	48	115	37
vughs	74	43	30	48	81	32	83
zones of oriented clay	19	22	50	16	128	75	56
charcoal	114	191	89	78	46	52	90
humus particles	92	87	123	123	143	122	93
living tissue	64	21	60	37	12	7	10
rock fragments	11	20	7	14	20	20	12
primary aggregates	39	50	37	55	11	10	19
secondary aggregates	52	193	38	93	56	110	77

tracers (Coutts *et al*. 1968). Morgan (1978) adapted splash cups, normally used in laboratory experiments, to measure splash erosion on sandy soils in mid-Bedfordshire, England. The results, summarised in Table 3.4, confirm the relationships between splash erosion, rainfall energy and slope angle obtained by other workers under laboratory conditions. Only 0.06% of the rainfall energy contributed to splash erosion. The major role of splash is to detach soil particles prior to their removal by overland flow, confirming Morgan's (1977) work on other soils where transport of particles by rain-splash accounted for less than 5% of the material being eroded from the hillsides. Thus, except in certain circumstances, erosion by rainsplash is subordinate to that by surface wash.

Table 3.4 Rates of splash erosion (from Morgan 1978).

Site	*Slope length (m)*	*Slope angle (deg)*		*Annual total (kg m^{-2})*
1	172	9	T	2.73
(topslope)			D	23.32
2	193	11	T	6.81
(midslope)			D	14.70
3	201	11	T	5.11
(lower slope)			D	22.79
4	178	8	T	4.93
(topslope)			D	28.42
5	195	11	T	3.59
(midslope)			D	30.47
6	209	6	T	3.02
(lower slope)			D	14.87

T = splash transport; D = splash detachment.

Surface wash

The previous chapter described how flowing water could be initiated on slopes either by rainfall intensities exceeding the local infiltration capacity (Horton overland flow) or by localised saturated conditions (saturated overland flow). It was also seen how microtopography influences the type of surface flow that takes place. Unconcentrated flow in thin sheets is only possible on fairly smooth surfaces. Emmett (1970) found that sheetflow or wash varied greatly in character and depth and was a mixture of laminar and turbulent flow. Kilinc and Richardson (1973) assessed flow to be supercritical laminar but flow rarely remains uniform and concentrations develop around even the smallest microrelief features.

The erosive capability of unconcentrated flow will be slight and only very fine material will be transported. This will be material already partially loosened by weathering such as by wetting and drying cycles, freeze/thaw activity or raindrop impact. Most natural surfaces are too rough to allow substantial amounts of uniform flow and where local flow concentrations occur there may be some erosion. But, flow concentrations are usually too local and too brief to produce true channels. Vegetation will inhibit overland flow and erosion will be concentrated at breaks in the vegetation cover. Bare scars in the vegetation cover can be caused by mass movement and is one way in which the two sets of processes interact and reinforce one another.

The more intense flows will erode small channels or gullies, the shallowest of which will migrate across the hillside so that the whole slope is affected. Rills are small channels only a few centimetres wide and deep and are very ephemeral features that are destroyed by a variety of processes; they are usually associated with silt or clay soils. Occasionally they may grow large enough to escape destruction and a gully is formed. Channels on sands and gravels tend to be more braided with coarse debris frequently deposited as bars in the centre of the flows. These, in turn, divert the flow into many channels. If master rills develop into substantial gullies, they will lead eventually to the creation of new rills on the gully sides when incision has reached a critical depth. Subsurface flow is also attracted and piping may be initiated.

There are great differences between rates of surface wash on vegetated and unvegetated slopes since vegetation is probably the most important single factor in determining the rate of transport. Vegetation intercepts precipitation, thus lessening the impact of raindrops, and prevents the formation of a compacted layer. Vegetation also improves soil structure and increases the infiltration rate. Once surface flow has commenced, vegetation interrupts overland flow and may physically bind the soil, inhibiting surface erosion. Thus, in humid temperate regions with complete vegetation cover and moderate rainfall intensities, rates of surface wash are extremely low. Carson and Kirkby (1972), using data from Young (1958) and Kirkby (1963), have estimated that on 80% of the sites examined, transport by wash was less than 0.20 $cm^3/cm/yr$. In New Zealand, on slopes covered by Tussock grass, Soons (1971) found wash rates ranging from 0.13 to 5.6 $cm^3/cm/yr$, depending on slope angle. In this situation, major storms will be increasingly important in producing soil wash and it is necessary to calculate magnitude and frequency statistics for these high energy events. This produces complex relationships between rainfall amounts, frequency of occurrence and soil wash. Values of soil wash increase dramatically if vegetation cover is reduced by climate or human activity. On bare slopes at Perth Amboy, New Jersey, rates of soil transport ranged from 200 to 500 $cm^3/cm/yr$ (Schumm 1956a). Even this figure was exceeded by the 1050 $cm^3/cm/yr$ on 20–30° slopes in the Sacaton Mountains, Arizona (Leopold *et al.* 1966). After vegetation cover, topography is probably the major controlling factor on the amount of soil eroded by surface wash.

Effect of topography

Three main components of topography affect soil movement processes. These are slope steepness, slope length and slope shape. Erosion potential is greater on steep slopes because of the increased downslope component of gravity and is greater on long slopes because of a downslope increase in surface flow depth. Slope length is really a surrogate measure for distance from the slope crest or from the point at which flow commences. Several empirical relationships have been obtained relating soil transport by surface wash to slope length and slope gradient. Zingg (1940) obtained:

$$S \propto x^{1.6} \tan^{1.4} \beta$$

where

$$S = \text{soil transport (in cm}^3\text{/cm/yr)}$$
$$x = \text{slope length (in metres)}$$
$$\beta = \text{slope gradient}$$

Musgrave (1947) obtained the relationship:

$$S \propto x^{1.35} \tan^{1.35} \beta$$

and Kirkby (1969) obtained:

$$S \propto x^{1.73} \tan^{1.35} \beta$$

Many other experiments have shown that soil loss and slope angle are related by power functions with exponents ranging from 0.7 (Neal 1938) to

2 (Hudson & Jackson 1962). Most of the values fall between 1.35 and 1.5 and the similarity between them is a good indication that power laws provide reasonable empirical models. The exponent value varies with slope steepness (Horvath & Erodi 1962, Roose 1972) and with slope shape (D'Souza & Morgan 1976). Smith and Wischmeier (1957), however, established a polynomial relationship:

$$A = 0.43 + 0.30S + 0.043S^2$$

where

$$A = \text{soil loss (in ton/acre)}$$
$$S = \text{slope (per cent)}$$

The topographic function (LS) used in the universal soil loss equation has the relationship:

$$\text{LS} = \frac{L^{1/2}}{100}(0.76 + 0.53S + 0.076S^2)$$

where

$$L = \text{slope length (feet).}$$

This has been modified by Wischmeier (1975) to take into account changes at specific slope gradients. It has also been modified according to the standard 72.6 ft long slope used in the universal soil loss equation. This results in:

$$\text{LS} = m\,\frac{\lambda}{72.6}\,\frac{(430\sin^2\theta + 30\sin\theta + 0.43)}{6.574} \quad (\lambda = \text{constant})$$

where m is 0.5 if the slope is steeper than 4%, 0.4 for 4% slopes and 0.3 for slopes of 3% or less. The LS-values are for uniform gradients but they can be modified to account for the effects of slope irregularities (Foster & Wischmeier 1974, Wischmeier 1974).

Relationships between slope gradient and rainsplash transport are more difficult to assess. Data obtained by Kirkby in Arizona showed that, for specific particle sizes, downslope movement by splash was proportional to the sine of the slope angle. Net transport rate, however, showed no systematic increase with slope gradient because increases of gradient were offset by increases in grain size (Carson & Kirkby 1972).

The lack of detailed information makes the study by Bryan (1979) very important. He has established relationships between entrainment by sheetwash and rainsplash and slope angle under simulated rainfall on slopes varying in angle from 3° to 30°. These results support the conclusions of Horton (1945) and Smith and Wischmeier (1957) that when high slope angles are involved, polynomial functions are a better approximation. Splash loss from surfaces without appreciable surface water increased with slope angle but the relationship became more complex as soon as a water layer was formed. Tentative conclusions reached by Bryan (1979) were that splash transport would reach a peak just before overtopping of surface roughness elements occurred and, thereafter, would decline. As slope angle increased the effect of splash on flow properties declined. Overtopping of surface irregularities seemed to occur at angles between 15° and 18° and, therefore, splash effect increased to these apparent gradients and then declined. Much of the wash-transported material was entrained by the splash processes and wash increased steadily with slope angle. Major differences between slopes could be explained by soil differences.

The majority of studies of this nature have been conducted on slopes with fairly uniform gradients. However, there are marked differences between convex, concave and straight sections. Soil erosion on convex sections increases rapidly as slope steepness and slope length increase downslope (Meyer & Kramer 1969). Concave slopes by virtue of their shape tend to counteract the increased potential of greater downslope runoff by gentler angles. Slope gradient and runoff potential move in opposition. But this assumes that slope shape is influencing the nature of the runoff whereas there is another school of thought that argues that slope shape, especially the concave lower sections of slopes, are shaped by the runoff processes. In the study by Meyer and Kramer (1969) the maximum eroded depth was least on concave slopes, followed by uniform slopes, complex slopes and convex slopes. Similar results were obtained by Young and Mutchler (1969). Uniform and convex slopes did not differ significantly in the amount of soil lost but concave slopes were eroded less. But the convex slopes, which are normally found on the slope crests, had less soil eroded than would be expected because of shorter distances from the slope divides.

These examples stress that slope systems must be treated as a whole, with the mutual arrangement of the specific components of slope shape being significant. Many slopes are convex–concave or convex–straight–concave in form but many are more complicated than this and the number of possible combinations is great. Each combination will possess different runoff characteristics, as was stressed in Chapter 1. This only considers the one-dimensional slope profile and the plan shape of the slope is equally, if not more, important in affecting runoff processes. In the previous chapter it was seen how contour curvature and variations in soil thickness affected the location and intensity of saturated overland flow. Soil erosion processes will be affected in a similar manner as shown in the interesting study in Poland by Jahn (1963). Jahn found that on the steep upper parts of convex–concave slopes the soil was so severely eroded that unweathered loess was exposed at the surface. In contrast, the lower slope portions were covered with slopewash material. This study is also invaluable because it demonstrates the major distinction between concentrated and unconcentrated processes. Information provided by soil profiles and sediments indicated aggradation in the concave sections and erosion in the convex sections. But, if intensity of erosion is determined on the basis of the size and quantity of rills, the reverse was true; rills being more numerous on concavities. Thus, line degradation (rill erosion) was greater on concave sections but so too was accumulation by undifferentiated surface wash. The threshold between the two sets of processes is clearly of fundamental importance.

The movement of soil on slopes by surface wash is a complicated process and it has only been possible to outline, in the broadest sense, some of the factors involved. But an understanding of the processes involved and the factors that govern these processes is fundamental to explain soil type and distribution within the landscape. The movement of soil and water is an integral part of the catena concept which is examined in Chapter 4, as is the subsurface movement of soil which is now considered.

Subsurface water erosion

Water moves more slowly within the soil than over the surface. Throughflow velocities rarely reach 5 m/h and are usually much less. Material is moved physically by rolling or in suspension and chemically by solution, but the rate of flow within the soil means that chemical action will probably be the more important mechanism. The quantity of material moved is also limited by the size and arrangement of the soil pores. Space does not permit a detailed summary of all the factors involved and emphasis will be placed on the function and effect of soil, and relationships to topography and landforms.

Subsurface wash

Subsurface flow is mainly laminar and the major physical force involved is a viscous shear along the margins of the flow. The magnitude of this shear is proportional to the cross-sectional area of the pores. Resistance to movement within the soil is mainly due to cohesion and this, in the finer particles, is a result of electrochemical forces. The flowing water will produce some mixing and will physically shear the clay and other particles, but a particle will only move if pore spaces are larger than itself. The horizon differentiation of a normal soil profile is important in influencing the size and arrangement of pores, although, because of compaction by the weight of the soil, pore sizes will generally decrease with depth. Larger voids always occur at free faces and removal of soil particles through these voids may lead to new voids and the gradual destruction of the soil framework. This process may be one way of creating pipes or concentrated flow within the soil. It is also very similar to the soil creep process advocated by Culling (1963), described later. Water flow is quicker in pipe networks, thus more erosion and transport in suspension will take place but possibly less chemical action.

There have been few experiments designed to measure the amount of material passing through the soil in suspension. Scharpenseel and Kerpen (1967), using radioactive labelled clay, demonstrated that what little movement did occur appeared to be in the form of a pulse. Much of the material was trapped in the upper soil layers and became permanently fixed. Other studies have also indicated that particle transport, even of clay sizes, is very slow through capillary soil pores. Evidence for particulate movement is provided by a variety of micromorphological techniques which allow features, such as clay skins around larger particles, to be identified.

Transport in solution

It is difficult to separate material in true solution from very fine particles carried in a colloidal state as the term solution is often used for both states. Solution is a very effective transport agent as judged from the solute load of rivers. Some of the material leached from the upper soil horizon on steep slopes is not redeposited within the soil profile. Rapid movement of water through large pores ensures a low residence time within the soil and a limited opportunity for chemical reactions. In contrast, water in small pores may be stationary long enough for chemical reactions to occur. The role of pore size with respect to chemical reactions has been described by Lai and Jurinak (1972) and Wiklander (1964). The major factors in the solute removal system are the opportunity for mineral–water interaction, the length of time of the interaction and the chemical reaction rates. The interrelationships of these factors produce a complex system of chemical removal as the work of Boast (1973) and Kurtz and Melsted (1973) has shown.

Differences in rainfall frequency and intensity will influence the removal of solutes. Trudgill (1977) has differentiated four types of rainfall: low intensity–low frequency, low intensity–high frequency, high intensity–high frequency and high intensity–low frequency. The low intensity–low frequency rainfall type will be solutionally inoperative because, although solution will occur in the soil, little will be removed from the soil. Where the frequency is higher, as in the second rainfall type, water is supplied constantly enough for slow flow through the soil to occur as well as for solutes to be removed. The third type of rainfall is the optimum for the removal of rapidly dissolving constituents but the opposite for the removal of slowly dissolving minerals. The fourth rainfall type will enable all the constituents to be dissolved as the soil residence time of the water is longer. This type may be more efficient than the second type because of a greater flushing effect. The relationship between climate data and solution rates enabled Scrivner, Baker and Brees (1973) to predict soil profile formation.

Measurements of solute loads in rivers show that removal in solution may exceed that of all the mechanical processes combined. But dissolved matter in river water will include material from channel erosion and, if limestone is present, that derived from solution in subterranean channels as well as that derived from slopes. Nevertheless, as the review by Young (1974) indicates, in many environments as much material is removed from slopes in solution as by all other processes. The rate of chemical removal may be sufficient, under certain circumstances, to influence the slope form and the long-term evolution of the landscape. Ideas concerning the action of chemical removal have been incorporated, by Carson and Kirkby (1972), in a series of slope development models. Process-response models show that for similar assumed rates of solution loss and processes of downslope transport, slope retreat is greater on slopes dominated by solution (Young 1963).

Wind erosion

Wind deflation is an important process in many parts of the world and it can be disastrous for agricultural productivity. Pedologically it truncates the topsoil removing the finer particles, including organic matter. This affects the water holding and infiltration properties of soils and may lead to rill and gully erosion. In other areas, the redeposited material buries soil and vegetation creating complex soil profiles. Wind erosion is greatest in arid and semi-arid areas, especially where man has upset the natural balance. Such areas include the Great Plains of North America, the fringes of arid Africa, India and Australia and the steppes of western Siberia. In Iceland, severe wind erosion has been caused by overgrazing (Thorarinsson 1962). Wind erosion may also be locally important in humid areas when conditions are right such as in parts of East Anglia (Pollard & Miller 1968), East Yorkshire (Radley & Sims 1967) and Lincolnshire, England (Robinson 1969).

A great deal of work has been undertaken on the relationships between the dynamics of the wind system and the physical properties of surface soil. Much of this work has been done by Chepil and his associates (e.g. Chepil 1945, 1951 and 1955; Chepil & Milne 1941) culminating in the very important paper by Chepil and Woodruff (1963). Much of the following account relies on the results of these studies. The movement of particles by wind is also very thoroughly dealt with in Bagnold's classic book *The physics of blown sand and desert dunes* (1941).

The important wind variables are velocity, frequency, magnitude and duration. Surface factors include vegetation characteristics, such as height and density of plant cover, surface roughness and soil moisture status. Soil variables found to be important are particle size and cohesiveness (Smalley 1970), aggregate distribution and the amount of organic matter. Soil moisture enhances particle cohesion and inhibits erodibility. Chepil and Woodruff (1963) have shown that the relative amounts of sand, silt and clay are crucial to the erodibility status of soils. It seems that the first 5% of silt and clay combined with sand is equally effective in creating soil clods, but the behaviour of the clods is different. Clods formed of clay and sand are harder and less prone to abrasion by windborne particles than those of silt and sand. Above 5%, the silt fraction creates more clods but they are softer and more readily abraded than those formed of clay and sand. The greatest degree of mechanical stability is obtained in soils having 20–30% clay, 40–50% silt and 20–40% sand.

The size and frequency of non-erodible particles have a marked influence on the wind erosion process. As wind erosion progresses there comes a point where the non-erodible particles completely shelter erodible material and a wind-stable surface is created. The final stage can be defined by the critical surface barrier ratio which is the ratio of the height of non-erodible surface projections to the distance between projections which will barely prevent the movement of particles by the wind (Cooke & Doornkamp 1974).

A number of equations have been proposed to calibrate the wind erosion processes. Chepil and Woodruff (1963) demonstrated that the rate of soil movement, q (in g/cm/s), was described by the equation:

$$q = a(D_e)^{1/2} \frac{\rho}{g} (V_*^1)^3$$

where V_*^1 is the drag velocity above an eroding surface (cm/s), D_e is the average equivalent diameter of soil particles moved by the wind (cm), and ρ/g is the mass density of air. The coefficient a varies with the size distribution of erodible particles, the proportion of non-erodible factors and the soil moisture status.

An equation, similar to the universal soil loss equation, has also been suggested:

$$E = (I, K, C, L, V)$$

where

E = annual erosion
I = soil and slope erodibility index
K = soil roughness factor

C = local wind erosion climatic factor
L = length along prevailing wind erosion directions
V = equivalent quantity of vegetation cover

Because of the complexity of the variables each factor has to be treated separately and computer programs are often required (United States Department of Agriculture 1970). The climatic factor has been assessed by Yaalon and Ganor (1966) in the following terms:

$$C = \frac{v^3}{(P - E)^2}$$

where v is the average annual wind velocity (mile/hr) at a standard height of 10 m and $(P - E)$ is Thornthwaite's (1931) measure of precipitation effectiveness. Using this equation, Yaalon and Ganor were able to define wind erosion zones in Israel which coincided quite well with the arid and semi-arid areas.

Thus, the main variables in the wind erosion system are well known and the use of increasingly sophisticated computers makes accurate predictions of soil loss possible. Various remedial practices can then be put into operation.

Mass movement

Types of mass movement

Mass movement is a term which covers the movement of material on slopes under the influence of gravity without the benefit of a contributing force such as flowing water, ice or wind. Mass movement processes merge imperceptibly with those of mass transport in which a transporting agent is involved. Mass movements, themselves, form a continuous series ranging from free rockfalls to the slow creep of material on very low gradients and it is this continuity of movement which makes the differentiation of individual types difficult. Classifications based on the lithology of the failure surface, the mechanism of slope failure, the morphology and geometry of the failure form and the type of material involved, have all been proposed. With this complexity, it is not surprising that great difficulty has been experienced by many workers in placing particular movements into individual categories. The simple division of Carson and Kirkby (1972) of slide, flow and heave movements, has much to commend it. A triangular diagram can then be used to classify the types of movement (Fig. 3.1). The diagram can also be used to show the moisture content and the relative rates of movement. In general, flows tend to be moist, slides dry and heave can occur at any moisture content.

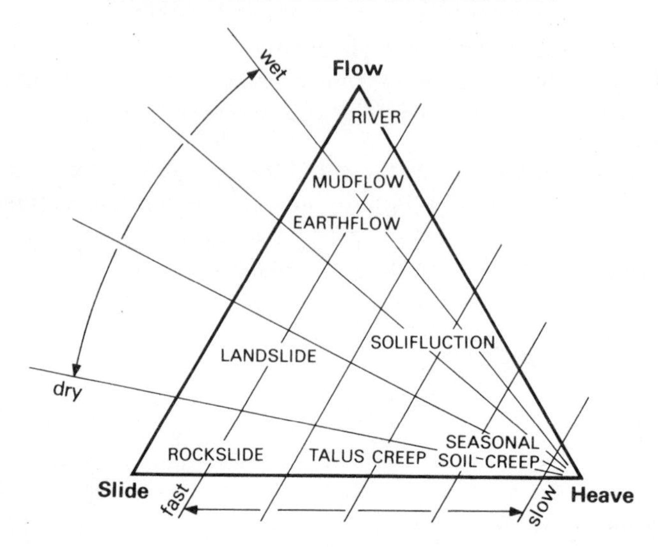

Figure 3.1 Classification of mass movement processes (from Carson & Kirkby 1972).

The greatest problems occur where there are combinations of sliding (slipping) and flowage forms and one has some sympathy with those workers who suggest that mass movements exhibit such a variety that rigorous classification is hardly possible. But classification is important, if not for a definite statement on process, at least to provide an acceptable and unambiguous terminology. The terminology initiated by Sharpe (1938) and modified by Varnes (1958) provides a good basis for the description of movement types and failure forms, distinguishing, as it does, between falls, slides and flows as well as taking into account moisture status, speed of movement and the type of materials involved. Ultimately, mass movements may be classified using combinations of morphometric and process variables but more information is required before this may be achieved. It is more important to assess the role mass movements play in shaping the landscape and the relationship between hillslope failure and weathering, soil formation and moisture distribution. Before that is attempted, a brief description of the more commonly occurring types of rapid mass movement, namely falls, slides and flows, is provided. Soil creep is treated separately at the end of the chapter.

Falls, which are usually superficial movements, involve the breaking away of material from steep slopes. They are largely governed in their size and location by the nature of the rock and its state of weathering. The most common causes of falls are high rainfall and freeze/thaw cycles. In Norway and Sweden, the highest frequency of rock falls coincides with the increase in freeze/thaw cycles in spring and the sudden thaw which loosens highly jointed rocks. Hutchinson's (1971) work on chalk cliffs of the Kent coast showed that falls were related to the average monthly effective rainfall and the average number of days of air frost per month. Falls can assume distinctive modes of failure; plane, wedge and slab modes being the most common (Hoek 1973).

Many of the larger rockfalls develop into rockslides which have been defined by Sharpe (1938) as the downward and rapid movement of 'segments of the bedrock sliding on bedding, joint or fault surfaces or any other plane of separation'. Some rockslides can be catastrophic and lead to considerable loss of life. A rockslide at Frank, Alberta, in 1903, involved approximately 20 km^3 of rock (McConnell & Brock 1904).

Landslides are relatively rapid failures that take place on discrete surfaces. Failure may occur as shallow planar slips, as debris slides or as deep-seated rotational movements. Rapid slipping on a relatively shallow plane, parallel to the groundsurface is the most common mode of failure on weathered slope materials and soils. Failure conditions are optimised when the soil is in a weathered or a residual-strength state, where the water table is at the surface and where water flow is parallel to the slope. This type of slide on straight steep slopes often controls the course of slope evolution. Short periods of failure are separated by long periods of weathering and slope evolution takes place under weathering-limited conditions. The spatial pattern on slopes appears random but over a long time period the whole slope might be affected.

Many shallow slides subsequently disintegrate and move suddenly downslope. These have been described in the literature as debris slides, debris flows or debris avalanches. They are often associated with heavy rainfall and special groundwater conditions. It seems likely that high pore pressures or water seepage are necessary for failure to occur.

Deep-seated landslides occur in materials, such as clays, where the rate of increase in shear stress with depth exceeds the rate of increase in shear strength, so that at a certain depth there is a critical surface where the mass is unstable (Brunsden 1979a). Cohesionless soils usually fail in shallow slips. Many of these slides occur on curved failure surfaces and are called rotational slides. There are three main modes of failure: single rotational slips, multiple rotational slips and successive rotational slips (Hutchinson 1967). Multiple rotational landslips are impressive landscape features and dominate the evolution of many escarpments and sea cliffs. Thus, in the British Isles, the coasts of Dorset, Hampshire, Kent and Yorkshire are classic sites for multiple rotational landslips as are some inland escarpments such as the Weald and Cotswolds (see later account of Bredon Hill).

Mudslides are slow-moving lobate masses of clay debris which slide on discrete boundary shear surfaces. They are especially common in overconsolidated clays and some glacial tills. Seasonal cycles of movement demonstrate that many are related to a seasonal rainfall pattern. This is certainly true of west Dorset (Brunsden & Jones 1974) but the pattern of movement of the Woollashill mudslide, on Bredon Hill is more complicated and is related to sediment supply as well as moisture characteristics (Gerrard & Morris 1981). Other types of mass movement, such as debris flows, which are transitional between stream flow and the drier forms of mass movement, may be locally important.

Causes of mass movement

Some of the causes of mass movement have been alluded to in the previous section. All materials existing on slopes are subjected to a variety of stresses and if these stresses exceed the shearing resistance of the materials, movement will occur. The causes of mass movement can be divided into those that produce an increase in shear stresses and those that produce a lowering of the shearing resistance. Processes causing an increase in shear stress are usually external to the soil–regolith–slope system. Geometric changes, such as an increase in height or steepness of the slope by erosion, will increase the total stresses on the system. The interaction between slope height and slope angle may also influence the type of failure that eventually occurs (Fig. 3.2).

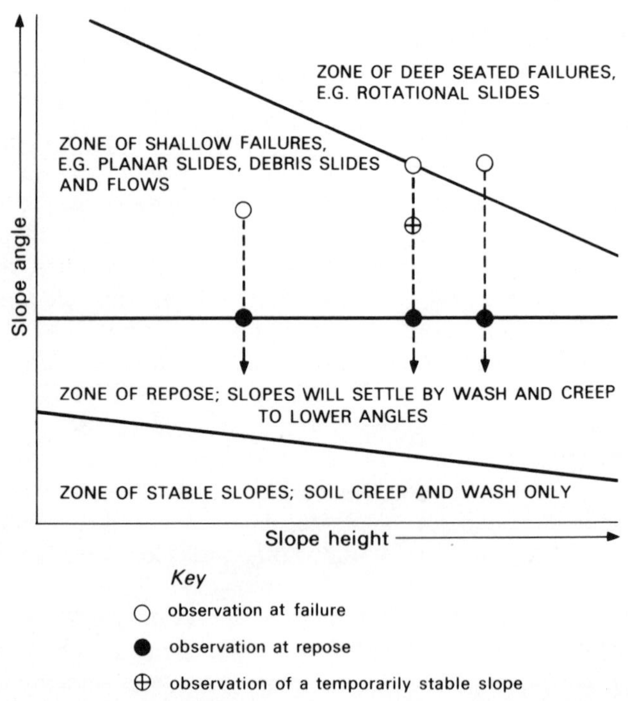

Figure 3.2 Differentiation of mass movements on the basis of height and angle of failure form (after Skempton 1953).

One of the major ways that shear stresses on slopes are increased is by the addition of material from further upslope. Very rapid loading can cause unstable conditions by raising pore water pressures so rapidly that drainage cannot occur. This is the process of undrained loading as described by Hutchinson and Bhandari (1971) and may lead to a rapid failure of the slope. Heavy rainfall will also raise pore pressures and is one of the reasons why many forms of slope failure are associated with torrential rainstorms. It also explains why there is usually a lag between the rainfall event and the slope failure as time is needed for the water to infiltrate, build up the pore pressures, and initiate movement. Infiltrating water will reduce the shear strength of slope materials in other ways. Cohesion is reduced in fine-grained soils by the elimination of surface tension as air is driven out of voids by water. The movement of water will also remove soluble cements and initiate weathering changes by hydration, hydrolysis and wetting and drying. There is a very subtle relationship between weathering, shear strength and the ultimate development of the slope.

Timing and effectiveness of hillslope failure

The important questions that need to be asked concerning the significance of mass movements are:

(a) What forms of mass movement are occurring or have occurred in the landscape?
(b) What is or has been the contribution of mass movements to the total denudation of the area.
(c) How quickly, if at all, does the soil and vegetation recover after a mass movement event.

These questions are being investigated in the Severn and Wye drainage basins by the author (Gerrard 1980). The most conspicuous forms of failure in this area have been large multiple rotational landslips on the major escarpments where competent beds of limestones and sandstones overlie clays and shales. This can be illustrated by considering the situation on Bredon Hill, Worcestershire (Morris 1974, Gerrard & Morris 1981). Bredon Hill is the northernmost of several outliers fronting the escarpment of the Cotswolds. Slope failure forms range in age from the Late Devensian (Last Glacial) period to the present day. At the moment the slopes possess varying degrees of stability. The upper slopes are characterised by multiple rotational landslips which gradually break up and feed debris into 'bowl-like' depressions. These depressions have, in the past, been the source for mudslides which moved through narrow valleys cut in the lower scarps. All except one of these mudslides are now inactive.

It has been assumed by many workers that here, as in many other parts of the British Isles, most large-scale mass movement activity took place in the Late Glacial period. This is an assumption that needs further investigation as the work of Chandler (1971) has suggested that several distinct phases of hillslope failure have occurred, one of these following deforestation during the Iron age. On Bredon Hill, mass movement appears to have gradually diminished in scale as climatic and biotic factors changed, as the slopes and, therefore, the failure systems became modified and as consumption of the cap rock at the top of the scarp reduced the water supply to the failure systems. There have been shorter-term fluctuations in activity, but the age of such changes is not easy to assess because of the rapidity with which bare sites become vegetated.

The geomorphological importance of a given event is governed by the magnitude of the force or energy involved, the frequency with which it recurs, the processes during intervening intervals and the work performed during these intervals. Although governed by topography, soils and vegetation, the relative timing and magnitude of mass movement events are the crucial issue when considering the effect of mass movements on the landscape. The timing and relative magnitude governs the effectiveness of the process, which is the ability to affect the form of the landscape. Much of the available information concerning this has been summarised by Wolman and Gerson (1978). Plotting the available information as the ratio of denudation during individual events of different return periods to mean annual

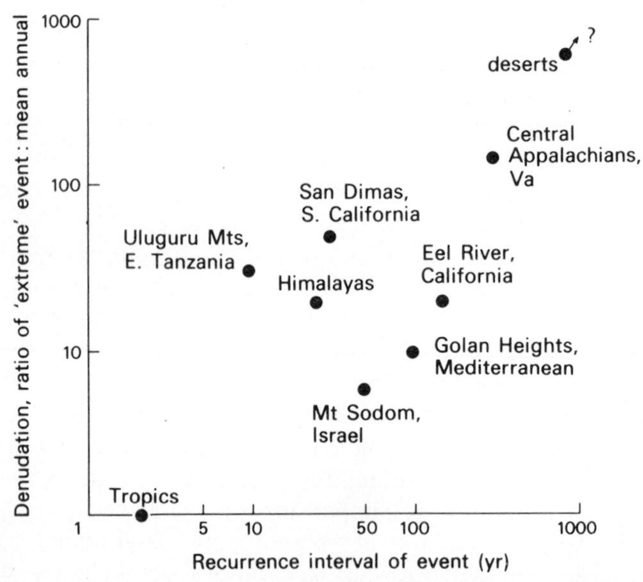

Figure 3.3 Relationship between denudation of hillslopes during large events of different recurrence intervals and mean annual denudation in various regions of the world (based on data from Brown & Ritter 1971, Gerson 1972, Hack & Goodlett 1960, Inbar 1972, Temple & Rapp 1972, Rice & Foggin 1971, Simonett & Rogers 1970, Starkel 1970).

denudation (Fig. 3.3) suggested the following conclusions:

(a) The relative denudation of a major storm in wet tropical mountain landscapes is close to the mean annual denudation and an event of such magnitude may recur almost every year.
(b) A rare event in an arid environment may denude many times the mean annual amount of material.
(c) The ratio of instantaneous to annual denudation does not vary systematically with climate.

Many hillslope scars are potential first-order channels. Whether a scar develops into a channel depends on the intensity of the failure mechanism and the rapidity with which soil and vegetation recovers. Slaymaker (1972) has noted how scars created by small debris slides produce sediment at a high rate and are potential extensions of the drainage net. Many of the numerous hillslope failures in the Uluguru Mountains, Tanzania following torrential rainstorms developed into prominent gully systems (Temple & Rapp 1972).

Recovery processes and periods are not well documented. Recovery appears to be rapid in wet, tropical regions (Table 3.5). In humid temperate regions scars remain fresh for decades. Scars created by the rainstorm of 1952 on Exmoor were still prominent 25 years later. Recovery depends, to a great extent, on land-use characteristics. In the Tanzanian example, noted earlier, most of the natural vegetation had been destroyed. There is strong evidence in Iceland, that not only has overgrazing made mass movement more likely but also it hinders recovery and accelerated erosion results. This is another indication of the delicate adjustment of the natural landscape in which soil formation plays a prominent part. The rapid and prominent forms of hillslope failure just examined have attracted much attention, but the slower and more widespread creep movements may be equally effective in shaping the landscape.

Soil creep

Soil creep is a general term applied to the slow downhill movement of soil and related debris by a variety of processes. Movement is usually so slow that it requires measurements over long time periods to assess its significance. Creep is perhaps a misnomer for true creep is only one of the mechanisms involved. This form has been called continuous creep. Other processes involved include expansion and contraction, heave, and many other processes acting apparently at random in the soil. This type of soil creep has been termed seasonal creep by Terzaghi (1950) because it is related to seasonal fluctuations in soil microclimate.

Continuous soil creep is usually caused by low shear stresses applied to soils on hillslopes by the force of gravity. But the stresses involved are very

Table 3.5 Estimated recurrence intervals of events producing mass movement scars and recovery times (from Wolman & Gerson 1978).

	Mean annual precipitation (mm)	*Recurrence interval (yr)*	*Recovery period (yr)*	*Reference*
S. and C. Appalachians, US	1000	100	25	Bogucki (1976)
Himalayas, India	2000–4000	20–25	—	Starkel (1970, 1972)
New Guinea	4000		25–30	Simonett & Rogers (1970)
Tanazawa Mountains, Japan	2000	5 (smaller) 100 (large)	25	Tanaka (1976)
Hawaii	2500	1 (139 in 3–5 yr)	3–5	Scott & Street (1976)
W. Andoya, Scandinavia	1000	50–60	–	Rapp & Stromquist (1976)
Uluguru Mountains, Tanzania	1058	10	2–10	Temple & Rapp (1972)

small and movement will only take place if the shearing stresses exceed the residual strength of the soil materials. Thus, this type of creep is restricted to clays and other materials that will deform at low stress values. In some soils containing high clay concentrations finite rates may be detected down to zero stress. Continuous soil creep is not likely to occur in coarse-grained soils because grain-to-grain contact is more important relative to clay content. Variations in particle size, bulk density and moisture content can all affect whether movement will take place. Measurements by Ter-Stephanian (1965) and Kojan (1968) have shown that such movements can occur at depths up to 10 m. Most rapid movement takes place in the upper layers and can be as much as 22 cm/yr. Such continuous creep movements commonly occur both before and after more dramatic soil failures as part of a sequence of progressive failure.

Normal soils are not usually affected by continuous creep but by the processes grouped under the heading of seasonal creep. All soils are subjected to the forces involved in expansion and contraction. Expansion can be caused by the freezing of water, by changes of moisture and temperature, by chemical changes associated with weathering and by the action of roots, soil organisms and burrowing animals. Seasonal creep is the result of the actions of expansion and contraction stresses combined with gravity stresses.

Davison (1889) was one of the first workers to recognise the significance of the expansion of surface soil during freeze/thaw cycles. He proposed a model of gradual soil creep by expansion normal to the soil surface followed by contraction in a direction between normal and vertical. But, as Carson and Kirkby (1972) point out, the process will operate in this way only if soil strength is large during the expansion part of the cycle and slight during contraction. However, observations of freeze/thaw and moisture cycles by Kirkby (1967) demonstrate that some sort of zig-zag movement does take place. There are sound reasons why non-recoverable downslope soil movements will occur during expansion/contraction cycles. Soil resistance to shearing stresses varies at different stages of an expansion/contraction cycle therefore creep will be greater during such a cycle than if the average rate was applied steadily. The direction of movement will always have a net downslope component because gravity stresses are in operation as well as expansion and contraction stresses. Expansion and contraction parallel to the soil surface also produces a greater downslope component to movement.

Seasonal soil creep is slight at depths greater than 30 cm because changes of soil microclimate become less with depth. In humid temperate environments creep is maximum at depths of 5–20 cm. The shallow depths involved mean that creep rates will be greatly influenced by vegetation and surface microtopography because of the effect of these two factors on microclimate and soil moisture distribution. Soil creep rates vary considerably from site to site making measurement difficult and statements of

Table 3.6 Estimates of soil creep rates.

Area	*Surface rate (mm/year)*	*Author*
Alaska	6.0	Barr & Swanston (1970)
Wisconsin	5.0	Black (1969)
Malaysia	5.0	Eyles & Ho (1970)
New Mexico	5.0	Leopold *et. al.* (1964)
Maryland	0.5	Leopold & Emmett (1972)
South Dakota	10–19	Schumm (1956)
Colorado	6–12	Schumm (1964)
Derbyshire	1–2	Young (1960)

average creep rates somewhat meaningless. Nevertheless, soil creep in humid temperate areas seems to be of the order of 1–10 mm/yr (Table 3.6). Accurate measurements are difficult to obtain. The most common methods involve the burial of markers such as thin wires or the insertion of flexible tubes or pillars. A full account of the more important methods is provided by Anderson and Finlayson (1975).

The most important initiation of soil creep in humid temperate areas is likely to be expansion and contraction due to soil moisture changes. In the early stages of the wetting cycle movement of soil is likely to be downslope but during the drying cycle the direction of movement may be sideways or uphill depending on the configuration and position of shrinkage cracks (Fleming & Johnson 1975). This effect will be influenced by the water absorption qualities of certain clay minerals and will be governed by the distribution and size of available voids. Because soil particles are close packed, displacements are determined by the characteristics of the pore spaces unless the forces are sufficient to force a particle through the neighbouring aggregate. This is the basis of the soil creep model proposed by Culling (1963). His model sees soil creep as being the result of random displacements of particles relative to the soil mass as a whole. Each particle in a natural arrangement possesses an envelope of pore spaces of variable form and random orientation about the centre of the particle. Some of the forces acting on the particle have no effect since they are opposed by the reaction of adjacent particles. A small proportion are successful in displacing a particle into a nearby void. The favouring of displacements in a downward direction will compact the lower layers of the soil and the percentage pore space will decrease towards the soil base inhibiting the further movement of soil. Further movement is checked unless the compaction is relieved. This can be achieved by the accumulation of surface material, by movement of the soil in the uppermost layers and by abstraction at the slope base by fluvial action. The 'holes' created in this manner at the boundaries of the system can then migrate upslope into the soil mass as particles move into the spaces created. This will result in a slow diffusion of particles from regions of higher concentration to regions of lower concentration which will eventually be in a downslope direction. There is very little available information on which to judge the importance of this type of creep but it seems to be of less importance than the other forms of creep described.

Terracettes

Soil creep rarely produces distinctive landforms but its effect can be seen in the build up of soil on the upslope sides of obstructions. But, under certain conditions, an accelerated form of soil creep may produce miniature terrace features (terracettes) that run parallel to the slopes. The first empirical study of terracettes was made by Odum (1922) who observed horizontal cracks in the turf cover on steep slopes and suggested that curved failure planes, concave to the ground surface, developed from these and that terracettes originated by miniature rotational slipping along these planes. Kirkby (1963) noted that cracks in the vegetation mat matched what one would expect if there was a uniform stretching of the soil layer and pointed to the importance of cohesion between soil particles and grass roots. Carson (1967), basing his ideas on a comprehensive study of slopes in the Exmoor and south Pennine areas of England, linked terracettes with the thickness of the soil mantle. He suggested that a critical soil depth of about 0.7 m existed such that below this figure soils were too thin to form terracettes and above this value they were too thick. The thinness of the soil seemed to impart strength to the mantle enabling it to 'cling' to the bedrock. Other workers (e.g. Young 1972a) have argued that terracettes are primarily associated with the trampling of sheep and cattle.

Terracettes are common in the Carboniferous Limestone slopes of the River Dove in Derbyshire, England. The slopes are steep (20°+) and are relatively straight and this has had a considerable influence on the type and thickness of the soil cover. Soils are extremely thin and exhibit poor horizon differentiation being dominated by a humic A horizon with little or no development of a B horizon. Soil is present in the C horizon only as a very thin sandy clay loam matrix between blocks of shattered limestone. Gerrard and Webster (1979) tested three main hypotheses of formation on these terracettes. The first hypothesis suggested that terracettes were the result of the periodic movement of the entire soil mantle such as by microslumping or sliding. The second suggestion was that terracettes were the response of the soil to repeated wetting and drying cycles and the third hypothesis argued they were the result of trampling by animals. Only the hypothesis of the redistribution of material by wetting and drying cycles stood up to rigorous field and statistical testing. The thinness of the soil was again seen to be crucial. These conclusions only apply to the area studied and it is quite likely that terracettes are the result of many processes. Studies of terracettes also suggest that detailed investigation of microtopography can provide a valuable insight into the processes active in the top 30 cm or more of the soil.

Conclusions

The movement of soil is governed by a complex suite of processes. The relative importance of these processes is largely a function of climate. Soil creep appears to be the dominant process in humid temperate regions while surface and subsurface wash dominate in tropical areas. Mass movements are important on steep slopes in all environments; they are all related, directly or indirectly, to topographic factors. Slope gradient is probably a major controlling factor and on most slopes this varies systematically with position. Soil types and specific soil properties can be expected to vary systematically with slope angle and position. This is the basis of the concept of the soil catena which is analysed in the next chapter.

4 The catena concept

Formulation of the concept

The realisation that particular slope forms were associated with particular soil sequences led to the formulation of the concept of the catena. Milne originally defined a catena as 'a unit of mapping convenience . . . a grouping of soils which while they fall wide apart in a natural system of classification on account of fundamental and morphological differences, are yet linked in their occurrence by conditions of topography and are repeated in the same relationships to each other wherever the same conditions are met with' (Milne 1935a, p. 197). Since then catenas have been recognised in a variety of areas and under a variety of climatic conditions, but the concept is one which has been subject to a great deal of discussion and controversy.

The real significance of catenas lies in the recognition of the essential processes involved in catenary differentiation and not in the formal appearance of its product. It is the interaction of soils and landforms and therefore soil processes and geomorphic processes which is the key to catenas and the reason why the concept has been so important in soil and landform studies. But the wide applicability of the concept is complicated by considerations of parent material variations and climatic differences. The temporal as well as spatial aspects of the soils are also important. Thus, before specific examples of catenas from different parts of the world are analysed, these issues need clarification.

The catena and the processes of erosion

Milne (1936a) was one of the first to include the processes of erosion as a major factor leading to the differentiation, under constant climatic conditions, of several different but related soils usually from a common original material. The example he used to illustrate this was a residual granite hill and associated slopes in East Africa (Fig. 4.1). A shallow dark grey loam (1) formed by weathering of the granite surfaces has worked downhill by creep and slow erosion to act, on the footslope, as the parent material on which a deeper soil (2) of the red earth group has developed. At the base of the red earth profile, where a temporary accumulation of seepage occurs in the wet season, a horizon of coarse granitic grit (3) in a black rusty ferruginous cement has formed. Occasional storm water running over the

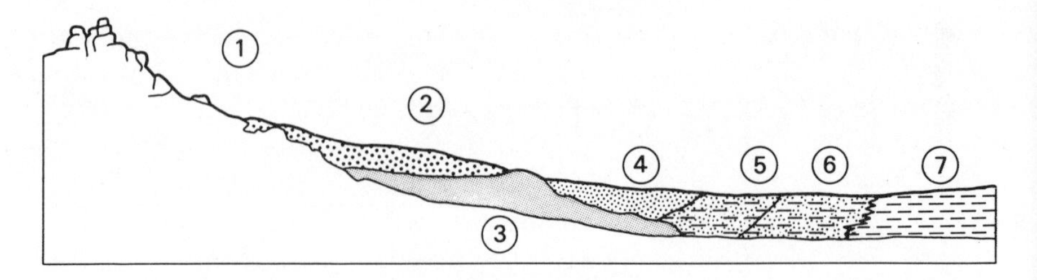

Figure 4.1 Soils of an East African catena (after Milne 1936a).

surface has gradually pared off the topsoil and the material has travelled differentially according to particle size, so that by a cumulative effect a zone of washed sand (4) has covered the footslope, with silty or clayey sand (5, 6) beyond it, and clay has accumulated on the level bottomlands (7). At all stages the erosion has been slow and non-catastrophic and the soils have borne their appropriate vegetation and been developing towards maturity.

Milne further suggested that the character and proportionate extent of the soils varies with the maturity of the topography, with the underlying lithology and with new cycles of erosion. Therefore, the physiographic and geomorphic evolutions of the landscape are both involved in the catena concept. The soil profile changes from point to point in accordance with conditions of drainage and past history of the land surface, and soil differences are brought about by 'drainage conditions, differential transport of eroded material and leaching, translocation and redeposition of mobile chemical constituents' (Milne 1936b, pp. 16–17). This concept is extremely important for the way it relates the soil to the processes operating and to the past history of the landscape. It is therefore very difficult to make any useful distinction between slope genesis and pedogenesis and this means that a better understanding of the soil should be sought in a geomorphological evaluation of the soil landscape. But, equally, a better understanding of the geomorphology of a region should be sought in a study of the soil.

Catenary differentiation

The differences between the soils of a catena are generally related to differences in their position and their drainage characteristics so that emphasis is placed on the difference between the freely drained upper parts of the slope and the imperfectly to poorly drained lower portions. This provides a continuum between those sites where the influence of soil moisture is at a minimum and those sites where maximum influence of soil moisture is felt. Slope steepness is one of the most important factors that causes a variation in soil moisture conditions as the steeper angles reduce the amount of water percolating through the soil and increase the removal, perhaps through accelerated erosion, of the upper portions of the soil profile. The essential feature is that soil and water can and do move downslope. For these processes to have their greatest effect the ground-surface must slope downward continuously from the crest to the base of the slope and it is incorrect to apply the term catena to landforms which lack this feature.

The main processes of catenary differentiation are surface wash, soil creep, solution and rapid mass movements. These processes, which have been examined in greater detail in Chapter 3, vary in their relative importance and effectiveness with climate and slope. Surface wash rates vary widely: in dry savanna areas, wash is very effective but in areas of higher rainfall the increased vegetation cover gradually reduces wash to a minimum near the savanna/rainforest boundary; at higher rainfalls, the trend is apparently reversed because the controlling influence of vegetation cover is already at a maximum whereas rainfall intensity may be increasing. Although surface wash under tropical rainforest occurs, its overall importance under these conditions is still largely unknown (Rougerie 1960). Most of Rougerie's observations were made in semi-evergreen forest and in a region where man-induced changes in the vegetation have been important. In tropical forests that have been cultivated, such as French Guiana, surface wash seems to be insignificant (Cailleux 1959). Measurements on experimental plots near Abidjan have also revealed little surface flow (Tricart 1972). The role of soil creep is still largely unknown in tropical rainforest areas and it is probably of much greater relative importance in humid temperate regions.

Early workers in East Africa, whilst ascribing varying importance to these processes, all agreed that they were significant in soil formation. Evidence for the potential of mass movements in these environments has been provided by work on the mechanics of the deep red clays of East Africa (Newill 1961, Coleman *et al.* 1964). In general, the importance of mass movement in the modelling of slopes in tropical areas has long been recognised and man-induced landscape changes can also be significant.

The downslope movement of material in solution is of great significance in catenary studies. Thus, soils are affected by the influx of soluble materials, especially bases, from higher up the slope and this leaching and redeposition of material constitutes a strong physical link between the members of a catena which is closely analogous to the link between the A and B horizons of a soil profile. This was first stressed in a classic early paper by Greene (1947). Considerable amounts may be removed from the slopes in this way especially under tropical rainforest conditions.

The relative importance of wash, solution, creep and rapid mass movements depends not only on climate but also on slope angle and distance from the slope crest. As was explained in Chapter 3, the rate of erosion by surface wash increases somewhere between linearly with slope angle and as the square of the angle, and approximately in proportion to the square root of the distance from the crest. At steep angles the rapid forms of mass movement become important although the critical angle at which they become significant varies with the type of bedrock and the regolith conditions. On gentle slopes in tropical regions chemical removal is the most effective process. At intermediate gradients surface wash is the most important process in climates such as those of savanna areas although in humid temperate regions it may be subordinate to soil creep.

Each catena is, thus, the result of the complex interrelationships between soil and slope processes and will be governed by the differing ratio of erosion to deposition occurring on different parts of the slope. From the pedogenetic point of view, all country which has relief consists of zones of removal, transference and accumulation, the limits of which can be peculiar to each transferable constituent or to each group of constituents of comparative mobility. This applies equally to the most simple of landscapes and to great geomorphological units. This erosion–deposition relationship can be quite complicated on individual slopes though it is usually the upper parts of slopes that lose material and the lower parts that gain it. This type of catena, where erosion on the upper and deposition on the lower slopes has caused a variation from a uniform soil cover has been termed an erosion catena by Ollier (1976). He cites the example described by Ellis (1938) from Manitoba where the lower B and C soil horizons have been gradually exposed by erosion at the top of the slope. A more complex situation has been described by Webster (1965) in Zambia where erosion by surface wash is greatest on the lower steeper parts of the slope leading to the preferential removal of fine soil particles and leaving a coarse-grained soil at the base of the slope.

Young (1972b, 1976) has distinguished between static and dynamic causes leading to catenary differentiation. Static causes are governed by site differences alone, irrespective of the position of the site, and include effects of slope angle and the depth of the water table. Dynamic causes are brought about by the position of the site with respect to the slope; they are mainly the downslope transport processes described above. On most slopes there is clearly an interplay between these two groups but it is conceivable that an extremely permeable parent material or very gentle slopes might inhibit downslope movement and then static causes will essentially control the development of the catena. These conditions are normally found on sand dunes, beach ridges or volcanic slopes such as scoria and ash cones. Conversely on steep slopes or on very impermeable rocks dynamic causes will be dominant, whilst on other slopes static causes may be dominant on one part and dynamic causes on another. Thus, if gentle crestal slopes exist, static causes may be reversed on the steeper slopes. This complex situation is well shown on loess slopes in Iowa described by Huddleston and Riecken (1973). In midslope situations the soil has inherited the combined initial sorting of the loess, the downslope sorting during slope evolution and the distribution of iron carbonates produced by weathering. The summit portions have escaped the erosive processes but both the shoulder and the toe portions of the slope show signs of the simultaneous interaction of erosive and pedological processes.

Soil changes within catenas

The result of the processes described above is to produce a series of changes in the soil properties from the upper to lower members of the catena. The variation in soil colour is one of the more obvious sequences and is typical of many West African catenas. Upland, well-drained soils are usually reddish-brown, the colour showing the presence of non-hydrated iron oxide in the soil. The iron is well dispersed and usually partly attached to the clay fraction, thus the clay itself appears red. On the middle and lower parts of the slope, drainage is slower partly because of moisture seeping downslope from the upper soils. These soils remain moist longer and dry out less frequently and less completely; this leads to an increasing degree of hydration of the iron. The red colour then changes to a brown or yellow one; the hydrated iron oxides are mainly limonite and goethite. The colour changes are not sudden; there is a gradual change from the original reddish-brown of the upper soils to orange-brown and then to yellow-brown and sometimes brownish yellow on the lower slopes.

On the lowest slopes, where the drainage can be very poor and where part or all of the soil profile is waterlogged, reduction of the iron and other soil compounds takes place. Under these conditions, bacteria obtain their oxygen from the oxygen-containing compounds and these are then reduced to other compounds. These waterlogged soils are usually bluish-grey, greenish-grey or even neutral grey in colour. In that part of the soil profile where the water table fluctuates mottling is likely to be produced.

Thus, differences in drainage are responsible for the gradual colour changes that are frequently seen in catenas. These drainage differences can be due to a variety of factors. In Indiana the hydrologic sequence has been shown to be correlated with surface slopes in medium-textured materials, with differences between land and water surfaces in porous materials, with the permeability of fine-textured materials and with flooding patterns in alluvium (Bushnell 1945). But in each case the gradations within the catena can be related to an oxidation–reduction balance in the same way as described in the West African situation.

Three different factors are clearly important in determining these sequences. The surface form of the slope is obviously important but so too is the form of the base of the weathered rock or regolith. The form of this weathering front is largely controlled by the type, intensity and orientation of the joints in the bedrock. This weathering front can be extremely variable and the relationship between the weathering front and the slope surface is of basic significance. To these two factors must be added the form of the water table. These three factors are connected in a highly complex way but are all of great pedogenetic and geomorphological significance. Whereas the form of the weathering front changes very slowly with time and the surface form somewhat more rapidly, the water table is subject to seasonal, annual and long-term fluctuations and also to changes imposed by the gradual change of the other two factors. The concept of slope thus needs to include a full appreciation of all these factors.

One of the ways of portraying catenas is by a series of soil profile diagrams representing the soil at different positions thereby allowing the changes to be seen clearly (Fig. 4.2). A slight variant of this has been used by Williams (1968) (Fig. 4.3). The types of changes possible have been outlined by Young (1976). In the simplest case a single horizon remains

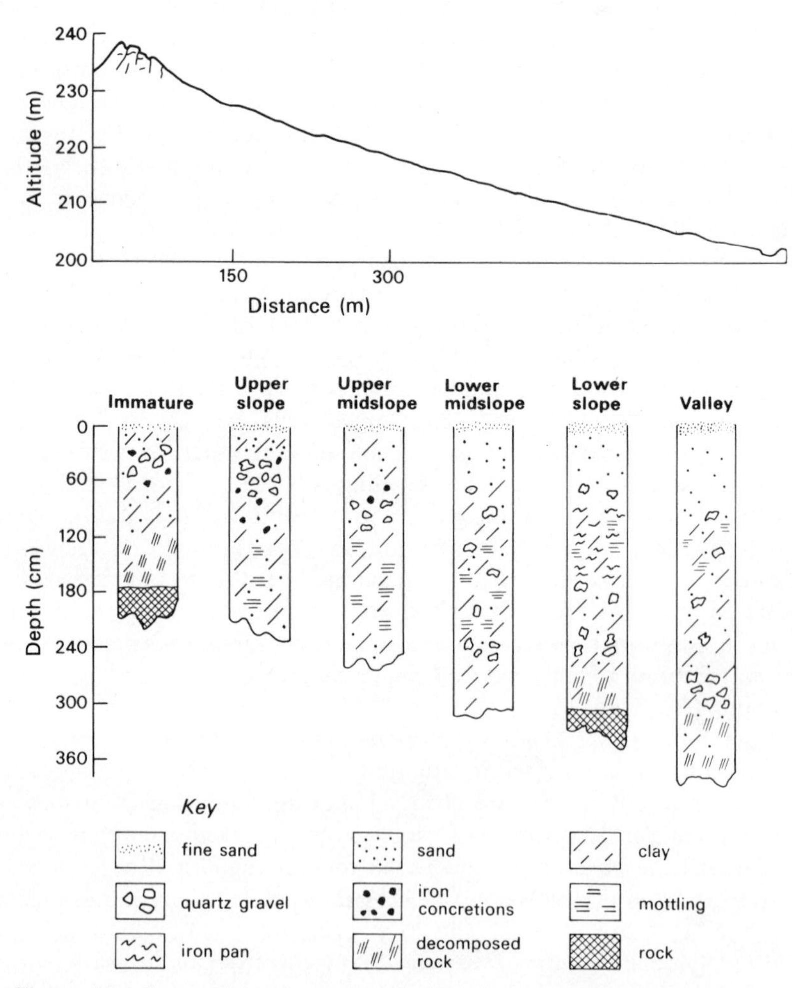

Figure 4.2 Sequential changes in a West African catena (after Nye 1954).

Relief	summit of fixed dune level–very gently undulating	dune margin gently undulating	dune remnant gently undulating	swale margins gently sloping	swale centre level to gently sloping	former lake margin level to gently sloping
Vegetation	*Acacia tortillis* subsp. *raddiana*; *Panicum turgidum*	*Acacia nubica*; *Panicum turgidum*; *Aristida funiculata*	*Capparis decidua*; *Acacia nubica*; *Acacia tortillis* subsp. *raddiana*; *Aristida* spp.; *Acacia seyal*; *Euphorbia aegyptiaca*; *Schoenefeldia gracilis*	*Leptadenia pyrotechnica*; *Ocimum basilicum*; *Aristida mutabilis*; *Ziziphus spina-Christi*	*Capparis decidua*; *Panicum turgidum*	*Aristida* spp.
Soils (• 5% $CaCO_3$; ⌇ 5% $CaSO_4$)	1: cm; S; 200	3: cm; SCL; 50; SL; 110; SC; 180; S; 200	2: cm; LS; 30; SCL; 150; SC; 200; L; 215	4: SC; cm 5; CL; 60; SCL; 140; L; 200; S; 225	5: cm; SC; 45; SCL; 140; C; 200	6: cm; SC; 25; SCL; 50; LS; 110; SIL; 155; K; 200
Topsoil colour	dark greyish brown	dark grey	v. dk grey-brown	v. dark grey	v. dk grey-brown	dk grey-brown
Subsoil colour	brown	dk grey-brown	dark brown	dk grey-brown	dark brown	v. dark brown
Topsoil % sand	84	77	72	70	57	57
Subsoil % clay	10	19	22	23	32	32
Subsoil ESP	0	32	23	1	53	62
EC in 2nd horizon	0.2	0.9	0.4	0.2	5.8	5.2

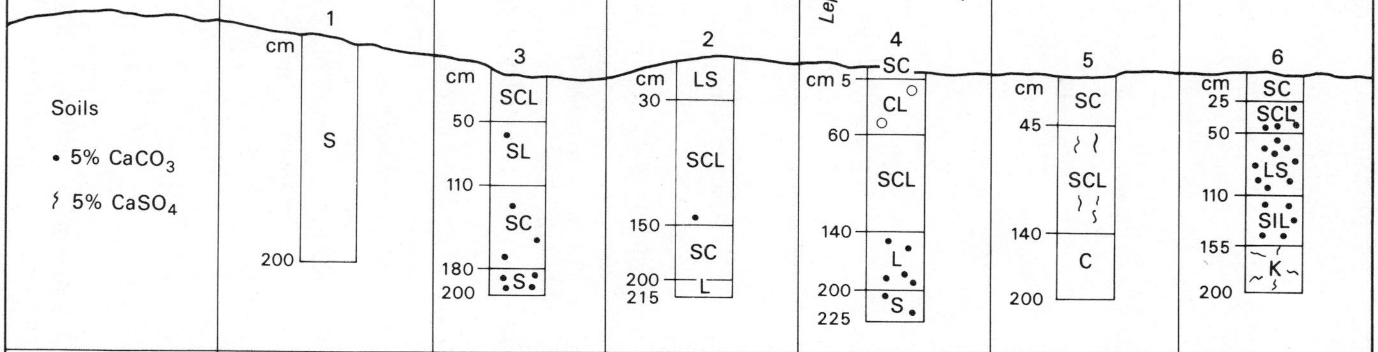

Figure 4.3 A dune catena in the Sudan (after Williams 1968).

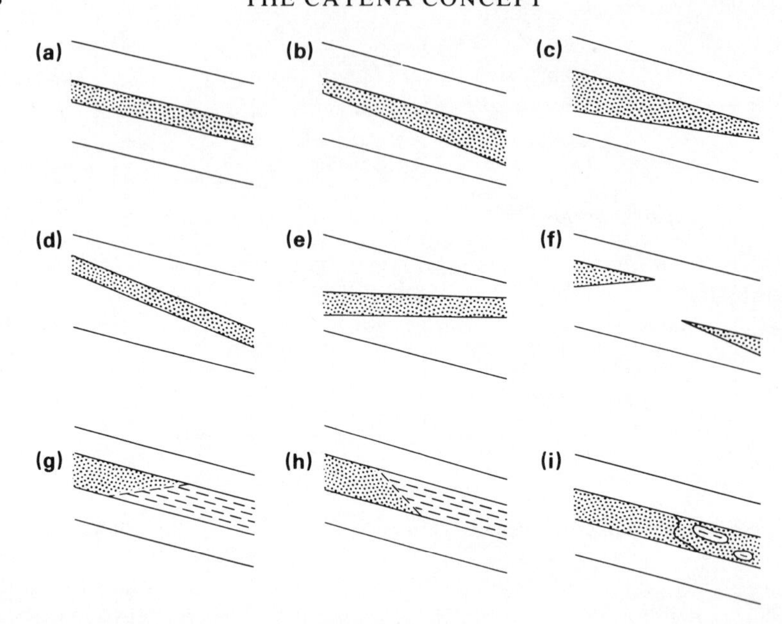

Figure 4.4 Possible horizon changes in a catenary sequence (from Young 1976).

unchanged (Fig. 4.4a), or it may thicken (b) or thin (c). It may also become deeper (d) or shallower (e). It sometimes ends completely and a new horizon commences (f) or it may be replaced by another horizon starting from the base (g) or top (h). The final possibility (i) is that a horizon may undergo a gradual change in properties whilst retaining its identity and continuity.

If all the horizons are analysed in this way three common situations can be identified: first, situations in which there are no downslope changes in successions, depths or properties of horizons; secondly, there may be parts of the catena where one or more horizons undergo gradual change; and thirdly, zones where rapid changes take place leading to substantially modified horizons over short distances. If the changes observed in catenas are analysed in this manner, soil and slope processes can be related in a more meaningful way.

Catenas on sites of geological diversity

There has been frequent discussion as to whether catenas should be restricted to sequences on one parent material. In the United States severe limitations are placed on the degree of variation permitted in the parent rock (Watson 1965). But this is an unrealistic limitation since parent material differences in the catena can occur even though the underlying geology is uniform. The underlying rock is often only the direct parent material of some of the soils, usually the upland ones. The rest of the catena will have developed in transported materials which, although they have been initially derived from the underlying rock, are now composed of weathered and partly weathered materials which have been transported and possibly sorted. The restriction to similar materials would mean that the soils on colluvial deposits would be placed in a separate catena from the soils on the adjacent upland. Clearly, this is unrealistic. Hole (1976), overcomes these problems by defining a catena as a group of soils developed from similar initial materials.

But this does not cover the situation where different geological formations outcrop on a single slope. Milne was aware of this problem as the following statement shows:

> Since the first recognition of these catenary associations, it has become apparent that we have to deal with two classes of them. In one, the parent material does not vary, the topography having been modelled out of a single type of rock at both the higher and lower level . . . . In the other kind, the topography has been carved out of two superposed formations, so that the upper one is exposed further down the slope (Milne 1935b, p. 346).

Many examples exist of this second type of catena. In parts of northern Nigeria the landscape consists of sandstone and ironstone capped flat-topped hills with steep scarps rising above an extensive undulating sandstone plain. The flat summits are capped with iron-impregnated sandstones or ironstones with little soil. The steep slopes possess a shallow layer of loamy soil over a rubble of sandstone and ironstone. The rest of the area is covered by deep orange-brown to red sandy clays with a brown mottled sandy clay loam in the depressions.

More complicated situations occur where the slopes intersect a variety of rock types such as the slopes developed on dolerites and shales described by Sparrow (1966). Each rock type may then develop its own catena, but since the upper rocks frequently fail to extend far enough downslope to reach poorly drained sites, the lower catena members are rarely present. If some recurrent pattern of parent material change with surface morphology exists this may be represented as a catena across a relief transect as in the Chiltern Hills, England (Fig. 4.5). The relationship between parent material and soils is complicated here by plateau and valley drift. Thus, the brown calcimorphic soils occurring on the moderate (8–15°) slopes are associated with colluvial or solifluction deposits containing varying proportions of loess-like limon and earlier formed clay-with-flints mixed with frequent chalk (Avery 1958, Ollier & Thomasson 1957).

Clearer relationships between parent material and soil types can be found in West Africa (Fig. 4.6). Alternating bands of softer schists and harder gneisses and quartzites form a series of ridges and depressions. A

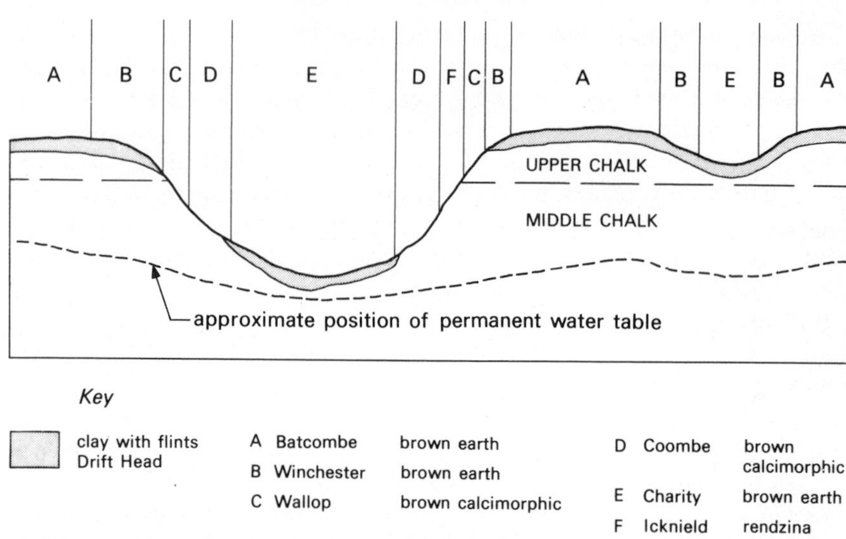

Figure 4.5 Relationships between soils, topography and geology in the Chiltern Hills, England (after Avery 1958).

thick ironstone cap (A) overlies the quartzites and quartz schists of the ridges. Soils at B contain quartz and ironstone fragments and may possess indurated subsoil horizons. Shallow pale brown gravelly loams (C) overlie weathered schists often with a stone line of quartz or ironstone gravel. Soils (D) on the gentler lower slopes are brown to pale brown gravelly sandy loams over mottled weathered schist, while the low ridges (E), underlain by gneisses and pegmatites, only possess very shallow soils.

In many instances the complex interaction between topography and geology makes it difficult to predict what type of soil will be found. Nevertheless, restricting catenas to one-parent-material situations is an unjustifiable limitation but it is incorrect to apply the concept to situations where soils are found, *in situ*, corresponding more or less exactly, with the underlying geological pattern, since in this case the effects of 'normal' erosion are absent.

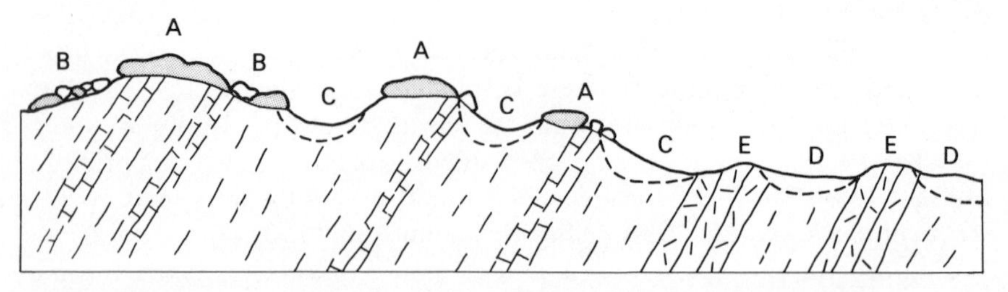

Figure 4.6 West African catena developed on alternating bands of hard and soft rock (after Ahn 1970, Pullan & De Leeuw 1964).

Catenas and time

The essence of catenas, as discussed above, is the relationship between soils and topography expressed in terms of slope angle and position. A certain amount of time is required before soils become sufficiently differentiated for a catenary sequence to emerge. There is often the implicit assumption that the soils have reached some sort of steady-state condition but it is notoriously difficult to decide when this condition exists especially when geomorphic processes are also involved. Curves for the build-up of most soil properties are fairly steep to begin with but after a time they flatten, indicating little change thereafter. But the time necessary to reach steady state will depend on the soil property, parent material and the kind of soil profile developing. 'A' horizon properties form rapidly whereas 'B' horizon properties form more slowly. Thus, it has been estimated that podzols in Michigan have taken more than 3000 but less than 8000 years to form (Franzmeier & Whiteside 1963) while laterites might date from the Tertiary or early Quaternary periods. Much of our knowledge of the time factor in soil formation has been obtained from dateable volcanic deposits. With time, carbonates are leached out of calcareous till, and iron is oxidised to greater depths with an associated change of pH (Bushnell 1943, Crocker & Major 1955).

Therefore, any analysis of catenas should take account of the past physiographic history of the area. As well as the soils changing with time the landforms would also have been changing, and for detailed catenary sequences to exist the relationships need to remain reasonably stable. Thus, the catena in any one locality is a complex interaction of landforms, soil and time. Therefore, the catena must be regarded as a dynamic phenomenon with a dimension in time and can be seen as an essential part of the processes of erosion and deposition. With this in mind, some examples of catenas from different climatic environments are now examined.

Catenas in different climates

In their detail all catenas are different but there are sufficient similarities to warrant a preliminary grouping on the basis of world climatic types, notwithstanding the doubt that has been cast on the concept of soil zonality. 'On examination of the catena–climate relationships of the world, we find a contrast between extreme and non-extreme situations. Distinctive soil–slope relationships occur in the extreme situations dominated by frigid or arid conditions . . . . In all the rest of the world, under non-extreme conditions, the processes of slope erosion, slope deposition and pedogenesis are almost inextricably interwoven' (Ollier 1976, p. 166). Some of these relationships are now examined in a few distinctive catenas.

(a) Tropical savanna catenas

Tropical savanna catenas exhibit a considerable variety of form but it is possible to classify them as catenas with rock outcrops (inselberg and pediment catenas), catenas with a hard laterite (plinthite) cap and catenas without rock outcrops. This classification, based on the work of Ollier (1959) and Moss (1968) is capable of further subdivision (Table 4.1). Although considerable variations exist, each catena is associated with a particular slope form (Fig. 4.7).

(i) Inselberg and pediment catenas. This catenary type is characteristic of much of Africa and is commonly developed on granite where hillslope angles seem to be partly controlled by the basal surface of weathering. The majority of the slopes leading away from the rock residuals are steep pediments varying from 8–10° in angle whilst the lower part of the catena may or may not possess an alluvial member depending on the often complex geomorphological history of the region.

Controversy centres on whether the slope forms are fossil and the result of pedimentation under arid conditions (Birot 1960) or whether they are being actively developed at the present time (Budel 1957, Cotton 1961). Allied to this are arguments concerned with the origin of the deep layers of weathered material and the varying importance of sedentary and colluvial and wash processes (Vine *et al*. 1954, Charter 1958, Moss 1963, 1965). One such catena, in Uganda, has been described by Radwanski and Ollier (1959). This sequence can be divided into three upland and two lowland components, clearly distinguishable at the soil series level. The upper series (1), called the Buwekula Shallow, occurs as a narrow belt surrounding the rocky inselbergs. The soils are shallow, compared with the other members, in that incompletely weathered rock occurs at shallow depths. The soil is essentially a loamy sand with abundant coarse angular quartz gravel and occasional fragments of feldspar. The Buwekula Red Series (2) occurs on the upper-middle and middle slopes and is usually the most extensive

Table 4.1 Classification of tropical savanna catenas (after Ollier 1959, Moss 1968).

(i) *Catenas with rock outcrops (inselberg and pediment)*
- (1) with extensive pre-weathering
- (2) without extensive pre-weathering

(ii) *Catenas with hard laterite*
- (1) hard laterite as an upper slope feature
  - (a) with massive laterite
  - (b) with concretionary or detrital fragments only
- (2) hard laterite as a lower slope feature

(iii) *Catenas without rock outcrops*
may be subdivided on the basis of underlying geology

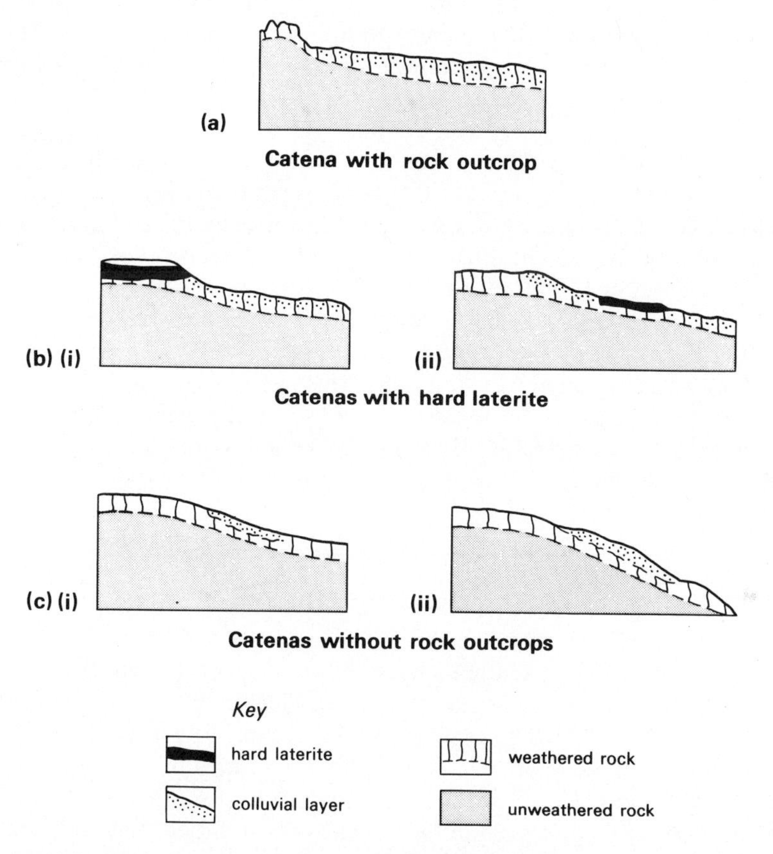

Figure 4.7 Basic features of tropical savanna catenas (after Moss 1968).

member. As the name suggests, it is mostly reddish in colour and of a sandy clay–loam texture. The Buwekula Brown Series (3) occurs on the low-middle and lower slopes and may be regarded as a variant of (2) in that it has been altered by drainage as influenced by topography. The changes between (1) and (2) are quite sharp whereas those between (2) and (3) are very gradual. The Buwekula Yellow-Brown (4) occurs on the slightly raised valley bottoms and valley slopes with the horizons showing evidence of the seasonal fluctuation in the water table. The Buwekula Grey (5) occurs on the valley floor and is often completely submerged in the rainy season.

The interesting aspect of this catena is the evidence it provides not only about the processes in operation on the slope but also about the past geomorphological history of the area. Detailed mineralogical evidence has indicated that there are three parent materials involved in the catena. The Buwekula Shallow has been derived from fresh or only slightly weathered granite; the Buwekula Red and Brown from intensely pre-weathered granite and the Yellow-Brown and Grey from alluvium derived from the pre-weathered granite. This is interpreted as providing evidence for a 'two-cycle theory' for the evolution of the landscape and pedological features (Ollier 1959).

(ii) Savanna catenas with hard laterite. The slope form is fairly constant with a flattened upper slope and summit separated from a straight or concave middle portion by a well marked convexity. The middle slope passes into a fairly straight lower slope of low inclination. The upper portion is associated with thin residual soils; the break of slope coincides with the hard laterite band and the middle slope is dominated by talus derived from the break-up of the laterite. The lower slope is characterised by sedentary soils or by finely divided talus. This soil and slope sequence is the result of the breakaway retreat of the hard laterite band. Occasionally catenas with hard laterite in a lower slope position are encountered (see Table 4.1).

(iii) Savanna catenas without rock outcrops. These are the classic African catenas as described by Milne (1947) in East Africa, Vine (1941) in Nigeria, Charter (1949) in Ghana and Watson (1964, 1965) in Rhodesia. Nye's (1954, 1955) study is included in this category because the rock outcrop is only a minor feature. These catenas generally possess smooth convex–concave slopes although stream incision frequently modifies the lower slopes (Fig. 4.7). The crest is usually occupied by a dark red sandy clay with a well developed structure which gradually changes into a yellowish-red sandy clay with weaker structure on the steepening convex slope portion. The upper part of the concavity is occupied by a dark brown sandy clay loam overlying a mottled sandy clay. The middle and lower parts of the concavity, with slopes of $1–2\frac{1}{2}°$, possess a grey sandy loam or loamy sand and the valley centres are filled with black hydromorphic clay. Variety of slope form and soil type within the general framework is produced by different parent rocks. Although a great deal of work has been undertaken in Africa, similar catenas have been described in the seasonal monsoon climates of India (Agarwal *et al*. 1957, Biswas & Gawande 1962, Gupta 1958), in Sri Lanka (Panabokke 1959) and in Brazil (Askew *et al*. 1970).

(b) Tropical rainforest catenas

Only a few examples of tropical rainforest catenas have been described (Delvigne 1965, Joseph 1968, Young 1968). The major distinguishing feature of this catena is the valley and slope form known as *sohlenkerbtal*, defined by Louis (1964), where strongly convex slopes intersect the level floodplain with little or no concavity. Because of this slope form only a two-member catena normally exists consisting of a freely drained upper member and a poorly drained soil on the valley floor. Textural contrast, unlike savanna catenas, is not strong and the valley heads commence abruptly with no distinctive soils.

(c) Catenas in arid and semi-arid regions

Arid and semi-arid conditions form one of the extreme conditions mentioned by Ollier (1976) as being significant in soil formation and therefore catenary development. But these regions also possess other differences which tend to set them apart. As elaborated in Chapter 3, slopes may be classed as weathering or erosion controlled depending on which set of processes is dominant. In many desert areas erosion is dominant and so soils are thin or non-existent. True soils are found only on the more stable surfaces, such as low-angle alluvial fans and pediments, and therefore tend to bear a very close relationship to landforms. Desert soils tend to be distinctive for other reasons. In general the clay content tends to be lower than in humid soils (Harradine and Jenny 1958) and consequently most desert soils have low exchange capacities (Scott 1962). Desert soils may also have distinctive mineral suites with montmorillonite and hydrous micas being the characteristic clay minerals (Ismail 1970).

The relief factor in arid areas is often critical. Cooke and Warren (1973) have noted three factors which set aside dry areas from more humid ones: first, the critical slope angle separating stable from unstable portions of the slope is generally more sharply defined in dry areas; secondly, where the water table rises above a certain well defined critical depth it will affect soil properties by capillary rise and saline or alkaline soils will result; thirdly, these two factors often mean that soils on different slopes and even on different portions of the same slope may be of different ages. The steeper slopes where erosion is greatest have the youngest soils whilst the lower angle slopes have the oldest soils (Gile 1967). Repeated phases of erosion and deposition on alluvial surfaces produce more complex situations (Gile & Hawley 1966).

But it does mean that there is a very close relationship between geomorphic processes, soils and landforms in desert areas. This can be illustrated by the soils and landforms of western Turkmenia as described by Lobova (1967). The landscape of western Turkmenia can be subdivided into three broad relief elements: the oldest and highest portion consists of elevated piedmont plains composed of Quaternary conglomerates; the next level is made up of younger alluvial pebble fans which grade into the third level which is a broad clay plain (takyr). The movement of water is critical to the type of soil found and this water movement is very much governed by the slopes and landforms present. In the upper parts, the water flows at a relatively rapid rate running along fairly deep channels and sometimes flooding the banks between the channels. In the middle portions, where the channels are shallower, the water movement slows down and often stagnates on flat depressions. It is here that the soil complexes are most extensively developed. Having reached the lower part of the takyr plain, the water stops due to the gentle gradient. Thus, the mode of movement, the infiltration rate and the duration of stay of the water are closely related to local gradients and to the types of rocks and these determine the local water condition of the soils. This variable aspect of water conditions may in itself lead to soils of different age as well as different type. Movement of water through the soil profile where there is rapid flushing speeds the process of soil development as has been observed on the upper more freely drained parts of slopes in Texas (Goss & Allen 1968).

The movement of water is also critical on the slopes of inselbergs where the water flows off the steeper slopes of the rock residuals and accumulates in the coarse alluvium of the plain where it leads to locally deeper weathering eventually seeping out onto gentler surfaces depositing fine sediment (Twidale 1962). In this way, the weathering products of the upper slopes are removed to the lower slopes. At the same time there is a change in clay mineralogy from the one-to-one clay minerals of the upper leached soils to two-to-one minerals of the often alkaline lower soils (Ruxton & Berry 1961).

For the reasons outlined above it is not surprising that simple catenary sequences such as that illustrated in Figure 4.8a occur. In semi-arid regions with a greater amount of available water the soils tend to be better developed but simple catenary sequences still exist especially where insel-

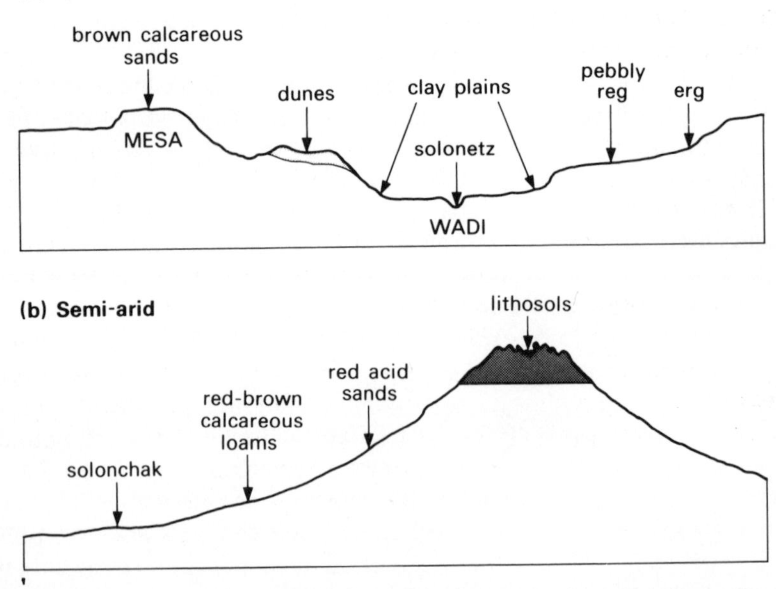

Figure 4.8 Characteristic catenas of arid and semi-arid areas (from Bunting 1965).

berg and pediment landscapes are developed (Fig. 4.8b). Soils and landscape development are therefore intricately related with new surfaces constantly appearing leading to a highly complex situation. These surfaces have been called pedomorphic surfaces by Dan and Yaalon (1968).

(d) Catenas in temperate regions

It is probably in the temperate regions of the world that the applicability of the catena concept is most in question. There are three factors that make the application of catenas difficult: first, the geological diversity makes simple relationships uncommon; secondly, many temperate areas are covered with numerous superficial deposits; and thirdly, the influence of man on the soils and vegetation has been tremendous and this has upset the evolution of any simple pattern between topography and soil. These points can be illustrated by examples from the British Isles.

Clarke (1954, 1957) has described a mixed catena that occurs on the Jurassic rocks in Oxfordshire. The rock succession is Northampton Sand which forms the hilltops followed by Upper Lias Clay, Middle Lias Marlstone and finally Lower Lias Clay at the base of the slopes. At least two soil types may be found on each geological bed providing a complex situation.

The problems created by superficial deposits have been mentioned earlier in the case of the Chilterns but many other examples exist. On the Haldon Hills of Devon soliflucted head deposits mantle the lower gentler slopes and give rise to a distinctive soil series, the Kiddens, comprising humic gley soils on the loamy head. In other areas of the British Isles the soliflucted deposits form terrace-like features with their own detailed soil–site relationships (Crampton & Taylor 1967).

Nevertheless, there are situations in temperate regions where the catena concept has been successfully applied. Most of these applications have been in cool temperate regions but catenas have also been described in warm temperate areas (Bricheteau 1954). The basis of the classification used by the Soil Survey of Scotland is basically a catenary hydrological sequence from the top to the bottom of the slope producing six separate soil series (Glentworth & Dion 1949, Glentworth 1954). A somewhat similar hydrological sequence has been used to describe the soils occurring on the Exeter Shale Hills in Devon (Clayden 1964, 1971). Well drained fine loamy brown earths of the Dunsford Series are associated with steep slopes, with more weathered gleyed brown earths and surface-water gleys occupying gentler slopes. Analogous sequences have been described on Exmoor (Curtis 1971), in the Mendips (Findlay 1965) and the limestone areas of Derbyshire and Yorkshire (Balme 1953, Bullock 1971).

Some of the simplest catena-like relationships in temperate regions occur on glacial tills (Acton 1965, Brown & Thorp 1942, Hall & Folland 1970, Muckenhirn *et al.* 1949), sand dunes (Matthews 1971) and loess (Hutcheson *et al.* 1959, Lotspeich & Smith 1953). In these circumstances, regular sequences are found with the extent of gleying depending on the topography, position and site drainage. Thus, with care the catena concept can be applied to temperate regions but the relationships are often extremely complicated.

(e) Catenas of tundra regions

Tundra regions provide the second of the extreme conditions that Ollier (1976) has suggested produce simple catenary sequences. The soils certainly reflect the climates in which they occur; they are mostly shallow and poorly developed and do not possess well defined soil profiles. If a traditional A–B–C horizon sequence does develop it may be subsequently contorted, displaced or obliterated by frost action and solifluction (Tedrow 1968). Some frost processes are clearly constructive in that they reduce the size of the soil particles and aid the formation of structural aggregates. But many of the processes are destructive as they lead to the physical displacement of the soil. Thus, it is only by grouping frost processes with pedogenic processes that the complexity of polar pedology can be understood. The presence of permafrost also ensures that many of the soils are poorly drained with gleying common.

The catenary sequences that exist simply reflect the drainage conditions (Fig. 4.9). Polar desert soils are the mature well drained soils of the ice-free polar regions (Tedrow 1966, 1974). They experience neither podzolic nor gley influences; the almost complete absence of vascular plants and the low temperatures and precipitation means that organic matter rarely enters into the soil system. The distinction between upland tundra and lowland or

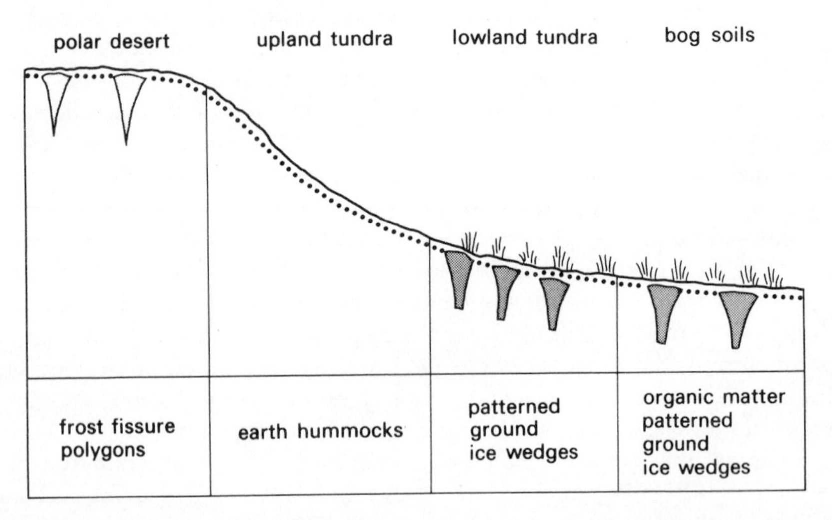

Figure 4.9 Soils and topography of the polar desert zone (modified from French 1971, 1976, Tedrow 1974).

meadow tundra soils is purely on the basis of drainage. Upland tundra soils are drier and occur on the upper parts of slopes. The characteristic microrelief consists of earth hummocks and small non-sorted polygons. Lowland tundra possesses more luxuriant vegetation and is often underlain by ice wedges. Bog soils occur in valley bottoms where the waterlogged conditions prevent organic matter decomposition and material accumulates to thicknesses of two metres. These bog soils are geomorphologically important in that they provide suitable material for palynological analyses and are capable of ^{14}C dating.

Conclusions

It is for the recognition of the systematic relationships between soils, certain landforms and geomorphic processes that the catena concept has been and still is of the utmost importance. The real significance of catenas lies in the recognition of the essential processes involved in catenary differentiation. The classification, genesis and geography of soils in catenary association are related to the evolution and elements of the landscape. Thus, the study of catenas has shown that soils cannot be analysed in isolation from the geomorphological systems of which they are an integral part. Catenas are best developed in tropical and semi-tropical environments, but can, with care, be identified in other areas. Although the concept is easiest to apply in areas with uniform geology, it has been successfully applied to areas of geological complexity. A recent extension of the catena concept has been the statistical analysis of detailed systematic relationships between slope and position and specific soil properties rather than generalised soil profiles as described in this chapter. This work is examined in the next chapter.

5 Soil relationships within drainage basins

The relationships between soils and slope position and slope gradient, described in the previous chapter, have largely considered changes in the generalised soil profiles. The advent of statistical techniques and the use of high speed computers enables these relationships to be treated in a more mathematical way. But it also means that much greater attention has to be given to the sampling and measurement schemes utilised to assess these relationships. Soils are extremely variable bodies and the measurement of individual soil properties, such as moisture content or bulk density, requires careful consideration.

Traditional studies of catenas have tended to examine single slope profiles but, with the aid of the computer, a large number of slope profiles can be handled at one time. This enables the sampling design to consider whole drainage basins and the variability within them of slope form and soils. A synthesis involving slope form, stream system and soils is possible and it is the aim of this chapter to examine some of the relationships that have been discovered.

Theoretical considerations

Many studies have shown that soil properties are related to gradient angle and to length of slope. This is partly the result of the interaction between slope form and the processes of erosion and deposition. Chapters 2 and 3 have emphasised that the movement of both water and material is governed by the geometric configuration of the slope. Thus, these processes can selectively add or deplete the soil of certain physical or chemical characteristics. But the relationships between soil properties and slope form are not necessarily simple and predictable. Some constant-angle slopes have been described with greatly varying soil properties and, conversely, soil properties have been found to be reasonably constant over slopes of greatly variable form.

Morphology also exerts an influence on the rate of soil formation and the degree of maturity of soils. Certain soil properties are related to the stage reached in the evolution of soil profiles. As soils develop, the depth of the profile increases, horizons become differentiated and a characteristic suite of physical and chemical changes can be discerned. But this sequence can be retarded on steep slopes.

A potentially large number of soil properties can be measured and the skill lies in choosing those properties related to either soil maturity or to the formative slope processes. The most useful chemical indicators are pH, organic matter, exchangeable cations and total exchangeable bases, and certain oxides and carbonates. Physical properties such as particle size, moisture content, porosity, plasticity, shear strength, bulk density and aggregation appear to be the most important.

It is usually assumed that meaningful relationships between slope form and soil properties will be the inevitable result of any properly conducted study. But realistic correlations will only occur if the processes of soil formation are in some sort of equilibrium with the surface and subsurface processes acting on the slope. No correlations should be expected if the landscape is very young morphologically or if erosive phases are extremely vigorous. A change of climate or a change in the amount and type of the vegetation cover will also upset the equilibrium of the system and a lack of significant correlations is just as meaningful an indicator of landscape status as is the highest statistical relationship.

The choice of soil properties to measure will be critical. It was noted in earlier chapters how soil properties vary in their rate of change as the soil profile develops. Values of pH and organic content develop and react very quickly to external changes, but clay content and exchangeable bases take a much greater amount of time to achieve equilibrium. Some soil properties will exhibit distinct correlations with slope form whilst others will not, because of this factor.

The other major methodological problem is associated with the measurement of slope form. Slope gradient will vary with the length over which it is measured and this must be borne in mind when considering soil relationships (Gerrard & Robinson 1971). Slope profiles are essentially curved surfaces and distinct breaks of slope are unusual but schemes, such as those of Ongley (1970) and Young (1971), have been devised to subdivide slopes into curved and straight sections. These methods are also affected by the size of the recording interval used (Gerrard 1978). The measurement of slope form is necessarily an abstraction and the gradient angles obtained are a function of the techniques employed.

A more intangible problem concerns the distances over which slope gradients should be measured. The soil is usually sampled at one point whereas the slope angle is measured over a set distance on either side of the soil sampling site. The question that needs asking is, over what distance should one expect the soil property to be related to the angle of the slope? The answer to this question hinges on the sensitivity of the system and is reflected in the spatial variability of the soils. Highly sensitive soil systems may react to microscale changes in surface morphology over distances as short as one metre. Less sensitive soil systems will be related to larger landscape components. A lack of correlation between soil properties and slope form may be because the measurement of slope form has been at the wrong scale.

The majority of studies have concentrated on slope profiles as the main sampling units. Soil properties have then been measured systematically along these lines. An alternative scheme is to identify one component of slope form, such as the steepest section or the crestal area, and to sample that section systematically within a drainage basin. Ideally, the two schemes should be integrated to provide a comprehensive account of spatial relationships. It is important to distinguish the types of slopes that exist in the landscape because water movement and soil processes are likely to vary with slope type. The most straightforward division is between valley-head slopes, spur-end slopes and valley-side slopes. Valley-head slopes are concave in plan form, spur-end slopes are convex in plan and valley-side slopes are generally straight. Slopes may be further subdivided on the basis of their positions in the drainage basin thus allowing slopes and soils to be related to basin characteristics if necessary.

The drainage basin as a pedogeomorphic unit

The unitary features of form and process exhibited by the drainage basin have long been recognised. In 1899, Davis was arguing that, although the river and hillslope waste sheets do not appear to resemble each other, they are only the extreme members of a continuous series. The topographic and hydrologic unity of the drainage basin provided the basis for the morphometric system of Horton (1945) which was modified and elaborated by Strahler (1964). The drainage basin provides a convenient and usually unambiguous topographic unit which can be subdivided on the basis of stream characteristics. This enables a nested hierarchy of both slopes and basins to be established. The drainage basin is also a functioning open system with respect to inputs of precipitation and energy and outputs of water and materials. The most widely used technique for describing streams is Strahler's (1952) modification of the ordering scheme devised by Horton (1945). Fingertip channels are specified as order 1 and where two first-order channels join, a channel segment of order 2 is formed. When two second-order channels join, a third-order segment is formed and so on. Although alternative ordering schemes have been devised, such as that of Shreve (1966), the Strahler system is still the commonest means adopted for differentiating streams within drainage basins.

Many relationships have been established between stream order and slope characteristics and, as soils and slopes are closely related, it would be expected that soils and stream order would be related. Strahler (1954), working in the Verdugo Hills, California, established that a general relationship exists between mean and maximum valley side slope angles and the gradient of the basal stream. Also, undercut slopes were steeper than slopes whose bases were protected by talus and slope wash. A high level of association between stream, slope and soil variables is also reported by

Chorley and Kennedy (1971). Again, a major difference was found between slopes that were being actively undercut and the opposing slip-off slopes. Most of the significant correlations on the undercut slopes were within the geometry group of variables implying that one of the most important factors was the rapid transport of debris to the stream. On the slip-off slopes, there were numerous strong links between soil and vegetation characteristics and features of the slope profiles. The conclusion reached was that on these slopes a more stable, debris production (weathering) situation existed.

The three-fold interaction within drainage basins, of stream–slope–soil, is a complicated combination of process-response systems. One of the simplest methods of unravelling this complexity is to examine slope–soil relationships and then to place these slopes, and their associated pedological and geomorphological processes, in a drainage basin framework.

Relationships between slope angle and soil properties

The considerable variety of slope form makes comparison between soils and slopes extremely difficult. For this reason, the majority of studies have been undertaken on simple slopes comprising a convexity, a maximum segment and a concavity. One of the earliest studies was by Norton and Smith (1930) on loess soils in Illinois, where they discovered an inverse relationship between slope angle and depth of the textural B horizon, and correlations between slope and soil structure, texture and consistence. Young (1963) has established several correlations in the British Isles: regolith thickness remained constant or increased slightly across the convexity and usually increased downslope on the maximum segments. But, Young found no systematic change in the degree of reduction over either the convexity or maximum segment except that the proportion of large stones increased on slopes over 25°. Young also found that regolith thickness and degree of reduction increased across the concavities. This has not always been found in other studies, but it is clear that there is a fundamental difference between soil relationships on convex and straight units and on concavities.

This distinction has been stressed in a series of papers by Furley (Furley 1968, 1971, Whitfield & Furley 1971). High correlations were found between soils and slope angle on convex elements and maximum segments but relationships on concave elements were much poorer. Generalised relationships for the convex and maximum slope zones are shown in Figure 5.1. Acidic soils showed a decrease in pH with increasing slope gradient whereas the relationship was reversed for calcareous soils. All soils, both acidic and calcareous, showed an inverse relationship between gradient and carbon and nitrogen content. For calcareous soils, percentage silt and clay declined with increasing slope angle.

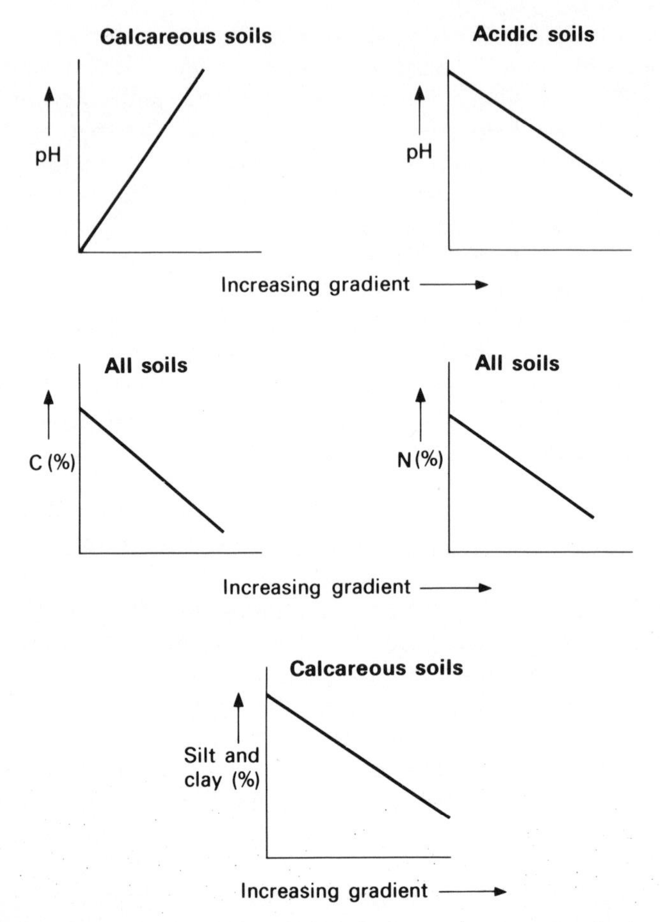

Figure 5.1 Generalised relationships between soil properties and slope angle (from Furley 1968).

These ideas have been examined on slopes in the Cotswolds (Jordan 1974). Most of the slopes have a simple convex–concave form and are ideal on which to test soil relationships. The soil properties analysed were pH, moisture factor, organic carbon, total nitrogen, cation exchange capacity, total exchangeable bases and various particle size grades. The results of regression and correlation analyses showed that only the total and upper slopes possessed any significant correlations. Not only were the relations more significant on the upper-slope portions but, in some cases, the form of the relationship was completely reversed on the lower portions. Thus, moisture factor decreased with an increase in gradient on the upper slopes but increased with increasing gradient on the lower slopes. Also, the impression obtained from this study was that gradient was not having a marked effect on the particle size of the soils. This has been found in many

Table 5.1 Soil depth correlations with slope angle and position on eight chalk slopes (from English 1977).

Slope	*Correlation coefficients* concave portion	convex portion	total slope
1	−0.34	+0.27	−0.31
2	−0.56	+0.37	+0.11
3	−0.53	+0.34	+0.03
4	−0.29	+0.26	+0.03
5	+0.16	−0.09	+0.14
6	−0.69	+0.59	+0.29
7	−0.66	−0.04	−0.06
8	−0.74	−0.13	−0.30

previous studies and Furley (1971) suggests that under such circumstances, there is little erosion of the mineral soil occurring and no signs of selective removal or deposition.

The results indicate that changes in gradient over slopes do appear to have a significant effect on the values of certain soil properties, but that this effect is not equally distributed over the entire slope. Most change occurs on the upper slope, especially at or around the convexity. A more constant distribution is found on the maximum segment and this may mean that this linear zone is one of transit rather than of erosion. Small changes in gradient have some effect on soil properties and the significant associations on the upper crestal sections lend support to the theory that soil maturity is most advanced on the gentlest of slopes.

The contrast between convexities and concavities is also manifest in the soil depth values on chalk slopes in the South Downs, England (Table 5.1). The concave sections show a strong tendency towards a negative relationship, although only two of the correlation coefficients are significant, whilst correlations on the convex sections are reversed. Even so, no fixed pattern emerges between soil depth and slope angle on all the slopes examined.

Effect of slope position

Many of the changes just discussed are also likely to be the result of the relative position of the soil sampling site. Slope gradient on simple convex–concave slopes is highly correlated with distance, especially if the slopes are separated into convex and concave units. Furley's (1971) results demonstrated that this is especially so if the entire slope is analysed rather than its separate components (Table 5.2). Of the 48 slopes analysed, on only seven was slope angle the dominant factor in explaining soil property variation over the complete slope profile. Slope position was the dominant factor on 34 of the slopes. When the slopes were subdivided into upper and

Table 5.2 Dominant factor explaining the variation in soil properties on chalk slopes (from Furley 1971).

Dominant factor	*Total slope*	*Upper slope*	*Lower slope*
slope angle	7	21	10
slope position	34	21	20
angle and position equal	7	6	17

lower portions and treated separately, interesting changes occurred. For the upper-slope portions, slope position and slope angle were equally dominant, but on the lower-slope portions, slope position was the major factor. Relationships were stronger also, between slope position and soil properties on the lower slopes.

On the basis of these and other results Furley (1971) has produced a model to explain the distribution of soil properties on slopes (Fig. 5.2). The basis of the model is that soluble minerals and exchangeable ions are leached from upper slopes, moved downslope and are deposited at the

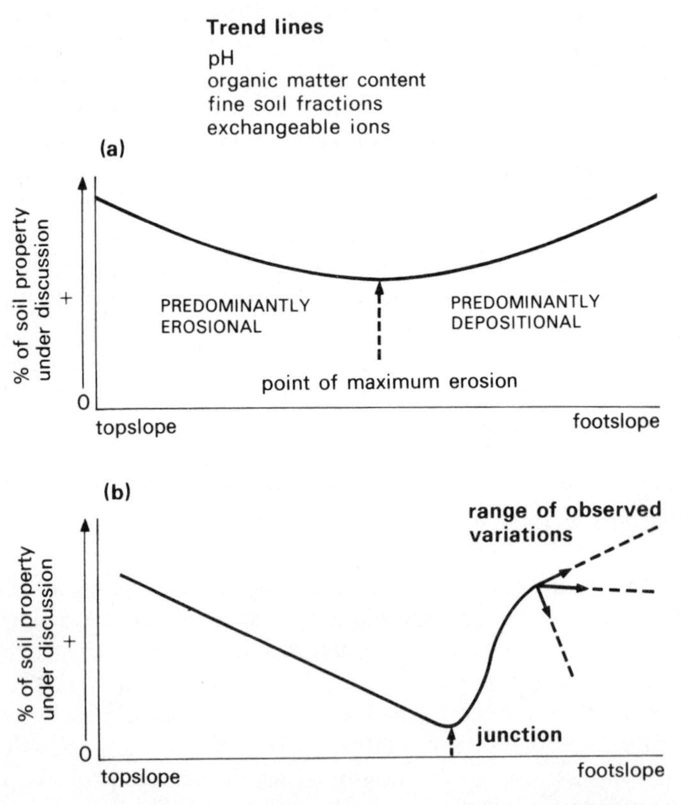

Figure 5.2 (a) Theoretical distribution of soil properties over slope form and (b) the distribution of certain soil properties on chalk slopes (from Furley 1971).

slope foot. The greatest concentrations of certain soil properties, such as organic matter, would be expected on the gentle slopes at the top and bottom of the slope. The different trends on the upper and lower slopes seem to reflect different processes: the upper slopes appear to be associated with processes of erosion and transport and the lower slopes with deposition and transport. This is similar to the non-cumulative and cumulative slopes of Nikiforoff (1949) and the aggrading and degrading surfaces of Crocker (1952). It is also not too dissimilar to the major division in the slope and soils model of Dalrymple *et al.* (1968). The lower slopes exhibit greater variability which may reflect erratic zones of deposition.

The junction between the two slope zones is not always sharp but is often diffuse and can oscillate in an irregular manner across the slope according to local variations in microrelief. It is also likely that the junction will fluctuate and migrate up and down the slope in time with fluctuations in the balance between erosion and deposition.

The common assumption made is that the concave slope portions are accumulation zones and that the relationships, as discussed above, are the result of deposition. However, this implicit assumption has been challenged by Young (1969). An accumulation zone is, by definition, an area where a net gain of material occurs, but most concavities, where examined in detail, are found to be bedrock features and not accumulations over sharp rock junctions. This means that the soil relationships must be the result of differential deposition and removal on a transit slope rather than gradual deposition.

The only situation where the lower-slope portions will be pure accumulation zones is in areas of interior drainage or small closed depressions. Examples of these depressions are described later on glacial deposits. Material moves off the slopes but is not evacuated and builds up on the lower slopes. Footslopes and toeslope sections, therefore, encroach on the backslope sections and concave elements come to dominate the slope system. One such example has been described by Walker and Ruhe (1968). Soil distribution patterns are concentric in plan about the centre of the depression. Sediment and soil trends along radial slope profiles plot as sinuous curves with the degree of sinuosity relating to the slope form. This produces the type of relationships shown in Table 5.3. The nature of the sorting mechanism is shown in the change of F : C ratio, which is the ratio of the percentage in the 16 to 250 μm range to the percentage in the 250 to 2000 μm range for the whole of the superficial layer. These soil–slope relationships were best expressed as polynomials. The review of soil–slope functions by Yaalon (1975) showed that many other polynomial functions have been established. In some instances polynomials provide a better statistical fit, but not always. Also, they are often more difficult to interpret in terms of the processes acting on the slope. However, whichever method is used, the relationships between soil properties and slope form and position are impressive.

Table 5.3 Soil property trends in relation to slope profile components in a closed system on calcareous drift (from Walker & Ruhe 1968).

	Slope-profile component				
Property	*summit*	*shoulder*	*backslope*	*footslope*	*toeslope*
mean particle size	minimum	maximum	minimum to maximum	decrease	minimum
F : C ratio	maximum	minimum	maximum to minimum	minimum	increase
organic carbon	maximum	minimum	increase	increase	maximum
depth to carbonate	maximum	minimum	maximum	decrease to zero	zero

Soil–slope relationships within drainage basins

In the general discussion earlier in this chapter two strategies for examining the spatial relationships of soils and slopes were suggested. One strategy was based on the slope profile as the unit of study and the previous section has outlined some of this work. But, this strategy is very time consuming and few studies have involved more than about twenty slope profiles. The alternative strategy is to concentrate on specific slope components and to sample these, and their associated soils, throughout the drainage basin. This is the strategy adopted by Arnett (1971) in a sixth-order drainage basin in Queensland, Australia. The use of stream order is arbitrary but is a means of examining the spatial variation that exists within drainage basins. Arnett (1971) found that mean slope length, mean angle and mean maximum slope angle all tended to increase with stream order. These are trends which have been found in many areas and reflect the opening out of drainage basins by streams enlarging their catchments. Other morphological characteristics, such as rate of convexity and concavity, were examined by Arnett. The mean rate of convexity increased with stream order up to the fourth order and then declined. The relationship between rate of concavity and stream order was more complicated and exhibited marked fluctuations.

Geomorphological processes acting on slopes are largely governed by these factors of slope angle, length and curvature and, therefore, they should also be related to position in drainage basins, as measured by stream order. This was found to be so by Arnett (1971). The occurrence of sites on which soil creep was dominant was complex (Fig. 5.3). Crestal sites exhibited a rapid increase up to order four where creep was dominant on 60% of the profiles. Creep was generally less important on both the maximum slope facets and toeslope sites and decreased in importance with increasing stream order. Slopewash was found to be important on all the components of lower-order slopes but decreased rapidly in importance as stream order increased.

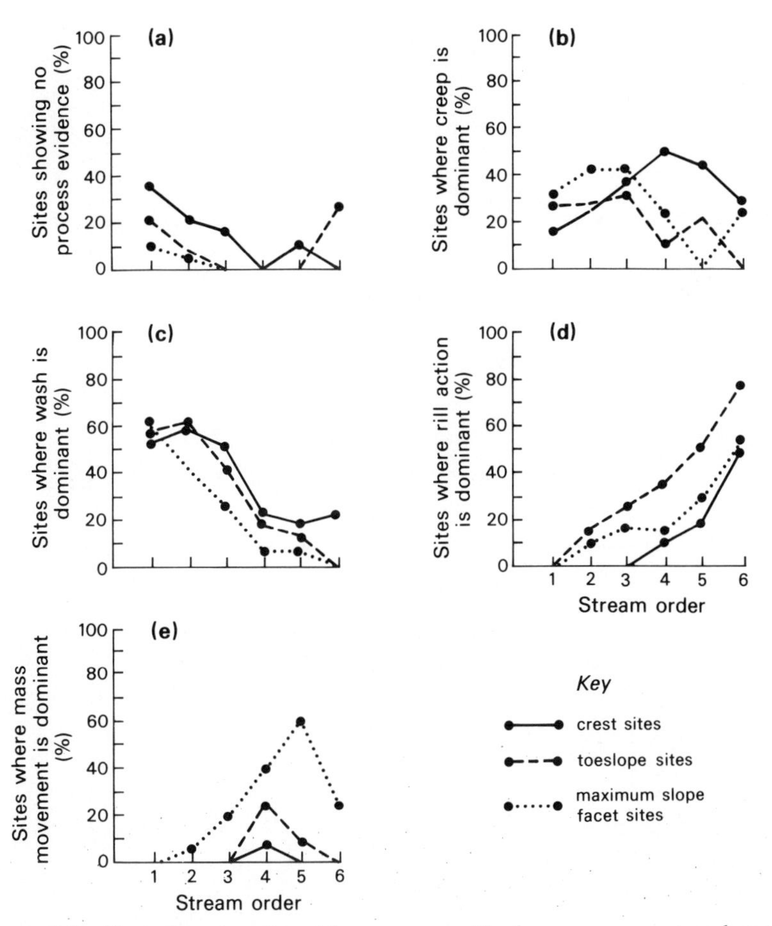

Figure 5.3 Variations in subaerial processes with slope component and stream order, Queensland, Australia (from Arnett 1971).

Rill action became increasingly dominant as the order of the slopes increased. Also it was always more important on the maximum slope and toeslope than on the crest slopes. No rill action was recorded on the crestal sites of fourth-order slopes. Mass movement processes were only important on the higher-order slopes and then, as would be expected, they occurred mostly on the maximum slope areas.

Straightforward relationships also existed between the morphological components and certain soil properties. Soil depth, B horizon thickness and percentage clay in the A horizon were found to be inversely related to both maximum slope angle and the rate of convexity. This also means that soil properties will vary systematically within the drainage basin. This was the fundamental point stressed by Conacher and Dalrymple (1977). The relative importance of the components in the nine-unit landsurface model

Table 5.4 Variations of soil properties within a drainage basin according to the components in the nine-unit landsurface model (from Arnett & Conacher 1973, reproduced by permission of the Geographical Society of New South Wales).

	Slope parameters					*Soil types*			*Landsurface units*
stream order	*length (m)*	*maximum angle (deg)*	*mean angle (deg)*	*convexity (deg/100 m)*	*concavity (deg/100 m)*	*crest*	*centre*	*toe*	*unit combinations*
1	132	16.7	9.4	16.4	37.0	deep red loam	deep red loam	deep red loam	1 : 5 : 2
2	254	24.1	16.9	30.0	41.0	red loam	red loam	acid red loam (gley)	1 : 5 : 3 : 2
3	273	27.4	19.0	37.0	33.0	shallow loam	skeletal loam	deep red podzol	1 : 5 : 3 : 5 : 8 : 9
4	351	31.4	20.0	45.0	24.0	skeletal loam	skeletal	deep red podzol	1 : 5 : 3 : 4 : 5 : 6 : 8 : 9
5	396	33.3	21.2	42.0	44.0	skeletal loam	skeletal	alluvial	1 : 5 : 3 : 4 : 5 : 6 : 7 : 8 : 9
6	476	30.9	16.0	40.0	51.0	skeletal loam	skeletal	alluvial	1 : 5 : 3 : 2 : 4 : 5 : 6 : 7 : 8 : 9

and the sequence in which they occur on a slope will depend on the position of that slope within the drainage basin. As the processes and the nature of the soil cover are all related to position and slope form, soil will also vary within the drainage basin (Table 5.4). This study, by Arnett and Conacher (1973), showed that drainage basin development can be examined in terms of the relations between the individual landsurface units. These interactions through time lead to a rational sequence of valley development as drainage basin expansion and integration takes place. This results in the characteristic landsurface unit combinations within each valley or stream order as portrayed in Table 5.4. Therefore, slope form, slope processes and soils create meaningful patterns. This is ample justification for treating the drainage basin as one of the most fundamental geomorphic units and for arguing for order in the landscape; order which is expressed as systematic and repeatable relationships between slopes, soils, position and intensity of stream activity. Conacher and Dalrymple (1977) conclude that the nine-unit landsurface model can contribute to both geomorphic and pedologic research at one or more of four distinct levels: the landsurface pedon and polypedon, the landsurface unit, the landsurface catena and the drainage basin. Maximum integration within the landscape occurs at the drainage basin level.

Conclusions

Good statistical relationships exist between many soil properties and slope form and position. It has not been possible to provide a comprehensive review of all these relationships. All that has been attempted is an assessment of some of the more straightforward of these and to highlight some of the methodological problems inherent in studies of this nature. The relationships are not sufficiently well established to enable the construction of efficient models, but, there appears to be a fundamental difference between the upper convex and lower concave portions. Whether this is simply a distinction between erosional and depositional zones is open to doubt and is something that warrants closer inspection.

The systematic variation within drainage basins, rather than on individual slope profiles, deserves more consideration. Quite often conclusions are based on a sample of relatively few slopes. Any study that tries to encompass whole drainage basins is valuable and this is one of the reasons why the hypothetical nine-unit landsurface model has been so influential. This model also possesses the flexibility that enables it to be applied to complex as well as simple slopes.

Although drainage basins can be regarded as the fundamental geomorphic units in the landscape, many distinctive landform assemblages occur in other contexts. These, such as erosion surfaces and coastal plains, possess distinctive soil associations which are examined in succeeding chapters.

6 Soils on erosion surfaces

Erosion or planation surfaces have been created by surface or near-surface wear on rock masses. They are reasonably smooth and approximately horizontal planes that cut across structural and lithological boundaries. They can be of any size but the term is usually restricted to large surfaces of low relative relief that are believed to be the end-products of cycles of erosion. The fact that they can be produced by a variety of geomorphological processes, such as subaerial erosion, marine erosion or chemical weathering, has given rise to much confusion and argument. The geomorphological literature is replete with arguments concerning the identification and origin of erosion surfaces. This is not the place to enter this discussion but the series of papers collated by Adams (1975) provides a fascinating insight into the development of ideas concerning erosion surfaces.

Much of the confusion arises because there is no unequivocal definition of an erosion surface and because similar surfaces can apparently be created by contrasting suites of processes. This is a classic example of equifinality whereby the same end-product can be achieved in a number of different ways. The main types of surfaces are peneplains, pediplains, etchplains and surfaces of marine erosion.

Peneplain was used by W. M. Davis as the name for a gently undulating surface of low relief produced at the end of an erosion cycle by processes of subaerial erosion. Towards the end of the cycle when all the slopes are very gentle the agencies of waste removal must everywhere be weak. 'The landscape is slowly tamed . . . and presents only a succession of gently rolling swells alternating with shallow valleys . . .' (Davis 1899, p. 497). Relief becomes less and less and an almost featureless plain, showing little sympathy with structure and controlled only by a close approach to base level, characterises the penultimate stage. The ultimate stage would be a plain with little relief, but perceptible inequalities of 30–50 m would probably still remain. These inequalities in relief will be sufficient to influence the fine detail of the variations in soil distribution.

Davis, although inventing the term peneplain, acknowledges that the idea came from the writings of Powell. Thus, Powell writes of mountains as being ephemeral topographic forms that ultimately would be reduced to low near-horizontal surfaces and 'the degradation of the last few inches of a broad area of land above the level of the sea would require a longer time than all the thousands of feet which might have been above it' (Powell 1876, p. 196).

Since its formulation, the peneplain concept has been heavily criticised, especially by workers whose experience has been in arid rather than humid temperate environments. The first major challenge was W. Penck's *Die Morphologische Analyse* in 1924. His conclusions were based on three assumptions. These were: slopes are established by the downcutting of streams and are steeper the greater the rate of downcutting; slopes once established retreat away from the stream parallel to the original declivity; and steeper slopes are denuded more rapidly than gentle slopes. As far as soils are concerned, original remnants of earlier erosion cycles remain unaffected longer in the Penckian model than they do in the Davisian cycle.

At the same time as Penck was introducing his ideas in Europe, workers in the arid south-west of the United States were describing pediments; gently concave erosion surfaces often mantled with superficial materials of variable thickness that occurred at the foot of the steep mountain scarps. It was soon clear that pediments were being formed by lateral planation by streams issuing from canyons and by rills cutting at the foot of the mountain slopes. Outliers and unreduced remnants were being denuded by weathering and transportation of the debris by rills. Pediments develop by the parallel retreat of mountain fronts and the ultimate cyclic landform is the **pediplain**, consisting of broad coalescing pediments (King 1953).

The effects of intense chemical weathering and the advance of the weathering front can produce a third class of erosion surface; the **etchplain**. The term was used by Wayland (1933) when suggesting that some planation surfaces in Uganda may have been created by the etching of a previously formed surface by deep chemical weathering followed by surface wash. Budel (1957) recognised the role of deep chemical weathering and wash and introduced the term double surfaces of planation (*doppelten Einebnungsflachen*) which are developed as the weathering front descends into bedrock, while surface wash removes the upper weathered zones. Adams (1975) argues that etchplains seem to require the presence or former existence of a previously developed peneplain or pediplain. Also, the deep contemporaneous weathered zone on a peneplain, if stripped away, might reveal a surface that could be considered an etchplain. The differences between the various erosion surfaces are probably not as great as many workers suggest.

Large, extremely level uplifted erosion surfaces, have also been attributed to the work of the sea. Except in those cases where marine deposits attest to their origin as uplifted coastal plains, it is doubtful if many erosion surfaces are the result of marine action. To produce a marine cut surface of any appreciable extent requires a steadily rising sea level for a considerable period of time. A rising sea level is necessary because, without it, marine energy is soon dissipated as the marine bench extends and the cliffs will not be attacked nor the material moved across the surface. What little is known of previous sea levels suggests that this situation is extremely unlikely.

Thus, erosion surfaces created by marine agencies are likely to be limited in extent.

Other specialised, but limited, forms of erosion surface exist. **Altiplanation** terraces are formed by the retreat of rock slopes by frost action with the material being removed by solifluction. In common with other erosion surfaces, they cut across different rock structures. The term **panplanation** was introduced by Crickmay (1933) to describe the process of lateral planation by rivers which develop a uniform surface of overlapping rock cut straths as divides are cut through. But it is doubtful if such a surface has ever been positively identified.

Age and status of erosion surfaces

Erosion surfaces take a long time to be produced and during that time external conditions might have changed. These conditions include crustal movements and climate, and many erosion surfaces are now isolated from the processes that created them. It must also be borne in mind that erosion surfaces are not necessarily everywhere synchronous. The following classification of erosion surfaces defining their current status has been produced by Adams (1975):

(a) *active surfaces* are still being shaped by their formative processes;
(b) *dormant surfaces* are those whose active shaping has ceased temporarily, perhaps by climatic change, and are expected to function again in the near geological future;
(c) *exotic surfaces* have formed under climatic conditions that no longer exist;
(d) *defunct surfaces* have been removed from the action of erosive processes by uplift or depression;
(e) *buried surfaces* have been covered by sediments not related to their shaping;
(f) *exhumed or fossil surfaces* are buried surfaces that have been exposed by the removal of a non-genetic cover such as later sediments.

Soils may provide part of the information on which to base the status of any erosion surface. Thus, exotic surfaces can be identified by a soil cover that indicates that there have been gross changes of climate. Also, the type and distribution of soils will make it clear when active erosion surfaces are being formed at the expense of dormant or exotic surfaces, as in many parts of Africa. But analyses of this nature require a thorough understanding of the way erosion surfaces develop and how soils respond to this development.

It is clear that, with respect to both the development of peneplains and pediplains, soil formation and distribution is governed by the factors that affect the stability of slopes. The ideas embodied in Penck's *aufbereitung* concept and the distinction made by Holmes (1955), between derivation and wash slopes, are instructive in this respect.

Aufbereitung concept

This account of Penck's *aufbereitung* concept relies heavily on the summary and assessment by Beckett (1968). As weathering progresses, a soil becomes reduced, in the sense that there is a reduction in its average particle size. The potential mobility of the soil increases as the particle size decreases and all reduced material above a local base level is 'metastable', i.e. vulnerable to removal. The maximum rate of natural denudation is the rate at which surface material which is almost, but not quite mobile, becomes mobile. Thus, on any particular gradient there is a degree of reduction beyond which soil is too mobile to remain *in situ*. Therefore the development of the landscape will be a function of this metastability of the soil; which is a function of the ease with which soil is detached and transported. But, Penck argues, landscape development depends also on the metastability of the particular site, which is a function of slope gradient and proximity to the next major break or change of slope on the slope profile. An encroaching pediment will thus affect the soil on the upper surfaces long before that soil is affected physically by erosion. The *aufbereitung* concept stresses that even on relatively uniform surfaces there will be sufficient differences to affect local rates of soil development. This is also implicit in the synthesis put forward by Holmes (1955).

Penck's argument is that the landscape develops by the upslope encroachment, upon each slope element, of the one below it of lower gradient and greater degree of reduction. This would lead to a landscape of concave slopes formed by slope retreat. However, the analysis by Beckett (1968) has shown that the relationship between gradient and degree of reduction applies only to those parts of a slope on which there is no accumulation of transported material. The relation applies to the convex and linear slope portions but not to the concave portion. If Penck's arguments are applied only to the convex and linear portions, the landscape must develop by crest-lowering and crest-rounding and lessening of gradients. If these conclusions are realistic then one is forced into 'the ironical position that Penck's argument, when applied only within its implicit limiting conditions and for the elements of a slope to which it can be shown to apply, provides support only for the so-called Davisian cycle of landscape development' (Beckett 1968, p. 19).

Derivation and wash slopes

Holmes (1955) argues that the slopes of a landscape can be classified as derivation slopes or wash slopes: derivation slopes correspond to scarps and wash slopes correspond to pediments. The derivation slopes are unstable and provide a source of sediment which is deposited on or transported across the wash slopes. Also, gross derivation or wash slopes have small areas of the other within them. As derivation slopes are potentially unstable areas, the proportion of derivation slopes determines the rate of denudation. The difference between derivation and wash slopes is not wholly dependent on slope gradient but also depends on the local factors, such as vegetation and climate. This implies that landscapes do not necessarily develop by continuous downwasting or backwasting, but that development will take place when slopes are unstable and cease when they become stable.

These ideas imply that the landscape can be divided up into three major zones: zones where material is being eroded, zones where material is being deposited and, perhaps, zones which are neither losing nor gaining material. The first two are equivalent to the 'sloughing' and 'accreting' zones of Butler (1959) (see Ch. 10). Continuous soil development will only take place on the third zone. The accreting zone will show sequences of buried soils while soils on sloughing zones might be kept perpetually youthful. But, the location of these zones on slopes will vary with time, thus sloughing zones will become stable and accreting zones may become unstable. The geomorphological end-product will be a relatively smooth erosion surface and it will only be pedological information that will show how the surface was developed.

Soil development and the formation of erosion surfaces

It is likely that soil development and distribution will be governed by the different evolutionary pattern of the various erosion surfaces. Mulcahy (1961) has outlined, in general terms, soil development in relation to a landscape evolving by the cutting of successive pediments (Fig. 6.1). The

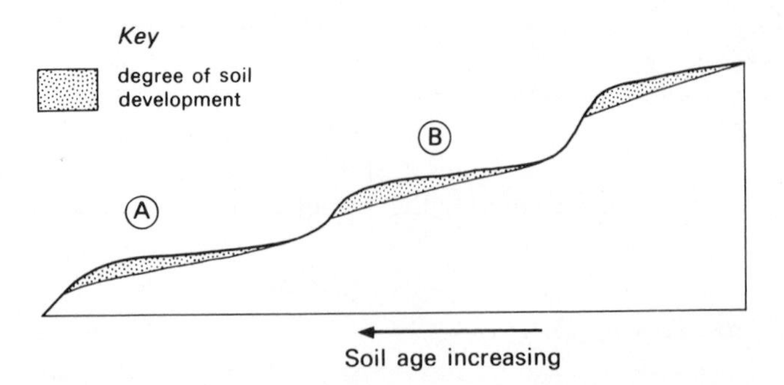

Figure 6.1 Soil development in relation to the retreat of scarps (after Mulcahy 1961).

landscape shows a series of pediments separated by steep scarps. The lower surface A is developing at the expense of B and is, therefore, younger. If soil age is equated with the age of the surface, the soil on surface B will be older and better developed than that on surface A. A stepped succession of soils should ensue and this will also be the situation in a region which is composed of a series of uplifted and partially dissected peneplains. Also, on any one pediment the outer edge is older than the sites nearer to the retreating scarp. This should mean that the soils will be better developed towards the edge of the scarp and less well developed near the scarp foot, while soils on the scarp face will be perpetually youthful. But a number of factors operate to upset this simple sequential development.

Appreciable soil development will only take place once the surface is no longer affected by severe erosive processes. In the case of pediment formation the whole surface may be affected all the time and not just the areas nearest the retreating scarp. The processes acting on pediments have been described in the following terms by Kirk Bryan (1922). As streams emerge from mountains, large particles are dropped and smaller ones are carried forward. The fine debris washed down by rains is moved forward by rill action to the larger streams, but because the supply of debris is small, the rills are not fully loaded and are effective erosive agents, reducing the height of interrill areas. The irregularities of the pediments are removed, with the higher parts being eroded and the lower parts infilled with debris.

Differential sorting of sediment on the surface will cause changes in texture, bulk density, permeability and porosity, which will affect the formation of soil. Thus, soil development will depend on the local configuration of the rill network. It also means that soils existing on erosion surfaces will not all be of the same age and may also be considerably younger than the surface itself. The criteria adopted by geomorphologists in the identification of erosion surfaces are not sufficiently critical to detect minor planations and the ages assigned to major erosion surfaces may bear little relation to the absolute age at any point. But, as Mulcahy (1961) points out, such minor planations and modifications may remove complete soil profiles, exposing weathered or even unweathered material on which soil formation starts afresh. The pattern of soil distribution and age relations is completely altered.

Stone lines

The term stone line was first used by Sharpe (1938) for a line of angular to subangular fragments which parallels a sloping surface at a depth of several feet. Parizek and Woodruff (1957) have emphasised that stone lines are three-dimensional features and proposed the term carpedolith—a carpet of stones in the soil.

Stone lines can be produced in a variety of ways. Biological activity and the reworking of material by termites will lead to a concentration of finer above coarser sediments. Normal pedologic activity will produce something similar by the breakdown of material to finer texture above coarser-textured material. Sharpe (1938) thought stone lines were produced by creep: coarse fragments become detached from veins and more resistant layers and are drawn along at the base of the creeping soil; they work their way downward in the soil profile because of the more rapid movement of the surface layers. But the studies of Ruhe (1959) have shown convincingly that, where stone-line surfaces of large areal extent exist, they are due to erosion by running water with the subsequent mantling of a lag gravel by finer-textured sediment. Stone lines point to the existence of former erosion surfaces.

Stone lines also indicate that the soil may have developed in more than one kind of parent material. The material beneath the stone line is weathered from bedrock whereas the material above the stone line is transported sediment. The material comprising the stone line may be different from either the material above or below it, having been transported in from different rocks occurring further up the slope. Stones not only indicate the presence of an erosional break but may indicate the extent of the processes that have taken place.

Pedological relationships

Many of the points discussed above can be amplified with a few specific examples. Many of the till landscapes of North America show a sequence of stepped levels as a result of multi-cyclic erosion of the landscape. One such area, in Iowa, has been intensively studied by Ruhe (1956). The highest surface is a relict of the Kansas drift plain that has not been changed by erosion since Kansan time. In terms of the classification outlined earlier, this is a defunct surface. But the situation is complicated by the fact that fossil soils or palaeosols (see Chapter 10) of Yarmouth–Sangamon age exist on the surface and have been buried by the later deposition of loess. So in places the surface is buried, in other parts the surface has been exhumed by later erosion and the time status of the surface can only be established by a detailed examination of soils and sediments. Morphology alone is not sufficient.

Cut into the upper surface is a pediment of Late Sangamon age in the sediment of which exists a palaeosol. The low level of the landscape is an Early Wisconsin pediment, cut into the Kansan till, below the Late Sangamon surface. No palaeosol is found on this surface indicating that loess deposition followed very closely after the cutting of the pediment. All these surfaces, and their respective sediments, have been subjected to erosion and sedimentation in Late Wisconsin–Recent time. This has had the effect of exposing the Yarmouth–Sangamon and Late Sangamon palaeosols and

Table 6.1 Soil properties on stepped erosion surfaces in Iowa (from Ruhe 1956).

Surface	*Soil*	*Thickness of solum (in)*	*Thickness of B horizon (in)*	*Clay in B horizon (%)*	*Soil horizon*	*Wrh index*	*Wrl index*
Recent	A	15	11	31.2	A	0.79	2.09
	B	32	23	32.2	B	0.92	2.13
	C	29	22	34.6	C	0.68	2.21
	average	25	19	32.3			
Late Sangamon	D	46	32	50.7	A	1.27	3.06
	E	70	56	49.1	B	1.12	2.49
	F	39	29	49.5	C	0.77	2.04
	average	52	39	49.7			
Yarmouth–Sangamon	G	87	70	51.4	A	2.11	4.85
	H	68	44	57.7	B	1.62	3.00
	I	85	62	50.7	C	1.28	2.57
	average	80	59	53.2			

surfaces so that these relict soils and surfaces are now part of the modern landscape. Although standard geomorphological techniques allow the general sequence of events to be established, it is the detailed information provided by soils and the pedologist that completes the picture. As surfaces become older, the thickness of the soil increases, the thickness of the B horizon increases, the clay content of the B horizon increases and the heavy and light mineral weathering indices increase (Table 6.1). Wrh is the ratio of quartz : feldspar and wrl the ratio of zircon and tourmaline to amphiboles and pyroxenes. The indications are that, although the vegetation at the time of soil formation was different on the individual surfaces, the soil differences are mainly a function of time.

Detailed pedological investigations also enabled Heine (1972) to correct some misconceptions about erosion surfaces in Germany. Although some true Tertiary soils were discovered, many of the supposed soil formations of the Tertiary period, that had been used to explain the morphologic development of the region, were found to be hydrothermal disintegration products. Also, many surface residual deposits and soils showed different age sequences because of the possibility of exhumed surface remnants.

Detailed analysis of soils and weathering products enabled Ollier (1959) to establish the sequence of erosion surface formation in Uganda. Ollier's premise was that present day soils were formed on pre-weathered rock. The sequence of events is outlined in Figure 6.2. Very deep weathering took place below the Gondwana surface to form a thick rotted layer. During the African cycle of erosion much of the weathered rock was removed by the growth of pediments and the parallel retreat of the steep slopes. But, the base level of erosion during this cycle was reached before all the weathered rock was removed and the surface is largely cut across

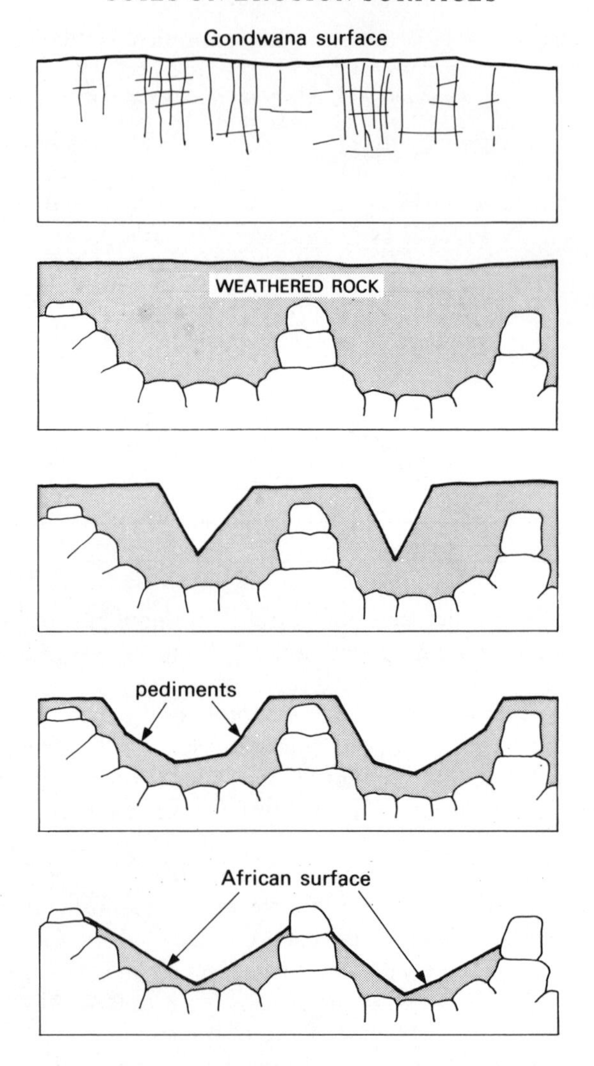

Figure 6.2 Two-cycle theory of African landscape development (from Ollier 1959).

this rotted rock. The problem was to establish that two cycles had been involved, i.e. a cycle of deep weathering followed by erosion and modern soil formation, and not one continuous cycle of weathering and soil formation.

Evidence used by Ollier (1959) was both pedological and mineralogical. Various features of the soil profile pointed to a two-cycle origin: the presence of stone lines in the soils indicates that a change has taken place in the surface conditions; the type of laterite in the profiles also supports a two-cycle theory. If laterite forms in weathered rock, *in situ*, it tends to be massive and vesicular, full of channels which are lined with layers of limonite. If laterite forms in upper, sorted layers of the profile it forms murram pisoliths. The laterites in the exposed profiles appear to be of this second type. Evidence provided by soil profiles certainly suggests a two-cycle origin for the landscape. The mineralogical evidence is less conclusive. Soils formed on the upper slopes are rich in mineral species whereas the lower slopes are relatively poor; the implication being that the upper soils are formed from the lowest zones of the weathering profile. This could be achieved by greater weathering on the midslopes than on the upper ones but, taken in combination with the pedological evidence, it is strong evidence for the two-cycle theory as proposed by Ollier.

Laterite and topography

Many of the concepts discussed so far are exemplified in relationships between laterites and planation surfaces. As already seen, the nature of the laterite was a crucial element in Ollier's two-cycle theory. Level or nearly level surfaces in tropical areas are often capped by laterite and laterite was thought to be a residual formation requiring a landsurface of low relief to allow the downward percolation of surface waters. Steep slopes allow rapid runoff and removal of weathering products whereas gentle slopes allow an ingress of water which removes the more mobile soluble constituents and causes the accumulation of the less mobile weathering products.

This concept agreed well with the traditional Davisian cycle of peneplanation as slopes are reduced to a point where vertical water movement through the soil and regolith is substantially greater than runoff. The laterite was assumed to develop with the landsurface and the end-product would be an erosion surface covered with a thick sheet of residual material. However, later ideas implied that laterite was a precipitate and only began forming after the planation surface had been created and after conditions of a stable, but fluctuating, water table had been achieved. Thus, Maclaren (1906), Woolnough (1918) and Wayland (1931) all concluded that a level erosion surface was necessary before laterite could form. This idea had far-reaching consequences as far as denudation chronology and the evolution of erosion surfaces was concerned since a thick laterite sheet was regarded as indicative of an erosion surface which had survived for a considerable period of time.

However, more extensive surveys have shown that laterite occurs on quite steep slopes, with angles in the range 7–10° being frequently noted (e.g. Pallister 1951, Mulcahy 1960, Trendall 1962). Laterite has even been reported on slopes up to 20° (De Swardt 1964). It has been argued that these slopes are not the original form of the surface but are due to post-incision modifications. These modifications may be due to cambering of the margins of mesas, accelerated erosion of the margins of mesas forming a convex waxing slope or the creation of detrital laterite as a link between high and low level laterite sheets.

Studies by MacFarlane (1971), in Uganda, suggest a compromise. MacFarlane regards laterite as a residual precipitate. Groundwater laterite is believed to accumulate as a mechanical residuum during the late stages of a downwasting landsurface. The precipitates form within the range of fluctuation of the groundwater table, which sinks as the landsurface is lowered by erosion. The precipitates accumulate as an increasingly thick layer in the lower parts of the soil. When downwasting has ceased, the water table becomes stabilised, the residuum is hydrated and a massive variety of laterite forms which has the appearance of a true precipitate.

The relationship between laterite and erosion surfaces is critical and has played a prominent part in the construction of most African denudation chronologies. MacFarlane (1971, 1973, 1976) has thoroughly reviewed the place of laterites in the development of theories of landscape evolution in Uganda. Wayland (1921) originally recognised a single peneplain, which he called the Buganda peneplain and which he associated with the African cycle of erosion. But subsequently he recognised two others, an older surface present on the resistant interfluves of south-west Uganda and a younger surface developed in the central lowlands (Wayland 1933, 1934). More detailed observations of the Buganda surface have shown that it possesses considerable relative relief and that some laterite sheets are apparently continuous through an altitude range of about 150 m. Thus, there is the problem of explaining why laterite, presumed to be a planation surface development, should occur at a variety of altitudes on one of the best examples of a laterite-capped planation surface.

This prompted MacFarlane (1976) to pose a number of questions. Is laterite formation restricted to surfaces of low relief? If the answer is yes, the Buganda surface is not one but two or even three surfaces. Can laterite form on a surface of high relief enabling a single Buganda surface to exist? Can laterite form synchronously at different levels, possibly covering surfaces at different ages? Can a single near-level laterite surface be differentially lowered, creating the impression of two chronologically separate surfaces? Can laterite form independently on separate interfluves to form an acyclic 'apparent peneplain'? To answer these questions the relationship between laterite development and landsurface development needs clarification and, as MacFarlane (1976) concludes, a closer study of laterite type and landsurface type should make a positive contribution to an understanding of landsurface evolution in the tropics.

Soils on stepped erosion surfaces

Periods of extensive erosion surface development and intermittent uplift have produced sequences of stepped erosion surfaces in many parts of the

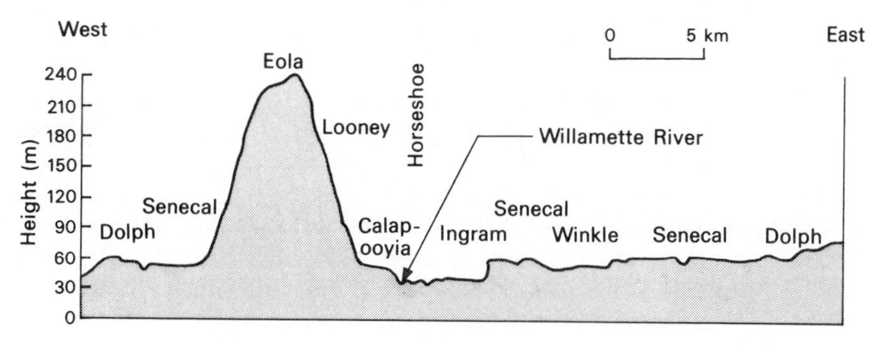

Figure 6.3 Suite of erosion surfaces in the Willamette Valley (from Parsons *et al.* 1970).

world. The time sequence of surface development provides either an absolute or relative means of evaluating soil development. Soil types might be expected to reflect the age and type of the surface and such a sequence occurs in the Willamette Valley, Oregon (Parsons *et al.* 1970). Seven major surfaces exist (Fig. 6.3). The Eola surface is the oldest stable surface in the region and is probably Middle Pleistocene in age; the topography is typically rounded and surface materials are deeply weathered. The Dolph unit exists as dissected flats, underlain by weathered gravel and bedrock, and includes numerous small pediments and straths; it is probably also Middle Pleistocene in age. The Calapooyia surface is extensive and extremely level; differences in elevation usually do not exceed a metre; surface drainage is poorly organised and sluggish and the surface may be of marine or estuarine origin; it is probably of Late Pleistocene age.

The Senecal surface appears to be a slight modification of the Calapooyia surface occasioned by minor incision of the drainage net; it must also be Late Pleistocene in age. The Winkle surface is one of the most extensive, and is the oldest surface associated with the present drainage systems. Subparallel bar and swale topography of old channels suggests braided overloaded stream channels in some localities and radiocarbon dates indicate an age of approximately 6000 years BP. The Ingram surface includes the higher flood plains of the Willamette River. The lower parts of this surface commonly flood and the oldest radiocarbon date for the surface is 3290 ± 120 years BP. The Horseshoe surface is the lower flood plain of the Willamette River and its major tributaries and is underlain by sandy alluvium and gravel.

The soils developed on the surfaces show interesting sequences. Organic matter distribution with depth shows a general decrease in organic content with increasing age of the surfaces. The weighted mean percentage of organic matter in the A horizons decreases from soils on the Horseshoe to those on the Calapooyia surfaces. It then increases from the Calapooyia to the Eola. This may represent greater accumulation of humus under forest whereas the soils on the lower surfaces were developed under grass vegetation. The soils of the younger surfaces have high base saturations. Soils with B horizons having clay films are first found on the Winkle and Senecal surfaces and thereafter become more prominent. Variations in soil types are also created by local differences of drainage and moisture status. Organic accumulation appears to be rapid in the Willamette Valley and the A horizons of the youngest soils may contain as much organic matter as soils on the older surfaces. Base saturation decreases progressively from younger to older surfaces. Also, cambic B horizons appear to form within 550 years but the development of argillic horizons requires between 550 and 5250 years.

Differences between soils on stepped erosion surfaces are not always simply the result of age differences, other environmental factors have to be taken into consideration. A series of stepped erosion surfaces occur in the Wahiaua basin, Oahu, Hawaii (Ruhe 1975). Although the dominant part of soil associations relates to a specific erosion level, most soil associations cross several levels in the sequence (Table 6.2). The soil association areas are concentrically banded with elevation which also corresponds with climatic zones. The differences in soils are likely to be due to differences in climate and not just to age differences. The same problem of isolating the relevant environmental factors was faced by Young and Stephen (1965) in Malawi. The ferrallitic soils of the high plateaux possess a much higher organic matter content in their upper profiles than the soils of the lower plains. This sharp increase in organic matter levels at higher altitudes was explained by the drop in the mean annual temperatures.

These studies demonstrate the problem of isolating the factors involved in soil formation. Erosion surfaces may represent a time sequence but other factors will also have changed through time.

Table 6.2 Correspondence of soil associations with geomorphic surfaces, Oahu, Hawaii (from Ruhe 1975).

Soil	*Geomorphic surface (%)*							
	5	*6*	*7*	*8*	*9*	*10*	*11*	*12*
Molokai	30.0	57.6	4.4					
Lahaina		39.8	50.6	9.7				
Wahiawa		2.3	26.8	46.7	18.5	5.8		
Leilehua				6.0	29.6	64.4		
Waipio						85.7	14.3	
Kunia		1.1	21.4	32.4	45.0			
Mahana					15.7	84.3		
Manana						41.7	56.4	1.9
Paaloa							25.0	75.0

Conclusions

The analysis and identification of erosion surfaces was common geomorphological practice in the 1950s and 1960s. But, as most of the studies were based purely on morphology, many of the results were inconclusive. The analysis of soils has added a new dimension to studies of erosion surfaces; similarly, erosion surfaces provide a chronological framework within which to study the soils. But soil properties and time cannot be directly related to the age of the surface. The surface may be appreciably older than the sediments and soils which mantle its surface. Also, it is the time a particular process has been active that is important and not necessarily the total time that soil material has been exposed to weathering. Time zero might not be the same for two measured properties. But, although a surface may have many kinds of soils these soils will have a common degree of soil development.

7 Soils of floodplains and river terraces

Characteristics of alluvial and terrace soils

River-formed landscapes are reasonably similar the world over in terms of both landforms and processes. This does not imply that soils from diverse river areas are identical but that the natural landforms and soil patterns are similar. This is true for both suites of terraces and the varied landforms of floodplains. There is a very delicate interaction between the geomorphological processes operative in river landscapes, the materials involved and, ultimately, pedological processes. Soil materials and drainage conditions show sharp boundaries related to major landform types (Fig. 7.1). Near present or former river beds, natural levees occur consisting of sandy sediments. These levees form the highest parts of the landscape and are, consequently, freer drained. Behind the levees lower lying areas occur formed of heavier-textured and impermeable silts and clays. Accumulation of organic matter in these backswamps is common. Terrace deposits are, in general, coarser grained and their greater relative elevation promotes freer drainage and waterlogging is less common. They are also usually beyond the influence of active river processes.

Levees and basins are universally important and this means that soil maps of rivers such as the Rhine, Mississippi, Indus, Tigris and Euphrates look remarkably similar. There are, nevertheless, major differences between the alluvial soils of these river basins. These differences tend to reflect the larger geomorphological and climatic systems of which the rivers are a part. A major distinction has been made between the alluvial soils of tropical and temperate areas (Edelman & Van der Voorde 1963). In this respect the provenance of the rivers is important. In temperate areas alluvial soils are generally rich in mineral nutrients partly due to the effect of glaciations providing powdered fresh minerals to be transported and deposited by rivers. Many tropical and subtropical rivers have their headwaters in deeply weathered igneous areas and their deposits consist of quartz and other resistant minerals.

Alluvial soils are usually thought of as being young or undeveloped. But not all such soils are undeveloped in the strict pedological sense since some changes that resemble soil formation may have taken place. Thus, some soils of alluvial swamps have distinct dark-coloured topsoils that have the characteristics of A1 horizons. Soils on river terraces are often called alluvial but since the majority of river terraces are of Pleistocene age, many

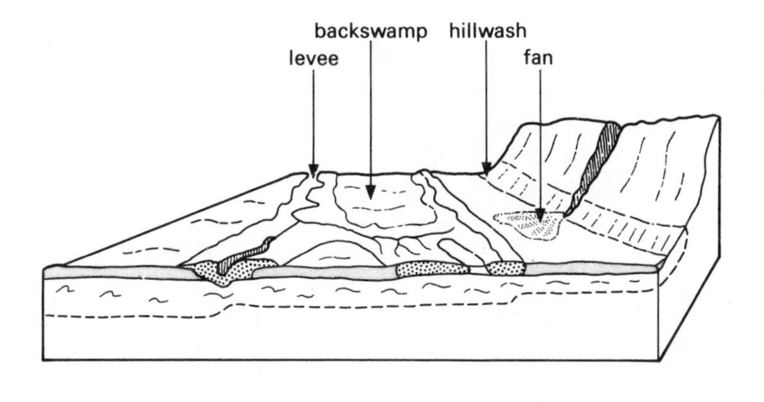

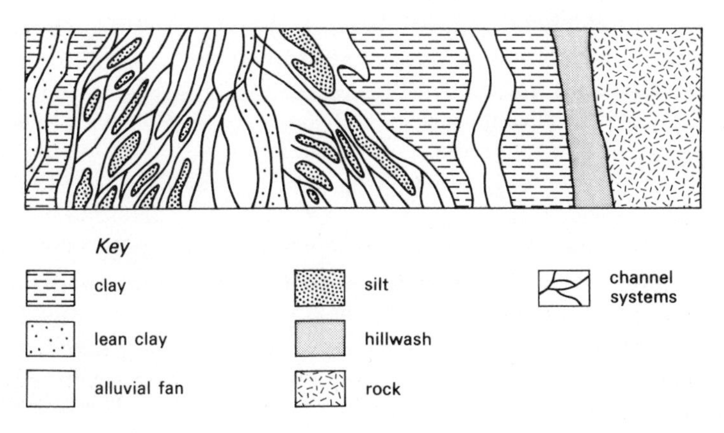

Figure 7.1 Landform and material relationships on the Awash River, Lower Plains, Ethiopia (after Currey 1977).

such soils are well developed. Although major differences between alluvial areas exist, the basic interrelationships between minerals, geomorphological and pedological processes provide a unifying theme within which to view the evolution of the soils.

Sedimentary and pedologic characteristics

Alluvial and river terrace soils exhibit characteristics of both sediment transport and deposition and soil formation. Sediment stratification is common and has a considerable effect on the development of pedogenic properties. Ruhe (1975) has drawn attention to this problem in the floodplain of the Missouri River. Within the channel belt the soils have light coloured horizons and their subsoils are stratified and show little pedogenic weathering. The soils in the meander belt have thicker dark coloured surface horizons and their subsoils show pedogenic structures. In the Wolf Creek floodplain in Iowa, ridge soils have little profile development but depression soils have clayey B horizons with strong subangular blocky structure. Both soils show sedimentary stratification but whereas ridge soils have little vertical organisation of clay, depression soils have good vertical organisation.

Failure to take effects of stratification into consideration leads to an overestimation of the rates of pedogenic processes and it is, therefore, important to be able to separate the sedimentological from the pedological characteristics. Several approaches to this problem have been suggested; the main principle employed being the disunity of the depth functions of soil properties (Foss & Rust 1962, Sleeman 1964, Oertel & Giles 1966). The method adopted by Raad and Protz (1971) is a variant of this theme. They identified sediment stratification by establishing statistically significant changes with depth in the values of the ratios of the percentage sand to percentage silt. This enabled prominent stratifications to be identified, clearly important in determining the rate and type of soil formation.

An interesting addition to this work has been suggested by Green (1974) based on the sedimentological work of Moss (1962, 1963, 1972). Using Moss's (1962) procedure, long (p) and medium (q) dimensions of grains down to a minimum length of 0.1 mm were measured. It seems possible to separate *in situ* soils from transported sediments by plotting the elongation function p/q against p for different grain sizes. Elongation function curves for an *in situ* granitic soil show that its quartz grains become increasingly equant with increasing size. The coarser particles of alluvial soils become less equant and more elongated with increasing grain size. This also seems to be a characteristic of bed load sediments. On this basis it is possible to distinguish transported from *in situ* parent materials.

Effects of flooding

Alluvial soils are often subjected to periodic flooding causing a variety of soil features. Gleying is often present and many seasonally flooded soils possess coatings of clay on the soil peds (Brammer 1964, 1966, 1971). These coatings are especially common in the seasonally flooded soils of East Pakistan where they are typically continuous, thick and grey in colour. They occur in the young floodplain soils of the Brahmaputra and Ganges alluvium as well as in some terrace soils. They have also been observed in the Guadalquivir floodplain soils of Spain, in northern Malaya and in the Indus plain. These coatings may have been mistaken in the past for clay skins, cutans or argillans and therefore overlooked.

Flood coatings differ from argillans in the rapidity with which they develop and, to a certain extent, in their composition. They consist, not only of fine clay, but also of silt and humus and, even in young floodplain soils, may be 0.5 mm thick. Their colour suggests that they consist of material from the soil itself and are not created by sediment brought in by floodwater. On the Ganges floodplain, where sediments in the floodwater tend to be calcareous, the coatings are non-calcareous in soils with non-calcareous topsoils. The coatings only occur in soils that are flooded for part of the year and are best developed in deeply flooded soils and least in floodplain ridge soils only intermittently flooded. Therefore, the formation of the coatings seems to be directly related to flooding.

After continuous submersion for about two weeks, the surface few inches of the soil become strongly reduced. Subsoil layers are, apparently, unaffected and remain oxidised. Topsoils that have undergone these seasonal alternations of reduction and oxidation for a long period will have lost most of their free iron by vertical leaching and will be in an easily dispersed condition. But it is still not clear how the dispersed topsoil moves to lower layers. It may occur at the start of the flood season when the topsoil will be saturated before lower layers and dispersed soil may flow by gravity down subsoil cracks and pores. It could also occur after flooding ceases when rains may wash soil down cracks opened up in the drying soil. But these conditions occur in a variety of non-flooded soils and seem not to result in the formation of coatings. There does, therefore, seem to be a relationship between coatings and flooding. The material in the coatings is finer than the adjacent soil mass. The coatings are often banded, indicating successive flows, but the clay appears to be non-oriented. It is considered by Brammer (1971) that the coatings move as thin mudflows possibly under hydraulic pressure from the weight of floodwater resting on the soil surface. Whatever their origin, these coatings appear to be specifically related to seasonal flooding.

Chemical composition and clay minerals

Alluvial soils in temperate regions often contain calcium carbonate and acid conditions are uncommon. In subtropical areas, with relatively dry climates, the calcium carbonate content of alluvial soils can be high but in the humid tropics many alluvial soils contain no calcium carbonate and acid conditions prevail. Exceptions to this rule do occur, such as the part of the Ganges–Brahmaputra delta which impinges on deposits rich in calcium carbonate. Because of the more acid conditions of tropical alluvial soils, cation exchange capacities are lower and exchangeable base ratios different from those of temperate regions. Also, due to the greater destruction of organic matter at higher temperatures, alluvial soils in tropical regions generally have a lower organic matter content.

The alluvial materials of the major river basins may have been transported considerable distances before being deposited. Thus, they are representative of the climatic and geologic conditions prevailing in all parts of the basin. This is exemplified in their clay mineral suites. Some alluvial deposits contain only kaolinite whilst in others the clays are largely montmorillonite. The relationships between climate, weathering, rock type and clay minerals are nicely portrayed in the alluvial soils of Sri Lanka and Egypt. Sri Lanka can be divided into wet and dry zones with a narrow intermediate band between. For the most part, the components in the alluvial soils of Sri Lanka are derived from clay and the associated minerals formed by the *in situ* weathering of the largely Precambrian igneous and metamorphic rocks. In the wetter south-western zone, the situation is complicated by the subsequent weathering of the soils (Herath & Grimshaw 1971). Gibbsite is common in the wet zone and can be attributed to the tropical weathering conditions. Secondary weathering frequently produces mixed layer minerals. The alluvial clay minerals of the dry zone have been formed by similar primary weathering processes but after transportation and deposition they have not been subjected to the same secondary weathering processes. These soils contain kaolinite and montmorillonite but gibbsite is absent. In the intermediate zone, minor amounts of gibbsite may be present together with montmorillonite.

Similar relationships occur in the soils of the Nile delta (Hamdi 1959, 1967, Hamdi & Iberg 1954, Hamdi & Barrada 1960). These soils are formed largely from the weathering products of the igneous rocks of the Ethiopian Plateau. The clay fraction of the upper layers of the alluvium is mainly composed of illite whereas in the deeper samples montmorillonite is common. It appears that over thousands of years submergence in groundwater alters the illite to a montmorillonite-like clay. Montmorillonite is the major clay mineral higher up the valley of the Nile (Hanna & Beckmann 1975). This montmorillonite could have been carried by the Nile from its upper basin or formed *in situ* by secondary weathering as the chemical status of the soils, such as high pH, abundant calcium and magnesium, provides conditions favourable for the formation of montmorillonite. It seems probable, considering the amount of montmorillonite present, that much was brought by the Nile but some has been formed in the soils. The illite and chlorite present probably originated from suspended matter carried by the Nile (Nabhan *et al.* 1969).

Floodplain landforms

Many of the characteristics of floodplain soils are related to the distinctive nature of the landforms. A very comprehensive review of floodplain geomorphology has been provided by Lewin (1978) and only the major elements are discussed here. The main landform types are illustrated diagrammatically in Figure 7.2, and although this is a composite diagram, each type can be frequently matched with actual examples. The complexity of

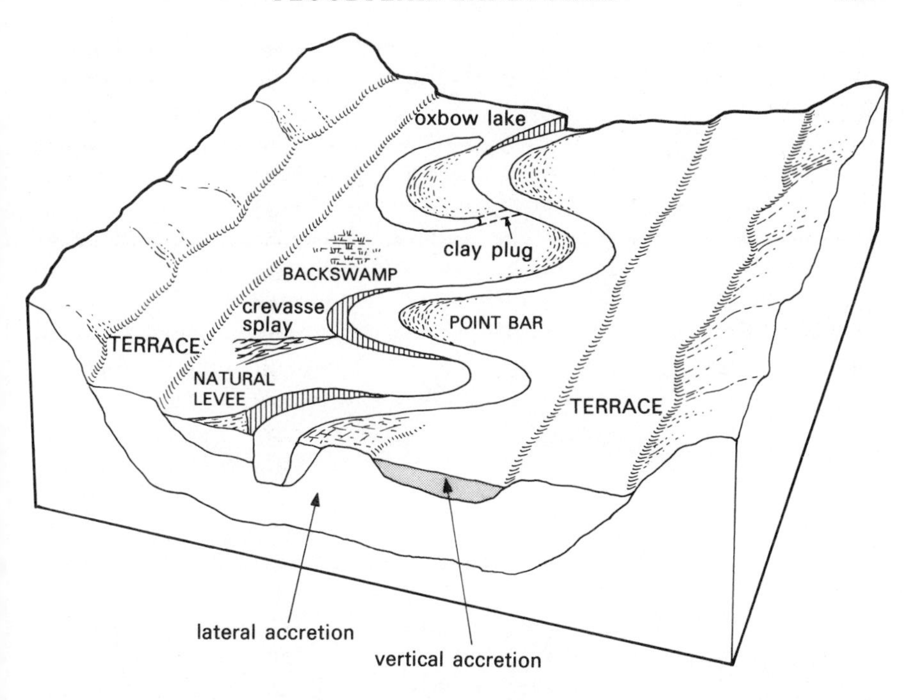

Figure 7.2 Landforms and deposits of a typical floodplain: Va, vertical accretion; La, lateral accretion (adapted from Vanoni 1971, Gregory & Walling 1973).

cut-off processes on the River Mississippi has been comprehensively described by Russell (1967), whilst crevasse splay development is well seen on the Seyhan River, Turkey (Russell 1967).

Each landform type is associated with a slightly different type of sediment and, therefore, the basic soil materials differ quite considerably. Point bars are built up of layers of coarse gravel with smaller amounts of sand. Levees are generally formed from the coarser materials carried by turbulent water. During river flows in excess of the bankfull stage, the water extends beyond the levees, becomes less turbulent and begins to flow as sheets. Bed load is deposited close to the channels whereas the suspended load, with the finer silts and clays, accumulates in the backswamp areas. The rate of sediment accumulation depends on the size and quantity of sediment and the frequency of flooding. Coarse material settles rapidly but finer clays take longer. In areas where flooding is infrequent, lateral accretion and channel deposition are most significant in the formation of floodplains. In the United States of America, Leopold and Wolman (1957) have estimated that 80–90% of floodplain deposits have been formed in this way and only 10–20% by the process of overbank deposition. However, in other areas such as the humid tropics, where fine-grained material is dominant and where flooding is frequent, overbank deposits assume greater importance. In Papua, especially along the Fly and Strickland Rivers, Blake and Ollier (1971) have shown that backswamps and overbank deposits are dominant.

Many of the general principles just described can be illustrated by taking examples from the major river systems of the world. One of the best documented is the Lower Indus Plain. The lower valley of the River Indus possesses an intricate pattern of channels, levees, cutoffs and sand bars. Occasionally, exceptionally high summer floods have allowed the river to shift its channel and establish a new route, but normally the annual floods simply overtop the levees causing flooding but no major course changes. These processes have created a number of distinctive landforms together with their associated deposits (Fig. 7.3).

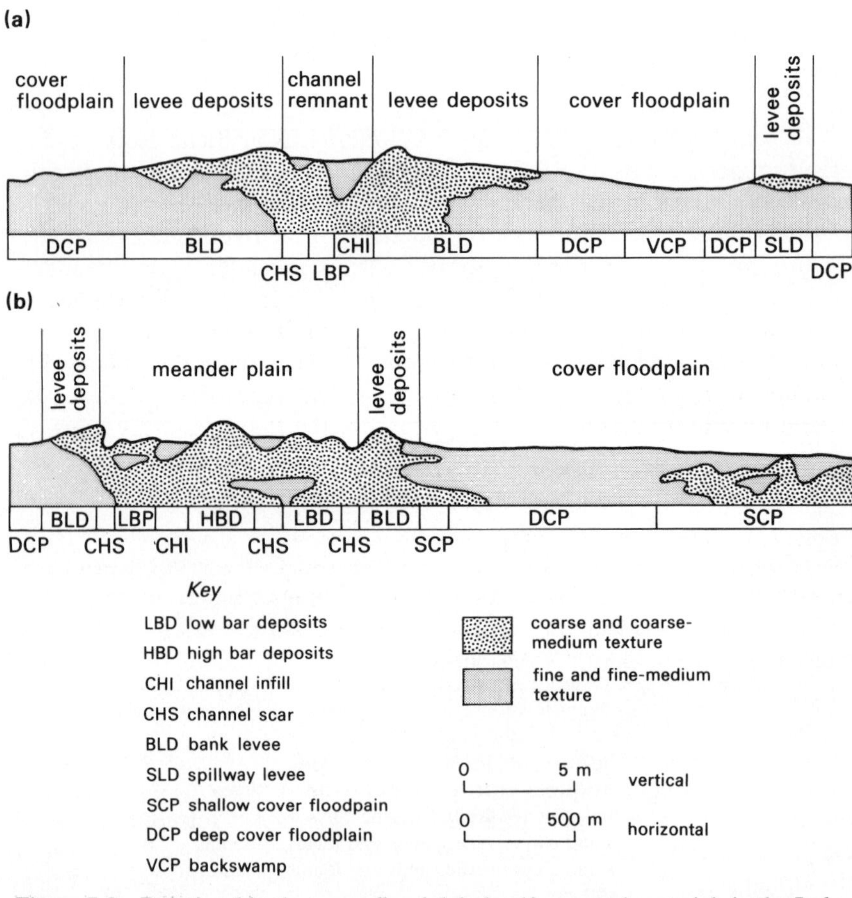

Figure 7.3 Relationships between floodplain landforms and materials in the Indus Plain (from Holmes & Western 1969). (a) A channel remnant surrounded by cover floodplains is separated by extensive levee deposits. (b) A meander plain is located near an earlier buried meander plain, now a shallow cover floodplain. The texture pattern in (b) is considerably more complicated than that shown in (a).

Table 7.1 Geomorphological components of the Indus floodplain (adapted from Holmes & Western 1969).

Geomorphological subregions	*Landform association*	*Deposits*
meander floodplain	meander plain channel remnant active floodplain	high bar low bar channel-scar channel infill
levees	levee forms	bank levee spillway levee flood levee anthropic levee
levee floodplain	levee floodplain	shallow cover deep cover backswamp

The present course of the Indus is contained by artificial banks and a large proportion of its flow is diverted into canals to feed one of the largest irrigation systems in the world. Alluvial deposition has, therefore, been considerably curtailed. Recent former courses of the river can be traced by the presence of distinctive landforms such as meander scars, meander scrolls and deserted channels. Two distinctive elements can be recognised: the broad floodplain of the major river was able to contain much of the annual floods restricting the development of levees (large and numerous meander scars are its main features); a second type of floodplain was formed by minor branches of the river – here the floodplains are narrow,

Table 7.2 Nomenclature for describing sediment characteristics in the Indus Valley (from Holmes & Western 1969).

Nomenclature	*Characteristic texture*
AL	dominantly coarse sand and loamy sand
A	mixture of sands and loams
Bd	sands and loams overlie silts and clays at depths > 100 cm
B	sands and loams overlie silts and clays at depths between 50 and 100 cm
Bs	sands and loams overlie silts and clays at depths < 50 cm
Xlm	complex but basically sands and loams
X	complex sequences of fine and coarse textures
Xhv	complex but basically silts and clays
Cs	silts and clays overlie sands and loams at depths < 50 cm
C	silts and clays overlie sands and loams at depths between 50 and 100 cm
Cd	silts and clays overlie sands and loams at depths > 100 cm
CdV	upper horizons dominated by clay
D	almost entirely silts and clays
Dv	clays probably dominant

Table 7.3 Relationship between texture and landforms in the Indus Valley (from Holmes & Western 1969).

	Percentage sites per textural group														
Landform association	*AL*	*A*	*Bd*	*B*	*Bs*	*Xlm*	*X*	*Xhr*	*Cs*	*C*	*Cd*	*Cdv*	*D*	*Dr*	*Total sample*
low bar deposits	41	27.5	0.5	4	–	4	2	–	14.5	6.5	–	–	–	–	200
channel scar deposits	26.7	26.7	–	6.7	–	6.7	33.3	–	–	–	–	–	–	–	15
channel infill deposits	0.7	–	–	–	0.7	–	1.3	5.7	2.5	24.8	9.6	–	35.0	19.7	157
levee deposits	10.2	21.3	5.5	33.1	7.1	12.7	21.6	–	0.8	–	–	–	–	0.8	127
shallow cover floodplain	0.4	1.8	–	0.4	–	0.4	10.2	11.1	5.8	53.3	8.9	–	6.7	0.9	225
deep cover floodplain	–	–	0.5	1.0	1.0	–	–	0.5	–	0.5	8.3	–	80.7	7.3	192
backswamp deposits	–	–	–	0.6	–	–	0.3	1.5	–	2.4	0.3	5.4	6.3	83.3	336

with bars and meanders restricted to a single channel. Annual floods easily overtopped the levees forming extensive cover floodplains. These major landforms and their associated deposits are listed in Table 7.1.

Texture of the materials

A detailed textural investigation of the various deposits of the Indus Valley has been undertaken by Holmes and Western (1969). They devised a symbolic nomenclature to distinguish both texture, comprising coarse, medium-coarse, medium-fine and fine, and depth relationships, i.e. whether coarse-textured material overlay fine or vice versa. The nomenclature used is shown in Table 7.2. An examination of the detailed textural classes shows that individual landform associations tend to be dominated by one or two classes. Thus, levees are dominated by class B, backswamp deposits by class Dv and shallow cover floodplains by class C (Table 7.3). This produces the general associations portrayed in Table 7.4. There is clearly a general relationship between texture patterns and factors such as elevation, relief, waterlogging, salinity, permeability and drainage. This generates a complex textural map but always the relationship between landforms and material is evident.

Similar relationships have been shown by Ruhe (1975) along the River Missouri (Fig. 7.4). Sites 4 and 8 are on natural levees and are dominated by sand and silt in the upper parts of the profile. Sites 5, 6 and 7, in the intervening basins, are dominated in the upper parts by silt and clay with a reversal occurring in the lower parts of their profiles. The lower sediments are channel accretion deposits whilst the upper sediments are the result of vertical accretion. Many other examples of similar relationships can be cited such as those of the Tigris and Euphrates Valleys (Buringh & Edelman 1955) and of the Llanos Orientales of Colombia (Goosen 1972).

Table 7.4 Characteristic textures of landform types in the Indus Valley (from Holmes & Western 1969).

Landform association	*Characteristic texture*
high bar deposits	AL
low bar deposits	A, AL, Cs, Xlm
channel scar deposits	A, AL, Cs, Xlm
channel infill deposits	D, Dv, Cd, CdV
bank levee deposits	D, AL, Bd, B, Xlm
spillway levee deposits	A, Bd, B, Xlm
flood levee deposits	Al, A, Bd, B, Bs, Xlm
anthropic levee deposits	A, Bd, B, Bs
shallow cover floodplain	CdV, Cd, Dv, D
backswamp deposits	Dv, CdV

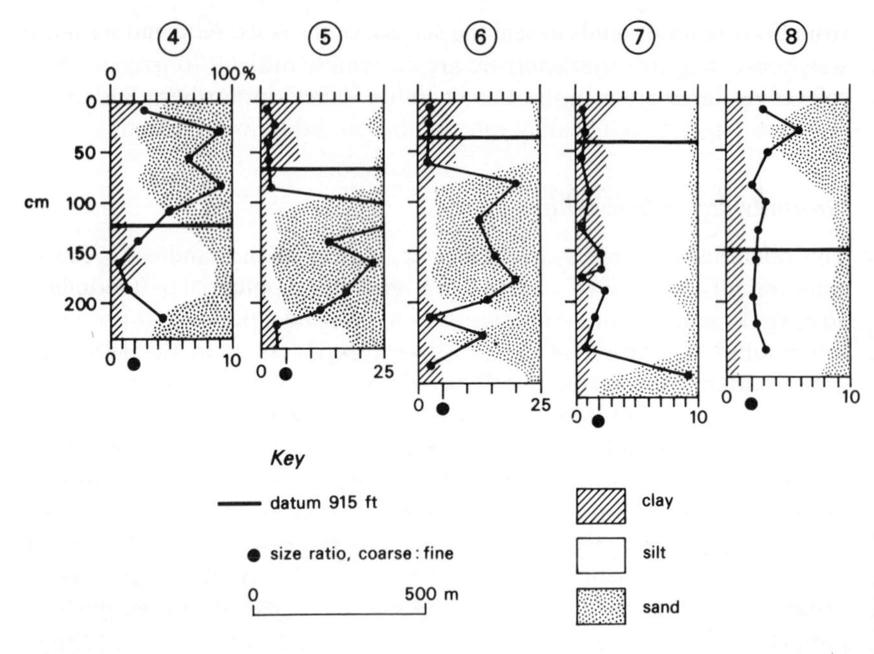

Figure 7.4 Soil changes with position and landforms on the Missouri floodplain (after Ruhe 1975).

Agricultural potential of floodplain soils

Once alluvial soils are drained they are usually very productive. Drainage of virgin alluvial soils is followed by great changes in soil conditions. This process has been termed the ripening of soils and entails a considerable loss of water and a contraction of the mass of the material producing numerous cracks. At the same time, air can enter the soil through the cracks and oxidation takes the place of reduction. Alluvial soils may be worthless in their unripe state but after completion of the ripening process they may be extremely fertile. Once ripening or initial soil formation has taken place, the soil can withstand considerable periodic inundation without losing its pedogenic structures.

As mentioned earlier, alluvial deposits are usually stratified. This stratification is gradually destroyed by the combined action of plants and animals which enter the soil once drainage has taken place. This biological homogenisation gradually reaches deeper layers and eventually the soil becomes mixed and develops an open structure with a heterogeneous pore system. Where biological homogenisation is limited so too are the agricultural conditions of the soil. Alluvial soils of arid and semi-arid regions present specific problems for reclamation. The deposition of thin laminae from flowing water tends to seal the surface of the soils. Arid and semi-arid soils possessing this characteristic are extremely difficult to irrigate. Such soils cover large areas in the Lower Indus Valley, in northern Sudan and northern Nigeria. Self-sealing can also be caused by wind action.

Groundwater relationships

The relationship between groundwater, materials and landforms can be complex but is vital when assessing the agricultural potential of floodplains. Irrigation can affect these relationships by causing a permanent rise in the water table as a result of the downward percolation. In the 1880s the groundwater level in the Northern Plains of Victoria, Australia, was reported as deep but now, since irrigation, it is within 1 m of the surface (Currey 1977). This is crucial because once the groundwater level reaches a critical depth, usually the root zone at about 1 m, crop growth is seriously affected. These critical depths will vary with each soil type because capillary forces vary, such that a water table may be raised by 3 m in clay soils but only 20 cm in sandy soils (Talsma 1963). An additional problem is caused by the uneven rise of the water table producing 'mounds' of groundwater.

Mound formation may be due to overintensive irrigation (Bouwer 1962). The permeable soils of abandoned, infilled river systems are susceptible to this problem. The soils adjacent to these infilled river systems may not be as permeable but a rise in the water table is still likely. A rise in the water table is also likely along channels as channel seepages cause pressure barriers which may locally raise the water table until it reaches the surface. Currey (1977) has described these features in the Lower Awash River delta in Ethiopia. He identified three systems: (a) a regional groundwater resource, under pressure, below an impermeable barrier, beneath the plains; (b) groundwater mounds developed on impermeable barriers; and (c) the Awash River groundwater mound developed in the floodplain as a result of river water infiltration. If the groundwater mounds can be identified preparations can be made to forestall their effects (Kirkham 1965).

Salinity problems

Salinity is a problem in floodplain soils. The salt content will depend on the soil type as well as its age and the climate of the region. Clay soils contain higher percentages of salts than sandy soils. Salt accumulates as water evaporates from lakes and swamps with the self-sealing processes described earlier considerably enhancing the ponding of surface water. Initially, the salt forms on the surface but this may be buried by the further addition of silt and clay.

Relatively young, reworked sediments in upland river valleys contain the least percentage of salt. Also, young abandoned stream sediments contain less salt than older sediments. The groundwater of major riverine plains is generally highly saline and the recognition that there could be damage caused by salt movement in an irrigation district is important to the long-term success of any project. In the irrigated areas of the Murrimbidgee Valley, Australia, surface salt has developed in a few clearly defined zones (England 1964). These are at the bases of stoney or gravelly hillslopes as a result of downslope seepage, at channel margins, in areas underlain by shallow aquifers and in low lying situations.

Similar relationships occur in the Loddon River Plains, Australia (Macumber 1969). Here, salinisation is closely related to the type of river valley and the presence of buried stream systems. In many places, saturated channel sands exist within 2–6 m of the surface covered by more recent clay accretion. Waterlogging of these sands is enhanced by large swamps formed outside levees of a former river. Elsewhere, the relationship between salinisation and buried stream systems is more complex. Shallow sands may have either a detrimental or beneficial effect on salt accumulation depending on whether they can act as a drain carrying salt from the surface. Peck (1978) has stressed that salinisation is also common in non-irrigated soils especially in Canada and Australia and is also related to soil type and topographic position.

Many of these problems have had to be overcome in the Mesopotamian Plains of Iraq. Their soil characteristics and irrigation problems have been extensively documented (Smith & Robertson 1956, Smith 1957, Harris 1958, Jacobsen & Adams 1958). Many of the soils are gypsiferous and this causes special problems. The soil profile consists of two contrasting layers: Mesopotamian alluvium overlying gypsiferous material. The alluvium is brown, fine textured and highly calcareous but contains no appreciable gypsum. There is, therefore, a sharp boundary to the underlying horizon. Gypsum becomes a problem when it is present in sufficient quantities to dominate the characteristics of the soil material. This seems to occur at a gypsum content of about 10%, with soils containing more than 25% gypsum providing a poor medium for plant growth (Smith & Robertson 1962). In spite of these problems, the alluvial plains of the large rivers of the tropics form a very large natural resource and there is no reason why such alluvial plains should not be as productive as similar plains in temperate regions.

River terraces

Terraces are abandoned surfaces not related to the present stream and are composed of two parts: the scarp and the tread above and behind it. The term 'terrace' is, therefore, usually applied to the entire feature, i.e. both tread and riser. A distinction needs to be made between terraces cut in bedrock and those comprising the former floors of alluvial valleys. The former is the 'strath' or 'rock-cut terrace' in which the riser consists almost entirely of bedrock capped by only a thin veneer of gravel. The other major type, the fill terrace, is composed entirely of sediment laid down during a period of aggradation. The term terrace is sometimes used to mean the deposit itself when alluvium underlies tread and riser. But it should be referred to as a fill, alluvial fill or alluvial deposit to differentiate it from the topographic form.

The sequence of events leading to the terrace features may include several periods of repeated alluviation and incision. Thus, it is possible to develop any number of terraces and, depending on the magnitude and sequences of deposition and erosion, any number of fills or different stratigraphic units could be deposited. Also, several alluvial fills could be present in the valley even when no terrace exists. In some cases the sequences are simple but very often the terraces and terrace sequences are complicated by hillwash deposits and, in much of Europe and North America, by the deposition of loess. The movement of soil and sediments across the tread and down the steep slope of the riser often makes the topographic features indistinct and the resultant soils very complex. The classic example of this is in the valley of the River Svratka at Cerveny Kopec, Brno, Czechoslovakia. Here a suite of five terraces has been largely obliterated by successive periods of loess deposition, soil formation and hillwash movement. It is estimated that about 900 000 years of loess deposition are represented. In situations such as this, soil relationships are quite complex.

Soils of river terraces

A good illustration of the relationships between soils and river terraces is that described by Walker (1962b) from Australia. A suite of four terraces exists in many of the steeply graded drainage basins inland of Nowra, New South Wales. The typical structure of these terraces is shown in Figure 7.5. Terrace 4 has a wide flat surface 10–12 m above the stream and is composed of layered sands overlain by silts and clays. Terrace 3 is narrower and occurs 3 m above stream level. It is essentially composed of loam and clay loam although there is a basal gravel layer. Terrace 2 occurs on the shoulder of number 3 terrace and is composed of evenly textured loams and clay loams. Terrace 1 is immediately adjacent to the stream and about 1–2 m above it. The sediments are extremely variable and consist of stratified sands and gravels with occasional bands of silt and clay. The terraces seem to represent simple phases of alternating stream entrenchment and aggradation. Radiocarbon dating suggests dates of 29 000 ± 800 years BP for terrace 4; 3740 ± 100 years BP for terrace 3, 390 ± 60 years BP for number 2 and a modern age for terrace 1. Walker (1962b) con-

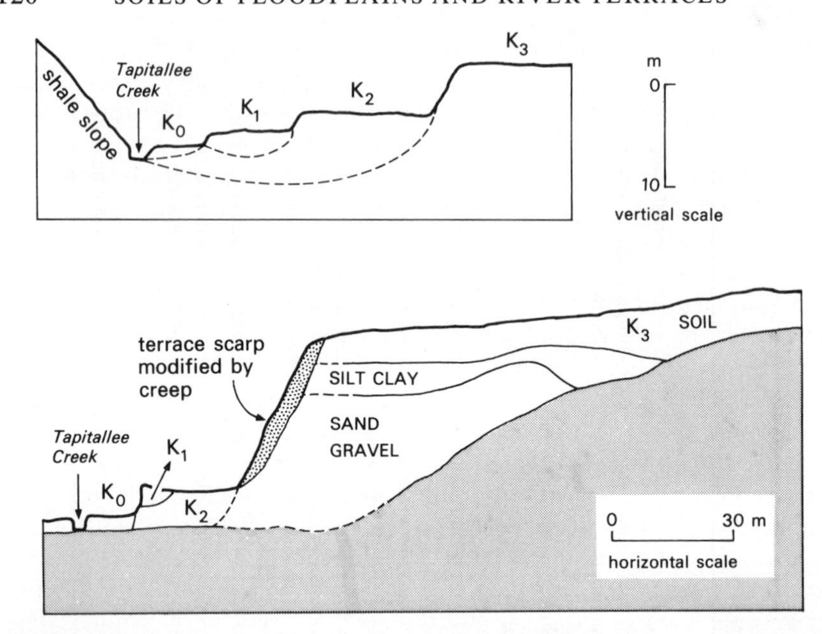

Figure 7.5 Terrace systems near Nowra, New South Wales (from Walker 1962b).

cludes that increased stream aggradation and terrace building were associated with changes to relatively drier climatic conditions.

There has been very little true soil formation on terrace 1. Depositional laminations are evident and faunal processes have not homogenised the deposits. Terrace 2 soils have a prairie type profile with only A and C horizons. The A horizon is a loam to clay loam with strong granular structure and abundant faunal activity. On well drained areas, faunal activity and organic matter have penetrated to about 1 m, below which depositional structures are evident. There has been very little alteration or translocation of mineral constituents. Soils of terrace 3 are grey-brown profiles with gradational A/B/C horizons. There is a gradual increase in clay content with depth and clay skins coat the voids in the lower B horizon. Soil formation has involved some segregation of mineral constituents. Red and yellow podzolic soils occur on terrace 4 with a pale, light-textured surface overlying a thick plastic clay B horizon. Segregation of sesquioxides has occurred in the lower A2 and B1 horizons and the B2 horizon colours are reds and yellows with grey mottles at depth. There is a strong segregation of mineral constituents and reduced faunal activity and organic matter penetration.

Although considerable attention has been paid to the stratigraphy of terrace sequences in the British Isles few studies of soils on these terraces exist. This may be because several major climatic changes have occurred during the formation of these terrace suites, which makes the relating of

Table 7.5 Soils on four terraces in the Kennet Valley, England (from Chartres 1980).

Site	*Depth (cm)*	*Colour (Munsell notation)*	*Texture*	*Other characteristics*
Furze Hill	0–60	very pale brown (10YR 7/4)	gravel with a sandy silt loam matrix	abrupt, irregular lower boundary
	60–120+	yellowish-red (5YR 4/8)	gravel with a sandy clay matrix	reddened mottles
Hamstead Marshall	0–120	light yellowish-brown	gravel with a silt loam matrix	clear, irregular lower boundary
	120–170	yellowish-red (5YR 5/6)	gravel with a sandy loam matrix	reddened mottles
	220–280	strong brown (7.5YR 5/6)	gravel with some sandy loam matrix material	evidence of fluvial bedding
Thatcham	0–50	light yellowish-brown (10YR 6/4)	sandy loam with occasional stones (flints)	distinct wavy lower boundary
	50/60–110	reddish-yellow (7.5YR 6/6)	sandy loam with common stones (flints)	faint reddish mottles
	110+	–	gravel	evidence of bedding at 2 m+
Beenham Grange	0–120/150	light yellowish-brown (10YR 6/4) to dark brown (7.5YR 4/4)	silt loam over silty clay loam	merging boundary with underlying gravels
	120/150+	–	gravel	evidence of fluvial bedding

pedological differences between terraces to time alone, extremely difficult. One notable exception to this is the study by Chartres (1980) in the Kennet Valley of southern England. The soils of four Quaternary terrace levels have been examined in great detail showing major differences between the deposits and soils (Table 7.5). The three upper terraces possess distinct colour and textural discontinuities within the matrix materials. The contact between these two different horizons on the Furze Hill and Hamstead Marshall terraces appears to have been disrupted by periglacial activity.

This study is important for the way it combines detailed analysis of the soils, including micromorphological techniques and heavy mineral assemblages, with geomorphological and geological consideration to produce a synthesis for the evolution of the complete terrace sequence. It is a prime example of the techniques of different disciplines complementing and reinforcing each other. The suggested sequence of phases of soil development is shown in Table 7.6. On the two highest terraces a phase of strong clay illuviation associated with manganiferous staining and rubification of the illuvial features represented the first phase of soil development. This was followed by disturbance of the illuvial features and then a second phase of clay illuviation characterised by the formation of strongly oriented egg-yellow ferriargillans. A second period of disturbance, accompanied by aeolian addition, and a third phase of clay illuviation completes the sequence. A great many features of relevance to Quaternary history may, therefore, be incorporated in polygenetic soil profiles.

The differences between these soils are essentially a function of time although the texture of the sediments has some influence. The terrace soils described by Corless and Ruhe (1955) in western Iowa represent a different situation as the terraces are mantled by loess and, because of this, formation commenced at approximately the same time. A well developed loess-mantled terrace occurs along the valley sides of the Nishnabotna River and is probably a remnant of a glacial outwash–alluvial complex. The same series of soils is found on the terraces and on the nearby uplands, therefore it appears that soil-forming factors have had a similar effectiveness on the terraces and the uplands. But differences occur as a result of slight variations in topography. Where runoff is inhibited on the flats and small depressions on the terrace surfaces, the A horizons become thicker and the B horizons become finer textured. This situation is reversed where gentle slopes exist and water can run off rather than accumulate.

Soil formation on river terraces is, therefore, a function of the distinctive landform–material assemblage and the age of the terrace. Where the terrace sequences are relatively straightforward and especially where they can be dated, considerable information is provided about the way soils and soil properties change with time. Conversely, analysis of soil properties is essential to the accurate elucidation of landscape history. Analysis of soils on terrace sequences therefore provides useful information for both pedologists and geomorphologists.

Table 7.6 Phases of soil development on terraces in the Kennet Valley, England (from Chartres 1980).

Furze Hill	*Hamstead Marshall*	*Thatcham*	*Beenham Grange*	*Possible time of formation*
aeolian additions	aeolian additions	aeolian additions	Terrace deposition	(Late Devensian)
cryoturbation: formation of involutions, disruption of existing soils	cryoturbation: formation of involutions and ice wedges, disruption of existing soils	cryoturbation: disruption of existing soil; less marked than at the two upper sites		Devensian
pedogenesis: lessivage of egg-yellow clays	pedogenesis: lessivage of egg-yellow clays	pedogenesis: lessivage of egg-yellow clays		Ipswichian
		terrace deposition under niveo-fluvial conditions		Wolstonian
cryoturbation	cryoturbation			
pedogenesis: lessivage and rubification	pedogenesis: lessivage and rubification			Hoxnian
terrace deposition	terrace deposition			Anglian or older

Conclusions

River floodplains and terraces, with their distinctive landform and material assemblages, provide an excellent natural laboratory within which to examine soils and pedological processes. In this respect great care has to be taken to differentiate sedimentological from pedological processes as failure to take sedimentary effects into consideration can lead to an overestimation of the rate of soil formation. Sequences of terraces are fruitful areas for the pedologist, especially if the terraces can be dated. This allows soils to be placed in a realistic chronology and conclusions reached on the rate of soil formation. The properties of the soils also provide the geomorphologist with invaluable information concerning past climatic regimes and stable/unstable phases in the history of the landscape. A knowledge of floodplains and river terraces, their conditions and soils, is additionally important because these are some of the world's most densely populated and intensively cultivated areas.

8 Soils of coastal plains and sand dunes

Materials in coastal systems

Salt marshes and coastal plains are composed of a variety of materials. These materials have been derived from various origins, transported at various speeds and converted to stable deposits at varying rates. Usually elements of marine, fluviatile and aeolian deposition are all involved. The type of material available for transport and deposition varies according to the texture of the rocks eroded. Thus, the generally soft rock coastlines of south and east England produce essentially silt deposits whereas the cliffed coastlines of much of north Scotland produce sand deposits. Rivers draining areas of predominantly basic rocks also provide many nutrients which favour the growth of salt marsh vegetation such as *Artemisia maritima* and *Carex divisia*. On other coasts varied geological frameworks and local energy conditions determine the mix of sand and silt sizes.

Much of the material in the coastal systems of the northern hemisphere are reworked glacial deposits which form an offshore store from which supplies are drawn to feed the depositional coastal system. Large tropical rivers produce great quantities of silt, usually originating in chemically weathered interiors, some of which is deposited on the river floodplains. But most of the sediment is transferred to the offshore coastal systems to be reworked many times before being finally deposited.

There may also be variable inputs of material related to seasonal climatic patterns. Kamps (1962), working in the Eastern Wadden of the Netherlands, reported an increase in clay content from spring to autumn. Increased flocculation due to high salinity and coagulation of particles by increased biological activity in the summer months results in the deposition of large quantities of mud. In autumn, salinity and biological activity decline and greater storm activity leads to a greater influx of silt and sand-sized particles.

The diversity of origins for coastal materials is shown in the evolution of coastal deposits along the Surinam coast, where both fine-textured clays and coarser sands are found (Augustinius & Slager 1971). These materials have reached the coast by many different pathways. It is thought that the clay originates from the Amazon River and has been transported in suspension along the north coast of South America by a variety of local currents (Reijne 1961). The sand deposits originate in parts of French Guiana, as well as the Surinam rivers and are moved by offshore and tidal currents. In addition, there is a variable input from wind action.

The interaction of the many processes acting in the coastal systems with the variety of materials ensures that a complex series of landforms is created. Many of these landforms are initially unstable media for both soil formation and vegetation growth but eventually, by either upwards growth by accretion or change in sea level, soil processes can be initiated. The sequence soil formation follows is then determined by the landforms and materials.

Coastal landform systems

Within the tidal flat complex, vertical tide fluctuations can be used to define geomorphological subenvironments and a number of zones can be identified emphasising the delicate relationships between landforms, sediments and sedimentary structures (Fig. 8.1). In temperate areas, tidal zones are characterised by a complex series of creeks and channels. The offshore marine zone possesses very gentle seaward slopes and is composed of coarse to medium sands. Shell debris may be locally abundant and the clay content increases seaward. The channels and inlets may be up to 600 m wide and 20 m deep near the major inlets, narrowing to 2 m wide and 1 m deep in salt marshes. Some anomalously wide, deep and bluntly terminated channels are often found behind beach ridges. They were probably connected to earlier inlets but are now filling with finer sediments. Because of the fast currents, channel sediments are coarser than the sediments in adjacent environments.

Bays are generally of two types: large, deep and open bays occur in the widest part of the coastal complex whereas small, shallow bays with less than 50 cm of water at low tide characterise the narrow inland parts. The physical structures of the sediments and biota composition vary with these different settings.

The zone between mean low water and mean high water consists largely of sand, especially in the vicinity of creeks. Some distance away from creeks sedimentation of mud and sand takes place and an unvegetated area of flat sand bars and mudflats forms which is dry at low tide. At mean high water marked changes occur. There is a drop in current velocity and the deposition of more clayey sediment occurs. The frequency of flooding also declines allowing the growth of vegetation which in turn speeds up silting, but, as the frequency of flooding is further decreased, the sedimentation rate also declines. There is a much more rapid upgrowth of sediment along the banks of creeks causing an eventual inversion of relief and the future soils of these levees will have a lower clay content and a better drainage. Periodic swings of tidal channels ensure large-scale recycling of sediments over comparatively short periods of time. Studies at Caerlaverock, Dumfries, Scotland, suggest that virtually all of a 1500 acre salt marsh has developed in less than 140 years.

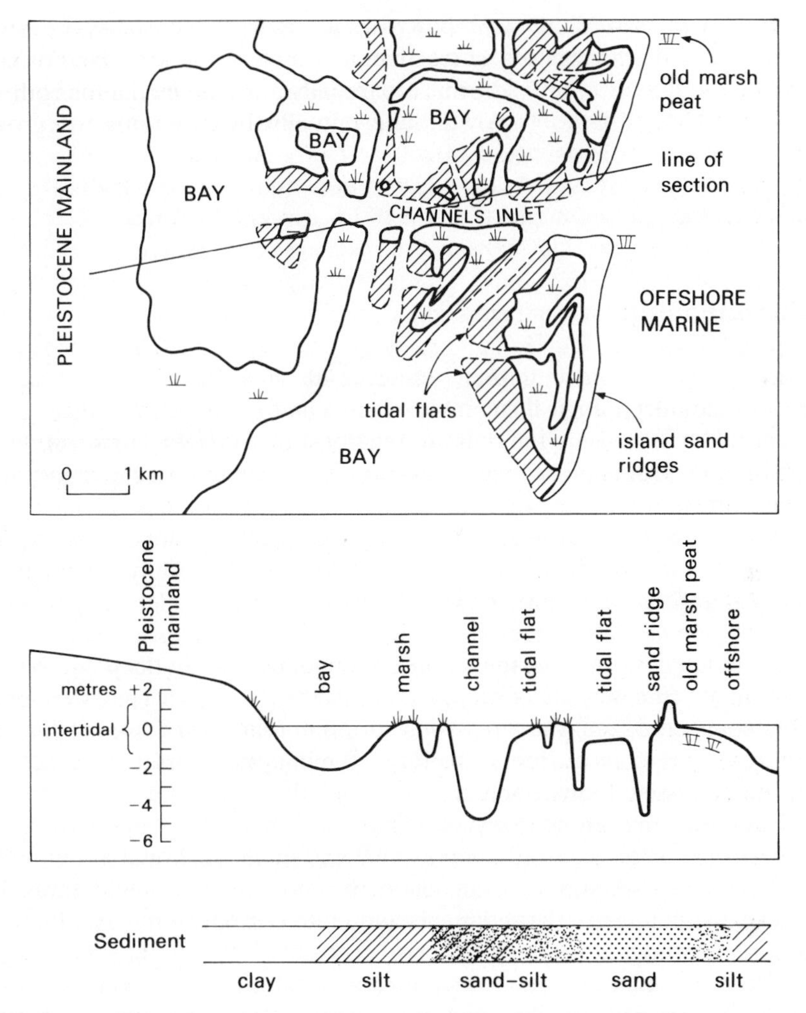

Figure 8.1 The major geomorphic subenvironments of coastal areas (from Harrison 1975).

Tidal flat organisms play a significant role in the process of accretion. Many filamentous algae have considerable silt trapping powers and in a series of experiments Ginsberg *et al*. (1954) discovered that a culture of the algae *Phormidium* could establish a surface mat of 4 mm of sediment in 24 h. Molluscs also have an influence on accretion either by providing surface roughness which enhances sedimentation (Gillham 1957) or by reconstituting clay into faecal pellets which settle quicker than unmodified clay particles (Kamps 1962).

The physical characteristics of the sediments change as the conditions change. In the bare mudflat stage, the material is anaerobic, scarcely consolidated with a limited permeability of the order of 10^{-4} m/d. The withdrawal of water brings about an irreversible dehydration and the soil shrinks and cracks. The sediments also undergo the process of consolidation, either under their own weight or from overlying sediments (Jelgersma 1961). This consolidation can affect the true rate of accretion as, under certain circumstances, the annual accretion can be compensated by the settlement of the sediments (Stearns & MacCreary 1957).

On tropical coasts, clays are concentrated in mudflats connected to the coast. In South America, these mudflats often consist of a sling mud which appears to be a gel which forms when there is a high concentration of fine particles (Diephuis 1966). The particles form a structure that settles as a whole and the sling mud gradually changes into an unripe clay by settling of the particles. As soon as the surface of the mud becomes higher than mean tide level, mangroves (*Avicennia nitida*) start to grow and further aid the depositional process by acting as a filter and slowing down the velocity of the currents.

Soil formation and salt marsh development

As accretion develops and the sediments remain above the water for longer periods of time, gradual changes in microrelief take place. With levee growth at the edges, the original convex contours of the open mudflat surfaces develop into concave surfaces. Eventually the relief levels off as the higher parts receive less material and the lower areas continue to receive sediment. Pioneer plants, which bind the deposits, are patchy at first and low vegetated hummocks develop, but as sediments accumulate, the plant cover spreads and becomes more varied. Depressions, starting as wide shallow channels, gradually develop into dendritic systems of creeks crossing elevated salt marsh. The properties of the resultant soils depend partly on the physical and mineralogical constitution of the parent materials and partly on past and present environmental factors. Parent materials are chiefly transformed by the leaching of soluble salts and native calcium carbonate, by oxidation, reduction and translocation of iron-bearing minerals and by the development of physical structures and the penetration of organic matter. In areas which are covered for most of the time no oxidation can take place and no soil formation occurs. Areas nearer the shore, especially the higher salt marshes and the creek ridges, are periodically dry and fissures form due to the shrinkage of the clay. But narrow vertical differences in altitudes result in considerable differences in submergence. As Gray and Bunce (1972) have shown for Morecambe Bay, England, the pioneer salt marsh zone has a mean submergence of about 350 tides, whereas the low-level saltings have a mean submergence of about 200 tides and the high-level saltings about 50.

Unconsolidated materials of loam and clay texture with appreciable reserves of calcium carbonate will favour the development of well structured soils if they are not permanently wet or saline for too long. Areas permanently above high water mark suffer fluctuating water tables. Low water table levels in summer allow extensive subsurface shrinkage and fissuring producing strong prismatic and angular blocky peds. The inhibiting effect of poor drainage on structure development is seen in soils developed on creek bed deposits which possess weak structure in the surface horizons and are structureless after about 30 cm. As the material cracks and fissures, stresses are set up which result in the formation of a surface soil considerably denser than might be expected. This stress is caused by unequal water extraction by the roots of pioneer vegetation and by uneven remoistening in the rainy season. To a certain extent this stress is compensated by plastic flow seen in the plasmic fabrics of the subsoil. The mechanism of this process is still largely unknown but, when the soil dries out, the salt content of the surface soil seems to increase considerably and it is thought that as water flows through the fissures and biopores, electrolyte concentration in the soil solution in the vicinity of the pores decreases, peptization takes place and part of the soil mass flows to the subsoil.

When land has been reclaimed and flooding prevented, soil development is largely governed by the seasonally fluctuating water table levels. Three zones can then be discerned in the soil: the first is below the lowest level of the water table and is a zone of permanent reduction; above this is a zone which alternates between conditions of aeration and water saturation and therefore between periodic oxidation and reduction; the third zone, nearest the surface, is waterlogged only for short periods and is never appreciably anaerobic. These zones are most clearly differentiated in porous, loamy or sandy materials as clay soils can have one or more impermeable layers which restrict the percolation of rainwater. Where soil and site conditions are suitable, rapid leaching takes place and salt contents are generally low. Saline soils tend to occur in poorly drained sites and near the coast where they are subjected to salt spray.

In the early stages of soil formation the bulk of the adsorbed ions will be associated with clay mineral lattices. The cation exchange capacity of the deposits will thus depend on the clay minerals present. Kaolinite has an exchange capacity of 3–15 mEq/100 g, illite 10–40 mEq/100 g and montmorillonite 80–150 mEq/100 g. Both sea water and sand are deficient in nitrogen but supplies in marsh mud are augmented by fixation of atmospheric nitrogen by blue-green algae. Thus, the nutrient content will vary with distance from the sea and with the vegetation type.

The influence of organisms in the early soil ripening phase is considerable. In the tidal flats and bays species such as *Ensis* sp., *Solen* sp., *Tegelus* sp., *Callianass* sp. and *Arenicola* sp. occupy discrete burrows in the high current areas of sandy sediments. As the sediment becomes finer, *Crassostrea* sp., *Mercenaria* sp. and burrowing worms become important.

Isopods, amphipods, worms and *Mercenaria* sp. are abundant in the very fine clay sediments; they aerate and thoroughly mix the sediments and prepare the material for soil formation. Organisms are also important in the later stages of soil formation. Thus, Green and Askew (1965) have attributed the high fertility of soils at Romney Marsh, Kent, to improvements in drainage caused by the activities of roots, ants and earthworms.

Infiltration rates in the early stages are low even in sandy marsh soils. This is partly the result of a lack of vertical structures but many other factors are involved. An index illustrating the changes that take place in the soil ripening process is provided by the *n*-value of Pons and Zonneveld (1965). The formula is:

$$n = \frac{A - 0.2R}{L + bH}$$

where A is the total water content in grams per 100 g of dry soil, L and H are the percentages of clay and organic matter in the dry soil, R is the percentage of mineral particles other than clay ($R = 100 - H - L$) and b is the ratio of the water-holding capacity of organic matter to that of clay. Values range from 0.3 to 0.4 for normal soils whereas soft, freshly sedimented muds have values between 3.0 and 5.0. Mudflats exposed at low tide have values of about 2.0 and lowest salt marshes 1.2 to 2.0.

Decalcification of marine soils

The leaching of calcium carbonate from the sediments is one of the more important processes in the early stages of soil formation. But investigations in the Netherlands have shown that the decalcification process is not simple and is made up of a number of components. In some cases older deposits were found to be less decalcified than younger ones. Zuur (1936) first focused attention on this problem and since then many workers have suggested that decalcification during upward growth of sediments can also occur (Edelman 1950, Bennema 1953, De Smet 1954, Van Straaten 1954, Zonneveld 1960). Furthermore, these investigations imply that calcium carbonate can also be lost during the transport of sediments. The amount of decalcification will depend on the amount of calcium carbonate present in the original sediments. Verhoeven (1962) demonstrated the existence of a $CaCO_3$ gradient in young marine mud along the North Sea coast and that the finer fractions contained a fairly constant percentage of $CaCO_3$. Bruin and Ten Have (1935) found only small amounts of fine-grained $CaCO_3$ and Doeglas (1950) could not find any difference in the particle size distribution of beach sand before and after elimination of $CaCO_3$. Thus, $CaCO_3$ is subjected during sedimentation to similar sorting processes as the other mineral particles and is not biochemically precipitated as was originally supposed (Edelman 1950, Bennema 1953, Zonneveld 1960).

During the period of upward growth of saltings, $CaCO_3$ is both supplied and leached out. With the appearance of vegetation the formation and decay of organic matter intensifies as does the production of carbon dioxide. Shrinkage cracks also increase the permeability. Zuur (1936) stresses the influence of permeability on leaching while Bennema (1953), and Zonneveld (1960) consider the reduction state brought about by the increase in carbon dioxide pressure responsible for rapid decalcification. Alternatively, Van der Sluijs (1970) concluded that variable conditions during silting were the most important causes of present day variations in calcium carbonate content and depth of decalcification in the marine clay soils of the Netherlands. This means that there should be a close relationship between decalcification, landforms and microtopography.

Soil–landform relationships

Many of the relationships outlined above can be illustrated with reference to specific examples. A good area within which to do this is Romney Marsh in Kent where there have been extensive investigations into the nature of the soils (Green 1968). The deposits and soil parent materials are complex but can be classified into a few major categories. The major sand deposit, the Midley Sand, is coarse textured, clay and silts are scarce and calcium carbonate is generally absent. It is exposed at several localities and forms a series of conspicuous banks which may have been a system of sand banks or dunes which suffered dissection and reworking during burial beneath the clays (Blue Clay) and younger deposits. The clays have a high, 2–50 μm, silt content and are the soil parent materials in the alluvium-filled hollows. Extensive deposits of peat occur at various depths and the presence of stumps indicates that they grew *in situ* during a period of low sea level (Gilbert 1933). Wood samples taken from the peat have a radiocarbon date of about 3000 BP (Callow *et al.* 1964) and samples, probably of birch, from the foreshore were dated at 3040 ± 94 and 3360 ± 92 years BP (Green 1968).

Since the formation of the peat, deposition has produced a variety of sedimentary patterns of contrasting age and complexity. The largest single element is the shingle cuspate foreland formed of successive ridges thrown up during storms (Lewis 1932, Lewis & Balchin 1940). Although the shingle is chemically inert, being largely composed of flint pebbles, a succession of plant communities has developed. The development of Romney Marsh during the post-peat period has been very complex with 'deposition of the finer materials under conditions determined by the ever changing configuration of the offshore beaches and the varying protection they provided from the full force of the sea, relative to fluctuations in sea-level, changes in river course . . . and drainage . . .' (Green 1968, p. 17).

Different landform assemblages or land types can be recognised which

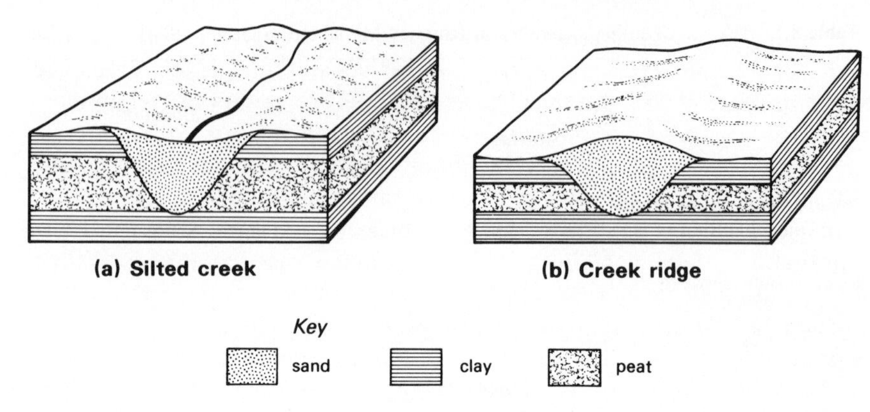

Figure 8.2 Creek ridge development on Romney Marsh, Kent (from Green 1968).

are also reflected in the soil associations. These relationships can be illustrated with respect to the decalcified (Old) Marshland. One of the most conspicuous features is the creek ridges which are essentially symmetrical in cross section and form complex dendritic systems. They are thought to represent a system of creeks cut into the thick peat deposits later infilled with clay, silt and sand (Fig. 8.2a). As the area dried out, falling water tables allowed the peat between the creeks to shrink leaving the deeper peat under the creeks unaffected. This led to an inversion of relief and former creeks became ridges (Fig. 8.2b). Local differences in the height and shape of the ridges are due to the different thicknesses of peat: low

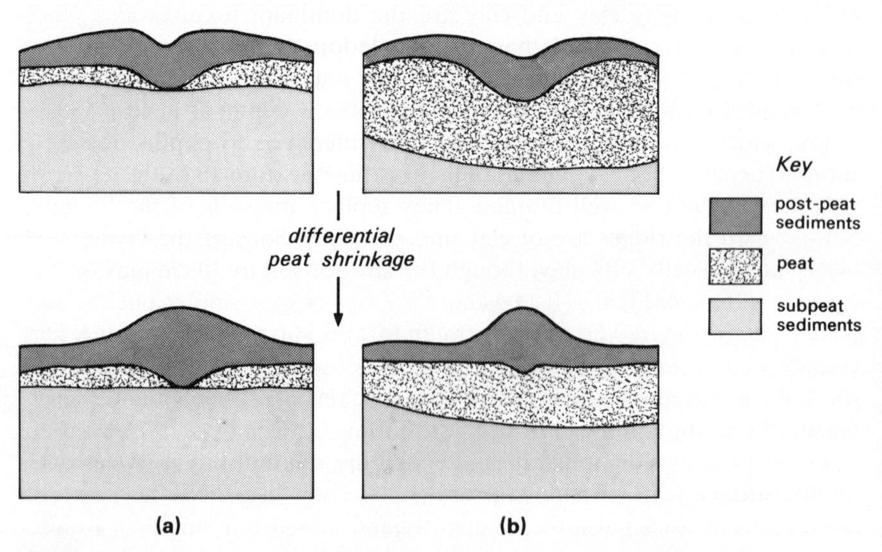

Figure 8.3 Formation of creek ridges of different size and shape (from Green 1968).

Table 8.1 Texture of soil associations on Romney Marsh (from Green 1968).

	Silt clay or clay	*Clay loam over silty clay or clay*	*Clay loam*	*Loam or sandy loam*	*Loamy sand or sand*
texture below 30 in similar or finer than that of B horizon	Dymchurch	Brenzett	Finn	Snargate	Midley
loam to sand between 24 and 42 in	Ivychurch				
thick peat between 24 and 42 in		Dowels			
thick peat above 24 in	Appledore				

ridges occur where the peat is thin (Fig. 8.3a), whereas the narrow ridges developed from deep creeks eroded in thick peat because of greater peat shrinkage (Fig. 8.3b).

The soil associations of the Old Marshland follow very closely the topographic features and can be differentiated on the basis of texture (Table 8.1). Two sections illustrating these relationships are shown in Figure 8.4. The Appledore Series comprises poorly drained, non-calcareous clay soils over thick peat which occurs at a depth of 30–60 cm. A typical profile has an Ag horizon, about 15 cm thick, of very dark grey humose clay with weak blocky structure. The Bg horizon is of non-calcareous coarsely prismatic clay. The Dowels Series consists of fine-textured soils over thick peat at 60–100 cm. Silty clay and clay are the dominant textures and, being higher, are better drained than the Appledore Series. The soils of the Snargate Series, which are dominant on the major creek ridges, are moderately well drained loams or sandy loams to a depth of at least 60 cm below which the proportion of sand often increases to depths of 3 m or more. The Finn Series contains soils of a finer texture than the Snargate and they are not so well drained. They replace the soils of the Snargate Series when the ridges are of clay and not sand. Soils of the Dymchurch Series are typically silty clay, though the surface soil to 30 cm may be clay loam or silty clay loam. The Ivychurch Series is very similar but the soils have coarser-textured horizons between 60 and 100 cm. The structures are coarser or less well developed compared to horizons at similar depths in the finer-textured soils. They are not plastic unless laminated and tend to occur where sandy lenses are near the surface.

These examples demonstrate quite well the relationships between sediments, surface features, drainage and soils. They also show that sea level changes have occurred quite frequently and have been sufficient to alter the local balance of erosion and deposition. Even with static sea levels there may be a gradual build-up of material and many coastal complexes

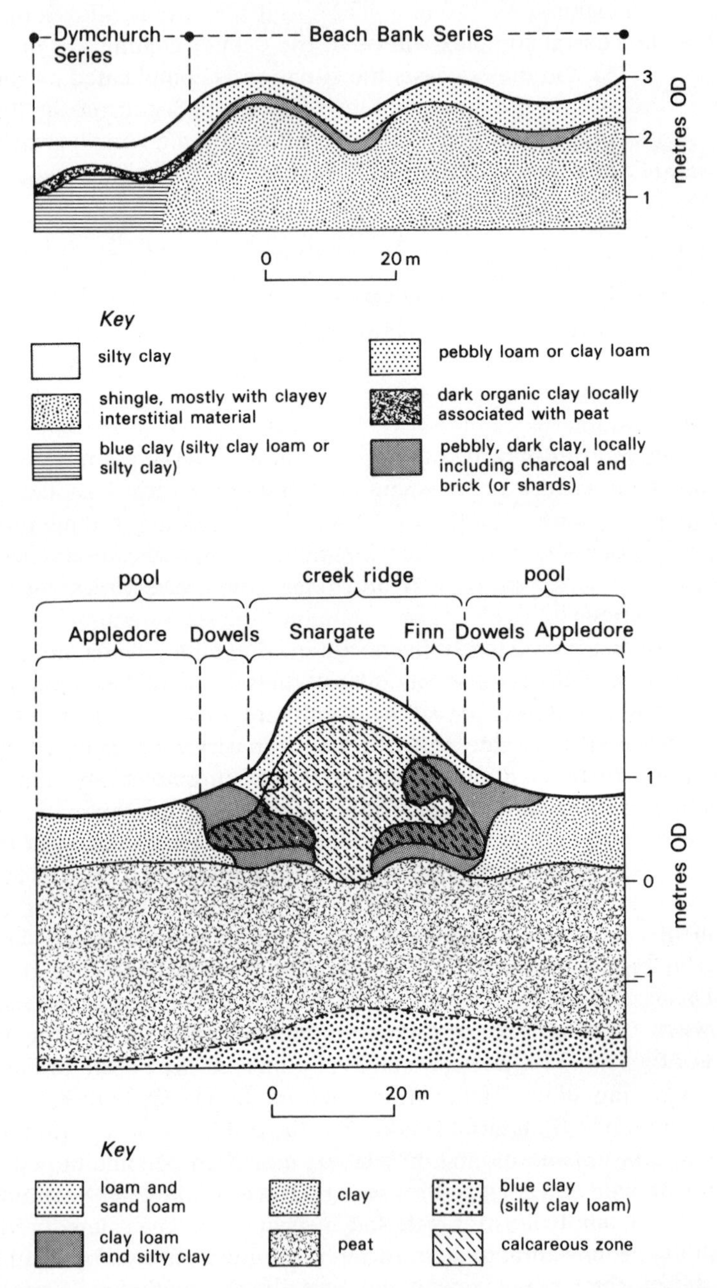

Figure 8.4 Soil–landform relationships from Romney Marsh, Kent (from Green 1968).

are being rapidly regressed. In the Delmarva Peninsula the rate of regression has been estimated at 10 m a year and if this rate continues the only record of the coastal complex will be in the deeper channels of the inlets (Harrison 1975). On many coasts the situation is complicated by the fact that a series of transgressions and regressions has occurred in the last 10 000 years. This means that soils are developed on a complex variety of materials in which several peat layers may be sandwiched between sand and silt beds.

Soils of coastal sand dune systems

Coastal sand dune systems are characterised by several distinct features. The dunes themselves often show a regular succession from the more active and unstable foredunes at the top of the beach to the older, more stable vegetated dunes inland. The other major element is the system of slacks which exists between the main dune trends. Once a coastal dune has come into being one of two things can happen: either a new dune forms to seaward or the dune grows to its maximum height and then erodes moving landwards. The first process may add ridge after ridge which eventually stabilise while the eroding dune system may remain unstable for years before becoming permanently fixed. Where prevailing winds are onshore the highest dune will be some way inland whereas the highest dune will be nearest the shore if the prevailing winds are offshore. Rates of dune movement can vary considerably but are often of the order of 3–7 m/yr.

The nature of the soil and vegetation has been extensively studied on dunes but less information is available on the slack environment. In the British Isles, the early work of Salisbury (1925) on the sand dunes of Blakeney Point, Norfolk, provided a focus for much later work and in that, and subsequent studies, distinct trends have been identified. Progressive leaching of carbonates occurs with increasing age and coupled with an increase in organic content there is a passage from alkaline to acid conditions. The rate of leaching is at first rapid but then declines as the amount of carbonate rather than the amount of rainfall becomes the limiting factor. The rate of leaching in the early stages depends on the nature of the shell fragments, being slower if the fragments are large. The process will be temporarily halted if material is added to the dune system by wind action and leached layers and organic-rich layers may then become buried.

A detailed study on coastal dune soils by Barratt (1962) in Northumberland, England, amply illustrates these general points. The saline foredunes are building around tufts of sand twitch (*Agropyron junceum*) and humic material is confined to pale grey patchy stains in the zone of maximum root development a few centimetres below the freshly accumulating sand (Fig. 8.5). The grey patches contain rotting leaves which are attacked by white and brown fungal hyphae. The main accumulating dunes above the level of

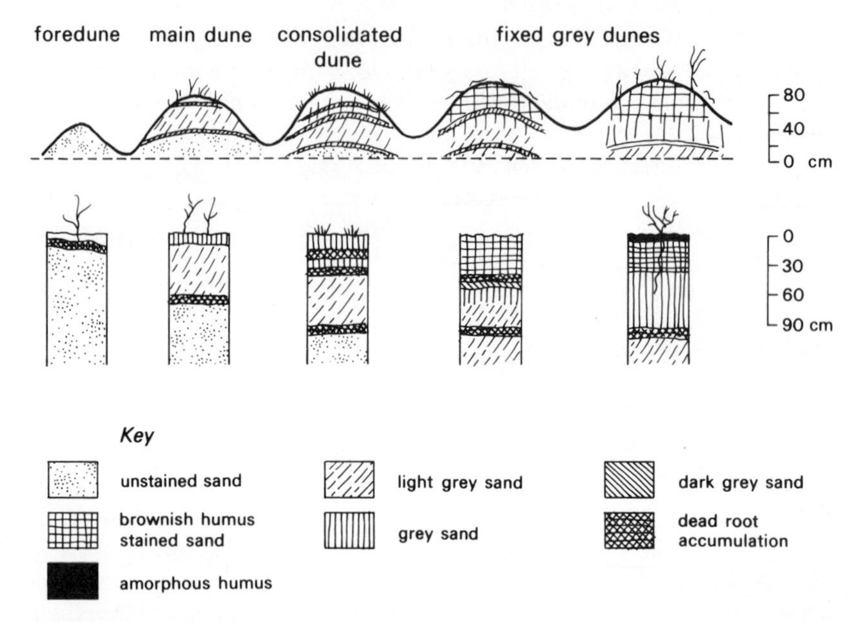

Figure 8.5 Dune development sequence in Northumberland (from Barratt 1962).

the highest tides are stabilised by marram grass (*Ammophila arenaria*). Dark grey, root-rich horizons 5–10 cm thick occur at vertical intervals of about 60 cm separated by pale grey sand. On the consolidated dunes sand is accumulating less rapidly and root-rich horizons appear at only 15 cm intervals. In the dark humic layers, fungal hyphae surround the grains of sand, binding them together in clusters, and play a vital role in stabilising the root-rich horizons. Vegetation cover is more substantial on the fixed dunes with mosses, lichens and low herbs and a dark grey-brown almost black topsoil up to 2 cm thick containing a mat of fine roots. In places, a vertical sequence of alternating light grey and dark grey horizons 1–2 cm thick extends below the surface to a depth of 8 cm. On the oldest dunes more substantial shrubs occur, the black-brown humic horizon is 8 cm thick and overlies a lighter brown layer.

The slight differences in soil moisture between the young and old dunes and between dunes and slacks control soil formation especially with respect to the oxidation of organic matter. Young slack soils therefore start with a considerable advantage especially as nutrients and other minerals also accumulate in the slack systems. This is ultimately reflected in the soil profiles and pH values. The rate of increase of organic content depends on the initial lime content of the dunes. On lime-deficient dunes, early colonisation by *Calluna* is possible with a concomitant increase in the rate of litter accumulation. More acid conditions then prevail, litter breakdown is inhibited and organic matter build-up is promoted.

Most coastal sand dune systems can be dated accurately only for several

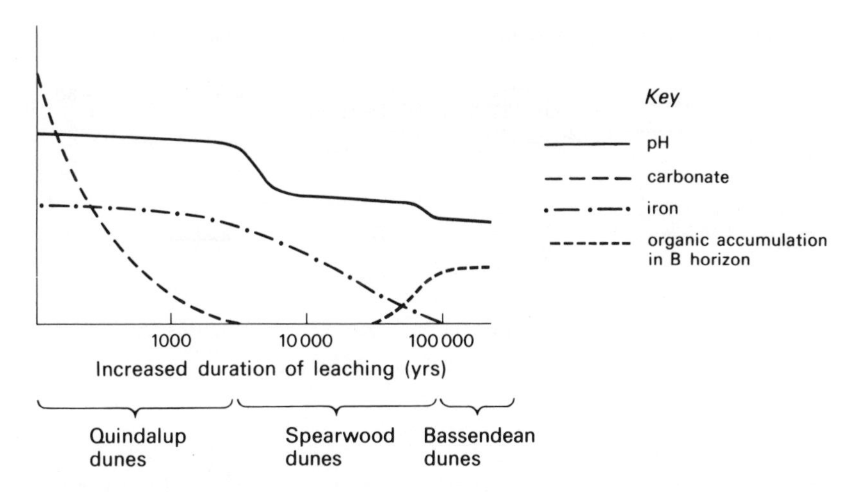

Figure 8.6 Podzolisation sequence on ancient dunes in Western Australia (McArthur & Bettenay 1960).

hundred years and information on long-term soil changes is, therefore, limited. But, in some parts of the world extremely old sand dune systems exist which can be dated reasonably accurately. One such system occurs on the Swan Coastal Plain of Western Australia where three major dune trends can be identified, the oldest being estimated at 200 000 years BP (McArthur & Bettenay 1960). Total carbonate removal from highly calcareous sand has taken from 100 000 to 200 000 years. Immediately following the total loss of carbonates the pH falls by about two units. There is also a progressive loss of iron with more effective removal taking place in the wetter and less well drained areas. The complete trends for the Swan Coastal Plain dunes are shown in Figure 8.6.

Conclusions

The development of soils on sand dunes and recently exposed marine deposits is a complex process. Both environments are potentially unstable and there is always the interaction between the developing soil profile and the process of erosion and deposition. Nevertheless, as the brief review in this chapter has shown, certain valid generalisations can be made. The distinctiveness of coastal plain deposits and landforms is frequently matched by the nature of the soils, as vividly seen in areas like Romney Marsh. This allows drainage and reclamation schemes in many parts of the world to be planned accordingly. Where coastal plain sequences can be dated with sufficient accuracy trends in soil formation can be deduced. Also, information obtained from the soil profile allows the identification of periods of geomorphic activity. The same is true of dune systems although the time scale involved is often different. In both environments surface stability is accompanied by the progressive leaching of carbonates, a decrease of pH and increase in organic content. Eventually a fully developed soil profile is achieved. Because of a certain similarity in materials and landforms many of the principles established in this chapter are applicable to areas composed of glacial deposits. These are examined in the next chapter.

9 Soils on glacial and fluvioglacial landforms

Glacial and fluvioglacial deposits exist as a continuous or patchy cover over a large part of the northern hemisphere. In these areas they often form the foundation materials with which civil engineers have to deal. For these reasons alone the study of soils developed on such deposits is important. The added fact that many of the more recent glacial events can be dated with reasonable accuracy means that information on the rate of soil development can also be deduced. Various names have been used for these deposits such as boulder clay, drift and till. Boulder clay is not a good term because many glacial deposits do not contain boulders and are very rarely composed purely of clay. Drift also tends to include fluvioglacial and glaciolacustrine deposits. Till is by far the most sensible general term to use for glacial deposits and is the one adopted here.

The integration of soil studies with the superficial geology and geomorphology of glacial deposits is beneficial to all. As Scott (1976, p. 51) stresses

> soils, . . . have been intensively studied in Canada, but only a handful of scientists have carried out any quantitative study of till, the parent material whose upper 1 or 2 m are altered to soil. Because of this approach, the effects of regional and local variations in till texture and composition have received an emphasis clearly secondary to climatic and microtopographic variations in the study of soil-forming processes, the relative emphasis probably being reversed.

Space does not permit a detailed examination of all the forms and processes involved in glacial and fluvioglacial deposition. All that is attempted is to highlight the regularities that exist in landforms composed of glacial and fluvioglacial material and to identify the close associations between these and the spatial patterns of the soils themselves and specific aspects of soil formation.

Glacial and fluvioglacial deposits

The characteristics of the deposits vary according to the properties of the environments in which they were transported and deposited. Sugden and John (1976) have argued that there are only three major modes of glacial deposition: material may be released from the ice in the basal zone or at the ice surface by melting, it may be transported on the ice surface and dropped by the melting of the ice beneath it or it may be transported between the basal ice and the solid rock or other underlying glacial drift. Studies of presently active glaciers suggest that the first two processes are the most important. These mechanisms produce tills with widely different particle size distributions, particle shapes, colour, porosity, permeability and compaction. This variability ultimately affects the pattern and types of changes brought about by weathering and soil formation.

Fluvioglacial environments are characterised by fluctuations in discharge over both long and short time periods. The deposits tend to be stratified and the particles are rounded or subrounded in shape. Both deposits and landforms are extremely varied, ranging from the narrow sinuous ridges of eskers to huge expanses of outwash sands or sandar. Any classification system and terminology used in connection with these forms and deposits may have to be amended as our understanding of fluvioglacial environments and deposits associated with existing glaciers is increased (Price 1973). Fluvioglacial forms and deposits can be differentiated on the basis of depositional environment and whether marginal or not to the ice.

Proglacial deposits tend to occur in smoother and more continuous sheets with the sands and gravels being well sorted and well stratified. Analysis of deposits in central Scotland by McLellan (1971) bears this out. Outwash sheets show consistently high gravel fractions whereas ice-contact deposits generally contain a wider range of particle sizes and are less well sorted with large cobbles in association with silt lenses. Strata are liable to be discontinuous and faulted and surface expressions are irregular with ridges, mounds and depressions rapidly alternating.

The type of deposit and landform and ultimately the soil pattern will depend on the former relative positions of the ice and the number of glaciations an area has experienced. Deposition in the wastage zone of the glacier is the most complicated because there will be processes of end moraine formation, some dumping of material, some lodgement, melt-out and flowage and ice push. The presence of fluvioglacial and perhaps periglacial processes will add to the complexity. Thus, the sequence of deposits found in formerly glaciated areas can be expected to be quite complex and this should be reflected in the soil patterns.

Landscapes of glacial and fluvioglacial deposition

The associations between landforms and materials and their relationships to position within or in front of former ice masses enables gross landscape patterns to be identified. It is, probably, at the intermediate scale where these patterns of depositional landscapes are most readily discernible. Prest (1968) working in North-West Territories, Canada, has shown that a

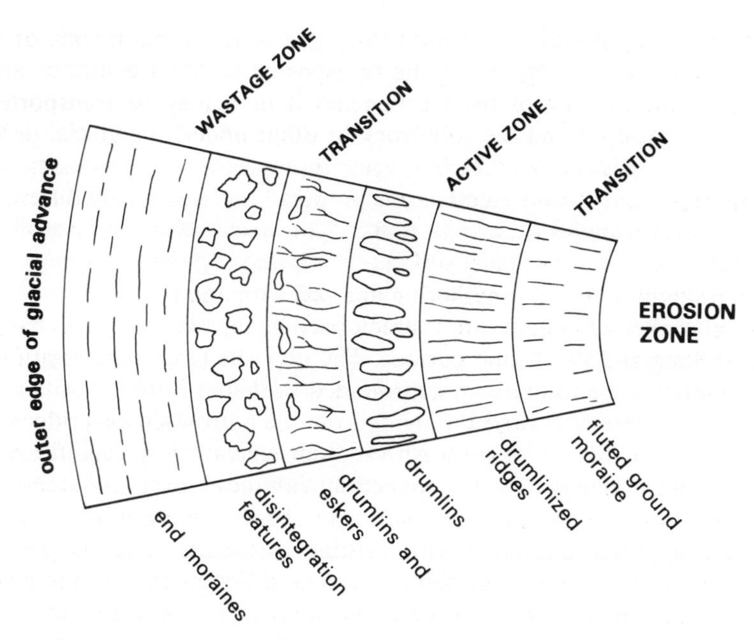

Figure 9.1 Glacial depositional landscape sequence (from Sugden & John 1976).

zone of drumlins gives way northerly to a zone of elongated drumlinoid forms, then to drumlinized ground moraine and finally to fluted ground moraine. Other workers have shown that at the outer wastage zone, parallel end moraines are conspicuous followed by a zone of ice disintegration features such as kettle holes. On the basis of these and many other consistencies, Sugden and John (1976) have presented a model for the types of depositional landscapes expected to develop beneath part of the periphery of a mid-latitude Pleistocene ice sheet (Fig. 9.1). In detail, the situation is more complex but valid generalisations can, nevertheless, be made. Thus, Ruhe (1950) has shown how till sheets of differing ages are characterised by different frequency curves of slope per cent, as the older the till the more integrated are the drainage networks and the steeper are the slope forms. This is reflected in the soils developed on the respective slopes. The distinctiveness of the landform patterns allows predictions to be made of the expected soil patterns. Some of these soil–landscape associations are now examined.

Soils on end moraines

A conspicuous pattern of swells and swales in a banded arrangement exists in many formerly glaciated areas. Gwynne (1942) has interpreted those of Iowa as being recessional moraines of Late Wisconsin age associated with the seasonal oscillation of a retreating ice front with partial overriding and thickening of material deposited during the season of melting. This landform pattern has a marked influence on moisture distribution and the soil types reflect this. The result is a banded arrangement of the major soil types (Gwynne & Simonson 1942). Soils of the Clarion Series occupy the swells and possess good natural drainage with three ill defined horizons. The A horizon (25–35 cm thick) is brownish black with an intermediate texture whereas the B horizon (10–50 cm) is dark yellowish brown. Soils in the swales belong to the Webster Series and have restricted drainage. A horizons are thicker (30–50 cm) and are black with a heavy texture and B horizons are dark grey and thinner (10–25 cm). In this instance recognition of the pattern of moraines has helped the mapping of soils.

On larger moraines such as the Des Moines lobe in Iowa (Oschwald *et al.* 1965), these differences in materials and drainage characteristics are sufficient to impart a catena-like arrangement to the soils, as suggested in Chapter 4. The relations between soils, such as those belonging to the Clarion and Webster Series just described, then become clearer. The similarities between areas is so great that Ruhe (1969) has formulated a generalised landscape model with related soil systems (Fig. 9.2). The larger moraines in the Vale of York, England, possess similar landform–soil associations (Fig. 9.3). Soils of the Wheldrake Series, which are well drained loamy brown earths, occupy the crests followed downslope in less gravelly situations by brown earths of the Escrick Series. These merge into acid brown earths (Kelfield Series) with, at the base of the slopes, groundwater gleys

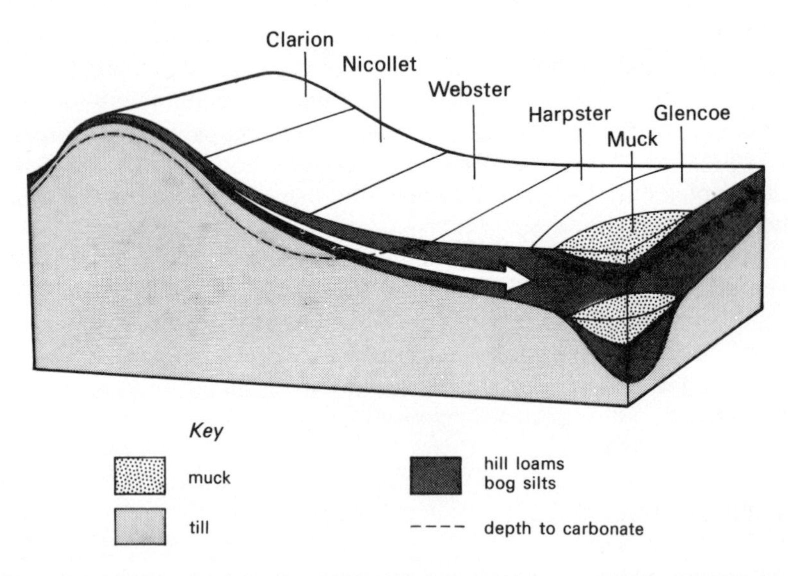

Figure 9.2 The Clarion–Nicollet–Webster soil association in Iowa (reprinted by permission from *Quaternary landscapes in Iowa* by Robert V. Ruhe, © 1969 by the Iowa State University Press, Ames, Iowa 50010, USA).

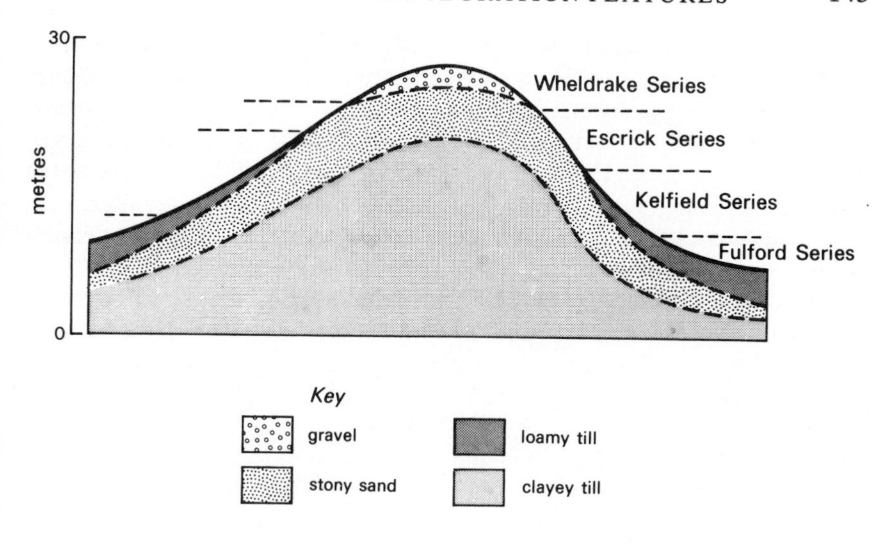

Figure 9.3 Soils on the Vale of York moraine, England (from Matthews 1971).

(Fulford Series). This sequence of soils is common on the larger end moraines of eastern England.

The soil associations so far described are well established and soil formation has probably been active for at least the last 10 000 years. In contrast, moraines near presently active glaciers provide excellent natural laboratories within which to chart the course of soil formation. In many cases it is possible to date these moraines extremely accurately and therefore specific time periods can be determined. Studies by Crocker and Major (1955) and Crocker and Dickson (1957) in Alaska have done much to increase knowledge of the rate of change of certain soil properties with time. In general pH of the top layers is reduced and calcium carbonate is leached out of the system. Nitrogen content decreases and organic carbon increases throughout the age sequences. Vegetation type also influences the speed of these changes with greatest change per unit time occurring under alder. More studies of this nature should enable valid generalisations to be made concerning the rate of soil development.

Soils on ice disintegration features

The final stage of till deposition in many parts of the world involved stagnation and ablation of the ice. The resulting landforms have been variously called 'knob and kettle', 'hummocky disintegration moraines', or more generally 'ice disintegration features'. The landforms consist of a chaotic jumble of knolls and mounds separated by irregular depressions. The knolls consist mainly of till but sand, gravel and crudely stratified drift occur, partially overlain by a layer of reworked drift. Slope stability during and subsequent to deposition and the interactions between slope, moisture distribution and soil formation are all important. The sequence of events leading to the soil features found in this type of landscape has been conceptualised by Acton and Fehrenbacher (1976). Their explanation is depicted in Figure 9.4. In phase 1, before the complete melting of the ice, slopewash of fines would lead to an accumulation of poorly sorted silts and clays in the depressions. Solifluction and other forms of mass movement could be expected to redistribute some of the till (phase 2). As the ice melts, topographic inversion takes place and these reworked sediments are now found

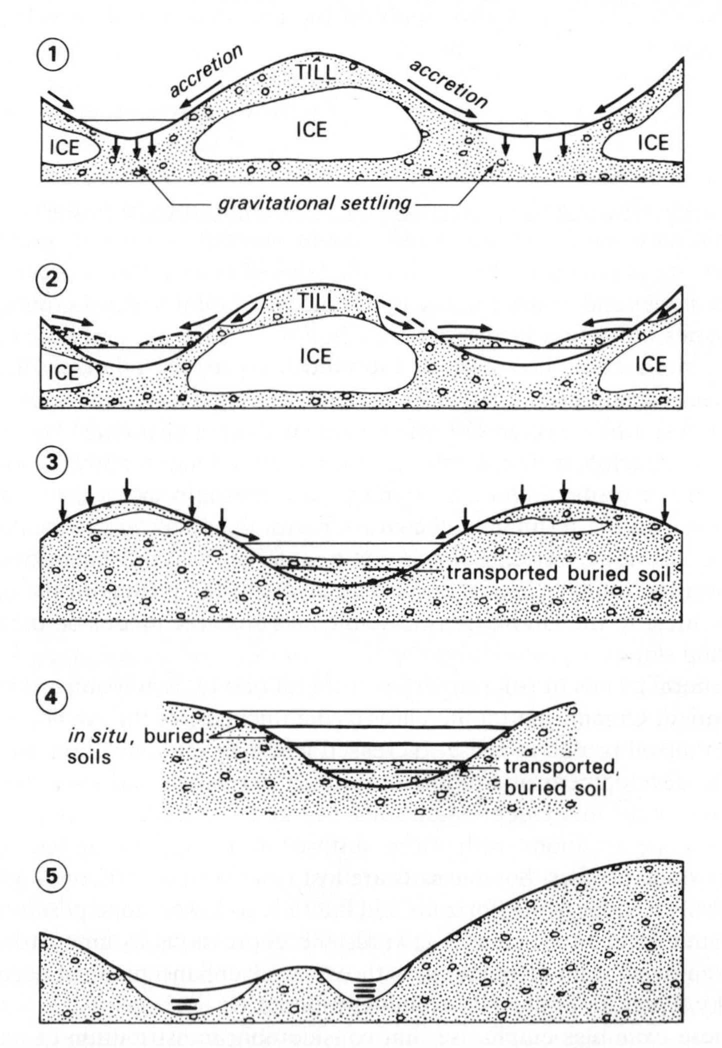

Figure 9.4 Origin of deposits and development of soils in hummocky disintegration moraines (from Acton & Fehrenbacher 1976).

on the summits (phase 3). Continued movement and reworking of sediments by solifluction and mass movement leads to the infilling of these new topographic lows and any soils that were in the process of formation might be removed or buried (phase 4). ^{14}C analysis for such soils in Saskatchewan has produced a date of 8410 ± 140 years BP (Martel & Paul 1974). This emphasises that these processes must have taken place very soon after the final ice wasting. Although periods of increased stability and instability allowed a sequence of organic-rich horizons to build up and to be later buried, slope stability eventually prevailed and a modern soil developed (phase 5).

These processes probably apply to the majority of soils developed on hummocky disintegration moraine as similar features are found in many parts of the British Isles. Such a sequence of soils in the Lancashire Plain has been described by Crompton (1966). Brown earths occur on the moderate to steep slopes of the hillocks with profiles which have A or Ap horizons of brown to reddish brown loamy sand with medium granular structure. The underlying horizons are of strong brown to yellowish brown structureless sand which is loose and incoherent. Layers of gravel and stones are common in these horizons. Gleyed brown earths occur on the lower slopes and in some of the better drained hollows whilst groundwater gley soils are found in the enclosed hollows where marked groundwater fluctuations exist. The soils on the hillock crests are relatively thin and represent continued removal of material during formation. Soils on the lower positions are often silty and banded with organic matter. These lower soils are developed almost entirely in accreted sediments and are of greater thickness. Erosional and accretionary processes appear to have a greater influence on the resultant soil characteristics than does *in situ* weathering. This is also the overriding conclusion to emerge from the exhaustive work in Iowa by Walker (1966). Successive layers in the centres of the depressions attest to the alternations in stable and unstable phases on the neighbouring slopes.

General trends of soil properties from hillock to depression can thus be identified. Organic matter increases as the thickness of the Ah horizon and the total soil profile increase. Increased leaching and eluviation, as shown by the development of Ae horizons, lower pH values and lower base saturation, occur in the depression soils. Marked Cca horizons are present in upper-slope positions with more diffuse accumulations in the moister lower-slope profiles. Soluble salts are lost from surface horizons and move vertically to underlying horizons and laterally to lower-slope positions, and prismatic structure increases towards the depressions as lime carbonates are removed from B horizons with eventual enhancement of secondary blocky structure in illuvial profiles exhibiting Bt horizons.

These examples emphasise that considerable redistribution of material has taken place in these landform associations. Hollows and depressions are the recipients of silts and clays washed off the surrounding slopes and it is easy to imagine that the soils and superficial materials are dominated by these movement patterns. But not every surface has been subjected to periods of instability and even on the more unstable slopes periods of relative stability have occurred. The processes of weathering cannot, therefore, be ignored. Alteration of the surface few metres of glacial and fluvioglacial deposits to produce essentially clayey weathered zones is to be expected, especially on relatively level stable landsurfaces. Thus, there are two main ways in which fine-grained materials can be produced from glacial deposits: one by *in situ* weathering changes, the other by erosion and subsequent deposition. The means of differentiating the two processes and materials have attracted attention for a long time.

Gumbotil and accretion gley

Many of the older (pre-Wisconsin) till sheets of North America are covered with grey tenacious clay masses. McGee (1891) was one of the first workers to draw attention to this material on the Kansan tills of Iowa. It was then called gumbo and although variously attributed to fluvioglacial deposition, colluvial processes or loess, McGee thought it was the residue of surface weathering. Kay, in 1916, in an extremely important paper, proposed the name gumbotil for this material. He defined gumbotil as a grey to dark coloured, thoroughly leached, non-laminated, deoxidized clay, very sticky and breaking with a starch-like fracture when wet, yet very hard and tenacious when dry, and which was chiefly the result of the weathering of tills.

The nature of the material and the course of weathering has been elaborated by Leighton and MacClintock (1962). Weathering would start promptly after deposition and progress through a series of stages as oxidation, leaching and eluviation took place (Fig. 9.5). In the early stages horizon 1, equivalent to a soil A horizon, develops and clay is eluviated. By stage 2 an oxidized but unleached layer (horizon 4) appears. Eventually leaching produces stage 3 and carbonates are gradually eliminated. Once the leaching of carbonates has occurred selective silica weathering becomes important and, with time, the characteristic profile of a gumbotil is thought to be produced (stage 5). The essential characteristic of this weathering sequence is that it occurs under conditions of poor drainage.

This sequence of weathering appears reasonable, given the physical and chemical properties of gumbotil, but some workers still argue that gumbotil has not formed *in situ* but is a fine wash deposit. Thus, Krusekopf (1948) argues that all of the characteristics of a gumbotil indicate that it is a water deposit, or lacustrine in origin, was deposited as a gumbotil and did not become so subsequent to its deposition. It was weathered and leached when deposited. Frye *et al*. (1960) have complicated the issue by outlining five possible ways in which gumbotil-like material could be developed.

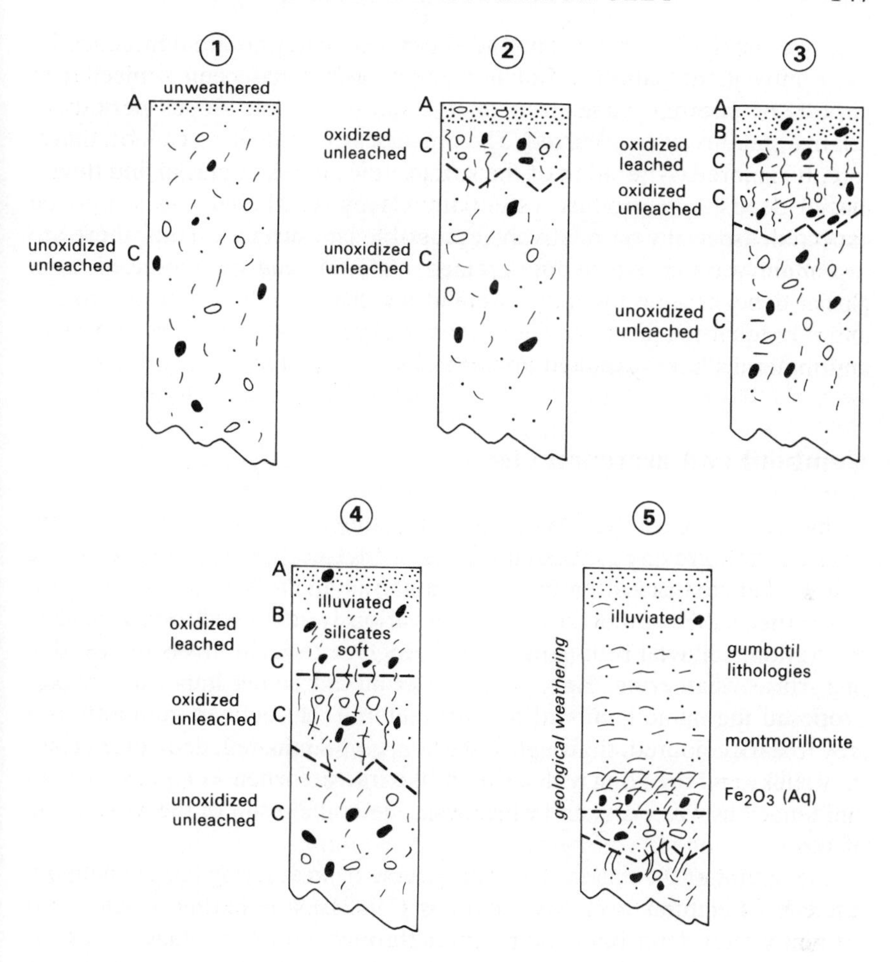

Figure 9.5 Course of weathering on glacial till (after Leighton & MacClintock 1962).

They are:

(a) accumulation in shallow pro-glacial lakes of the finest constituents of the debris load carried by the glacier;
(b) slow accretion of fine-textured sediments in swampy or marshy places on a till plain, the materials being derived from weathering of the adjacent slightly higher parts of the till plain surface and moved by sheet wash;
(c) slow accumulation in marshy environments of fine-textured aeolian sediments intermixed with sheet wash accretion;
(d) soil profile developed in a situation of high water tables where processes of accretion and *in situ* weathering are both operative; and

(e) process of gleying in a developed soil profile where initial low permeability of the parent material and low topographic relief combine to create poor drainage.

It is readily apparent that a variety of very similar superficial materials but of widely differing origin exist on ancient sheets. Because of this it is perhaps wise to restrict the term gumbotil to clay masses that have formed *in situ* under conditions of poor drainage. Gleyed material that has accumulated in depressions should be called accretion gley. It is important to be able to distinguish between these materials because of the different information they provide concerning the evolution of the landscape. The presence of gumbotil, formed *in situ*, implies a reasonably stable environment for a considerable length of time. Alternatively, identification of accretion gley demonstrates that there has been redistribution of surface materials.

It should be possible, by using a combination of features, to discover the specific origin of any of these materials. A useful summary of these distinguishing features has been provided by Birkeland (1974). Gumbotil should be massive, without stratification and should be leached of carbonates. Accretion gley would be expected to display prominent layers of contrasting particle size as well as a series of humus-rich layers. The contrast with fresh till underneath should be sharp in the case of accretion gley and gradual with gumbotil. Chemical decomposition and clay mineral alteration will show an orderly arrangement with position in gumbotil profiles whereas the clay minerals in accretion gley deposits will exhibit a disorderly arrangement of different stages of weathering.

The development of the 'classic' gumbotil profile takes a considerable amount of time but even weathering that has been in operation for only a comparatively short period can produce appreciable changes in the upper parts of tills. These changes can be so pronounced that it appears that two tills exist rather than one till with surface weathering. This has been the case in eastern England where Catt and Penny (1966) have shown that many of the features of the Hessle Clay, a supposedly separate and distinct Devensian deposit, that were thought to be diagnostic, could have originated by changes brought about by Postglacial soil development. The Hessle Clay should be regarded as merely a deep weathered mantle on whichever of two tills occurs at the surface at a particular location, thus, invalidating it as a stratigraphic unit.

The changes brought about by weathering, especially in clay mineralogy, also cast doubt over the use of specific clay minerals as either stratigraphic indicators or as till source indicators. Thus, Quigley and Ogunbadejo (1976) have shown that the high smectite contents in the surface tills of parts of North America do not reflect a different till sheet nor a different source area, but *in situ* oxidation and leaching that has removed all the original chlorites and carbonates respectively. Detailed understanding of the weathering of tills is, therefore, essential to a correct interpretation of materials, stratigraphy and Quaternary history.

Geotechnical properties

Glacial and fluvioglacial deposits are of special engineering significance in much of North America, Northern Europe and Asia. The geotechnical properties of such deposits are also important for considerations of slope evolution and landscape development. Because of their mode of deposition or material composition many slopes in glacial deposits are either unstable or potentially unstable. The work by Skempton (1953) on the evolution of slopes on the Shotton Boulder Clay in north-east England is a good illustration of this. Many individual landforms, such as drumlins, are also potentially unstable because of a combination of forms and materials and the effect these have on the subsurface movement of water. Because of this, the significance of glacial landforms to civil engineering projects is now almost universally accepted.

Natural slopes in till are assumed to exist at quite steep angles. Strength characteristics of intact till are normally high but variations in the till mass reduce stability. Some of these defects may be caused at the time of formation, such as desiccation or freezing following deposition. The presence of fossil ice wedge casts can impart considerable weakness and many slope failures in glacial materials in England have been attributed to this characteristic (Hutchinson 1974). Blocks of till collapse in units bounded by the vertical planes of weakness formed by the casts. The influence of fissures on the shear strength properties of clayey tills in central Scotland was discovered by McGown, Saldivar-sali and Radwan (1974) in their investigation of shallow slips. Similarly, Klohn (1961) records slopes in British Colombia which have their stability controlled by thin zones of highly plastic slickensided clay. Highly fractured till possesses complex hydraulic properties which influence groundwater flow systems (Grisak *et al.* 1976). If the clay content is high the till will tend to possess a high cohesion, relatively small angle of internal friction and because of lower permeability will have a small coefficient of consolidation. With small clay concentrations, tills will have low cohesion, larger angles of internal friction and large coefficients of consolidation.

Variation of till parameters is large but it is still possible to relate, in a general way, the geotechnical properties of tills to their mode of formation. Melt-out tills retain a grain size distribution typical of debris in transport and their state of consolidation depends on sediment overburden pressures and the effects of drying and freezing. The lodgement process may cause the nucleation of boulder clusters and in some cases different grain size fractions are non-randomly distributed producing a potentially more compressible structure. They are mostly heavily overconsolidated with horizontal shear joints or stress-release joints. Flow tills may be similar to melt-out tills except that a flow fabric has been overprinted onto an englacial one. Some flow tills possess a great variation in grain size composition and can be enriched or depleted in fines. Their complex history of drying and wetting, freezing and thawing also produces complex variations in their state of consolidation. Bulk permeability in glacial deposits will be increased by the presence of continuous sand and gravel bodies, whilst compressibilities will be decreased. The converse will be the case with the presence of clay lenses.

In an earlier section the chemical and physical changes brought about by weathering were stressed. Weathering also causes fundamental changes in geotechnical properties such that systematic changes with depth are often apparent. Some of these have been listed by Quigley and Ogunbadejo (1976). They are:

(a) *compaction*: the surface soils compact to a maximum density of 8–15 lb/ft^3 less than the deeper unweathered material especially if leached of carbonates;
(b) *Atterberg limits*: the liquid limit increases from 20% at 2 m depth to 52% towards the surface with a corresponding increase in activity from 0.4 to 1.0;
(c) *swell potential*: measured swell potential (per cent swell under 1 lb/in^2 loading) increase from zero at 2 m depth to 7% for carbonate-free weathered surface soils;
(d) *residual friction angle*: the residual angle is reduced in surface soils to about 18° compared to 27° for unweathered soils;
(e) *fissuring*: extensive near-surface fissuring and horizontal clay platelet parallelism produces a lower bulk strength.

Because of these strong connections between till genesis and geotechnical properties an understanding of a till sequence is an invaluable aid to the engineering geologist and to the geomorphologist interested in the evolution of landforms in such materials.

Pedological and geotechnical techniques and investigations considerably enhance the geomorphological and geological examination of till provenance and stratigraphic history. Conversely, geomorphological concepts are invaluable in assessing the significance of particular soil features such as stone lines, humus layers, etc. and demonstrate that a considerable redistribution of material and many landscape changes have occurred since the last glacial period. Soils and landforms exist in tandem and must be treated as such.

10 The stratigraphical importance of soils

General principles

Soils can provide much information concerning the evolution of landscapes. Soil development takes time, therefore a soil represents a standstill in geomorphological history. The presence of soils may be the only indication that there have been periods of stability within cycles of erosion and deposition. The nature of the soil may also give an indication of environmental conditions during the period of soil formation. Calcium carbonate concretions, iron pans, clays such as kaolinite and various exchangeable cations can provide valuable insights into specific environmental conditions. However, correlations between soil properties and environments are not sufficiently established to permit unequivocal conclusions to be drawn.

Soils of greatest use in this respect are those which have been buried under later deposits and have had their characteristics essentially fossilised. It is for this reason that buried soils have a vital role to play in Quaternary sciences, since they frequently provide the only record of time breaks within the stratigraphic record. It is necessary, when using soils as stratigraphic tools, that features of the soil profile that are mainly sedimentological in origin can be distinguished from those whose origin is pedological. This is the same problem as that encountered in an examination of alluvial soils (see Ch. 7). This uncertainty means that soils should not be used solely, and to the exclusion, of other criteria. A stratigraphical approach to the study of soils should begin with the materials observable in the field leading to an investigation of processes and, perhaps, concluding with some account of the history of soil development. However, the last stage is not without its problems, as later sections will show. A stratigraphical approach also facilitates the coordination and synthesis of information from related fields of the Earth sciences.

Soils used for correlation purposes are called soil stratigraphic units. The American Stratigraphic Code (American Commission on Stratigraphic Nomenclature, Article 81, 1961), defines a soil stratigraphic unit as a soil with physical features and stratigraphic relations that permit its consistent recognition and mapping as a stratigraphic unit. As stratigraphic relations are the crucial elements, any soil stratigraphic unit may, and probably will, consist of several distinct pedologic units. The soil should be studied as a mantle; a mantle that can be traced over wide areas. The pedological properties may vary but the stratigraphic relationships are constant. To be efficient as a soil stratigraphic unit a soil must have features that are pedologic in origin and that display a consistent relationship to other units in the stratigraphic succession. For this reason it is more realistic to think in terms of type transects rather than type sites. Thus, one of the conclusions of the INQUA Commission of Paleopedology (Yaalon 1971) was that profiles should be traced laterally to determine their spatial variation. This plea for a type transect has also been made by Follmer (1978) for the Sangamon soil of North America, which is probably the most widely known and best studied of all buried soils. This transect would be, in essence, a palaeocatena and should contain the complete range of drainage and topographic conditions common to the soil stratigraphic unit. In the case of the Sangamon soil, this should include a poorly drained, organic-rich accretion gley profile, a poorly drained *in situ* profile, an imperfectly drained profile and a well drained profile.

Correlations over short distances are essential to a detailed reconstruction of landscape development. This is achieved largely by the analysis and interpretation of buried soils. Morrison (1967) proposed the term 'geosol' for the basic soil stratigraphic unit but it has yet to be universally accepted. The widely used term palaeosol is the one adopted here. There is a considerable literature on palaeosols and all that is attempted in this chapter is to highlight some of the methodological problems involved in their identification and interpretation. More comprehensive treatments have been provided by Morrison and Wright (1967), Yaalon (1971) and Mahaney (1978) while Valentine and Dalrymple (1976) have produced an excellent summary of Quaternary buried palaeosols.

Pawluk (1978) has argued very strongly that emphasis in the study of buried soils should be placed on the pedogenic rather than the pedologic profile. The pedogenic profile consists of the interactions within and among the processes contributing to the dynamics of the soil body. Concentration on the pedogenic profile allows palaeoenvironmental conditions to be based on energy relationships rather than matter alterations. Since several morphologically different soils may form within the same pedogenic setting, because of material and other differences, concentration on the pedogenic setting is less prone to error. Evidence for processes rather than effects should be sought.

The great variability in pedological properties makes long-distance correlation difficult and perhaps unrealistic. Changes in energy factors, materials and geomorphological frameworks over even relatively short distances, make it imperative that as many sections as possible are analysed. Thus, Richmond (1962) has shown how, in Utah, a buried brown podzolic soil at high levels changes through a brown forest soil to a sierozem at lower levels. Well developed buried peat beds may grade gradually into organic silts and then to purely mineral deposits over distances as short as a hundred metres. The stratigraphical relations are constant but there has been a gradual facies change and genetically different soils can occur at different levels. Thus, the suggestion by Firman (1968) that soil stratigraphic units may be traced across soil and climatic zonal boundaries, poses numerous problems. Likewise, transcontinental correlations based on soils with the greatest development, such as that by Richmond (1970), between the interglacial deposits of the Rocky Mountains, the Sangamon palaeosol of mid-west North America and similar deposits in Europe are open to doubt. Some of the techniques employed in making these correlations are now examined.

Types and relationships of palaeosols

A palaeosol is a soil which has been formed on a past landscape. This landscape may be buried or exposed. Buried palaeosols occur where the landsurface has been covered by younger deposits, whereas relict palaeosols occur on surfaces that have never been buried. Palaeosols formerly buried but now re-exposed by erosion are termed exhumed palaeosols. Relict palaeosols have remained exposed on the surface since it was formed. Buried palaeosols have their characteristics largely fossilised by the surface accumulation of various sediments. Some secondary changes may occur, such as deposition of iron, manganese or calcium carbonate, and organic matter may be oxidised, but the changes are normally minor. Several potential relationships between buried, relict and modern soils are possible.

A weakly developed relict palaeosol will have its characteristics altered by a subsequent stronger pedogenesis. Therefore, weakly developed palaeosols may only be identified when they occur beneath younger deposits. As they reach and merge with the surface their characteristics will be obliterated by a stronger soil (Fig. 10.1a). Alternatively, if the buried palaeosol is strongly developed, pedogenesis during later soil-forming intervals may be unable to alter its characteristics. The situation displayed in Figure 10.1b will then arise. Combinations of these possibilities produce complex relationships (Fig. 10.1c).

Other possible relationships exist and have been termed composite, compound and subdivided palaeosols (Morrison 1978). Detailed examination of the soils might provide evidence of more than one episode of pedogenesis within the same profile. Such a palaeosol is composite (Fig. 10.2a). The sequence of events can be determined but the length of time between pedogenic events is indeterminate, although the stratigraphic relations between the various events may be discovered by tracing the soil to sites where the soil-forming events are clearly separate. In Quaternary stratigraphy it was commonly assumed that one palaeosol was associated with one interglacial, but it is now clear that several phases of soil development can occur in the same interglacial. Relict palaeosols are always polygenetic to some degree but many buried palaeosols are also

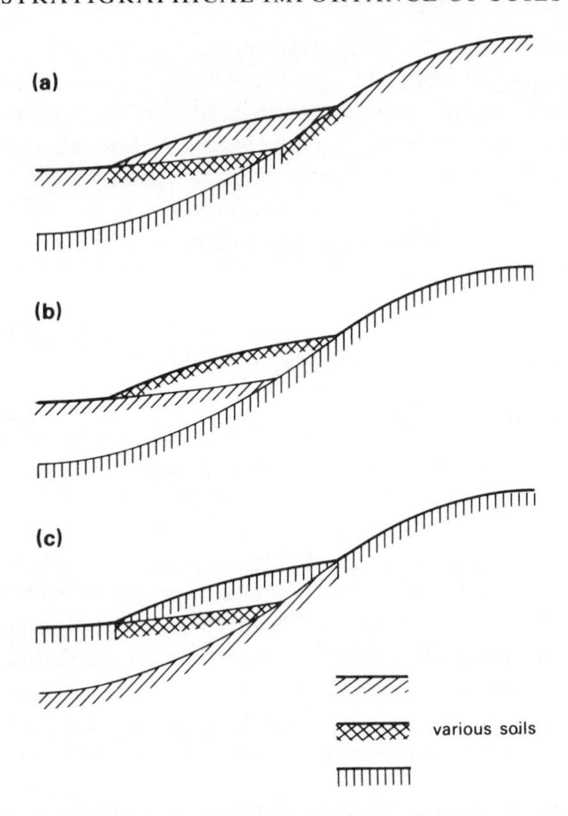

Figure 10.1 Hypothetical relations between fossil and modern soils.

polygenetic. Good examples are the Paudorf soil of Austria and the Sangamon soil of North America.

Multi-storey soil profiles are those where more than one soil profile occurs in close vertical succession, but are separated by sediment, so that the individual soil profiles do not overlap. These have been called compound palaeosols (Fig. 10.2b). Palaeosols that usually occur as single composite soils may be traceable to places where they are separated by sediment into two or more soil profiles (Fig. 10.3); these are called subdivided palaeosols. It is clear that what one worker calls a subdivided palaeosol may be described by another worker, in a different area, as separate palaeosols. Morrison (1978) has suggested that this has been so with the Paudorf soil. This palaeosol was thought to represent a Late–Middle Würm interstadial but it has now been shown to represent a time span from the start of the last Riss–Würm interglacial to the beginning of the main Würm glacial stage. Subdivided equivalents of the Paudorf soil are common in Czechoslovakia.

The similarity between buried and relict palaeosols presents many problems. Birkeland (1974) suggests two mechanisms whereby this similarity

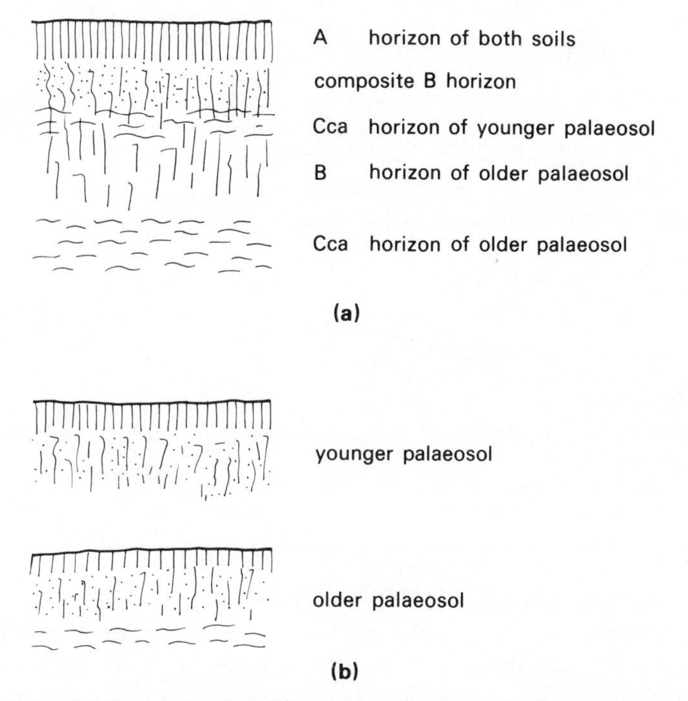

Figure 10.2 (a) Composite and (b) compound palaeosols (from Morrison 1978).

may be achieved. During periods of fluctuating climate, soil formation could occur in a stepwise fashion, where rapid development takes place under optimum climatic conditions. A curve of soil development with time such as that depicted in Figure 10.4 (curve A) would be produced. Climatic change at time I retarded soil development and surface processes buried part of the pre-existing soil. Because little soil development takes place between I and II, the surface soil that formed between O and II will be similar to the soil that formed between O and I but which has been buried between I and II. Soil development during time interval II–III should produce a more strongly developed soil profile than in the buried profile. Another possible explanation for the similarity between surface and buried

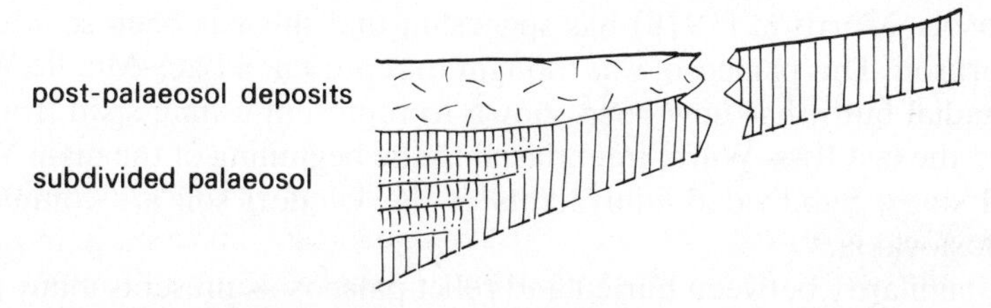

Figure 10.3 Subdivided occurrences of a single palaeosol (from Morrison 1978).

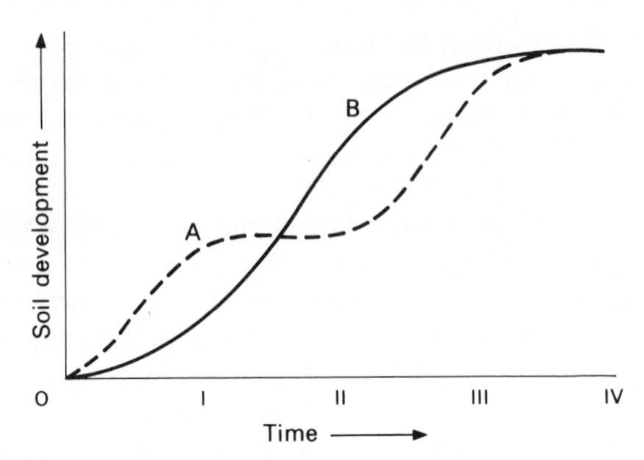

Figure 10.4 Hypothetical curves for soil development under (a) a fluctuating climate and (b) a constant climate. (From *Pedology, weathering, and geomorphological research,* by Peter W. Birkeland. Copyright © 1964 by Oxford University Press, Inc. Reprinted by permission.)

soils is that both have reached a steady state in development so that little further change is possible (Fig. 10.4, curve B). In areas where major climatic fluctuations have been frequent, this explanation is less likely because, although some soil properties seem to achieve a steady state relatively quickly, others need longer time periods. The first explanation accords with the view that appreciable soil development only occurs during interglacials and is considerably inhibited in glacial times. But evidence from high Arctic and Alpine areas shows that soil formation is far from inhibited. Therefore, the flattening off of curve A (Fig. 10.4) is too pronounced and a considerable dilemma still exists. Another major problem is that comparison between surface and buried soils should be between soils from similar topographic positions.

The mode of burial is often overlooked when assessing the pedological features of buried soils. In many instances burial is quite sudden, such as by slope or glacial deposits. But the possibility that the soil and vegetation can continue to develop and incorporate the burying medium must not be overlooked. Many buried soils occur in loess deposits and it is conceivable that soil and vegetation would not be inhibited unless the rate of deposition was particularly great. The interpretation of fossil soils is, therefore, still beset with numerous problems.

Identification of palaeosols

The unequivocal identification of palaeosols in deposits of similar composition is difficult to establish on field evidence alone and one is forced to agree with Ruellan (1971) that the identification of a buried soil in a single section is rarely simple. Valentine and Dalrymple (1976) argue that some of the difficulties stem from the looseness with which terms such as soil, regolith and weathering zones are used. But it is the nature of the soils themselves that produces the greatest problems, namely, the ephemeral nature and susceptibility to change of many soil features and the similarity of many soils to sediments. In many buried soils the A horizon may be absent because of erosion, yet it is largely the properties of the A horizon that are important in soil classification. This problem was encountered by Bruce (1973) in New Zealand loessic deposits. The A and B horizons had been stripped off prior to the deposition of succeeding loess and the morphological structure of the majority of the palaeosols was comparable to that of the subsolum horizons of the present soils.

A great many techniques can be employed in the identification of palaeosols as indicated in the report of the Working Group on the Origin and Nature of Palaeosols (1971). A simple division can be made between field techniques utilising observable characteristics and more detailed laboratory techniques. Accurate assessment requires a combination of both these approaches. Colour has been used by many workers, e.g. Butler (1958) in New Zealand and Kobayashi (1965) in Japan. But, colour can be deceptive and colour changes can occur with comparative rapidity. Raeside (1964) has used colour but in combination with structural features, root traces and clay skins. Various morphological characteristics have also been used: Simonson (1954) employed a combination of structure, cementation and clay and sesquioxide accumulation. Decalcification has been one of the most commonly used field indicators and has been used extensively to differentiate till sheets in North America. Gile and Hawley (1966) relied on the evidence of decalcification in differentiating soils on alluvial fan environments in New Mexico.

Laboratory techniques are being employed increasingly to identify palaeosols. Studies of compounds in which phosphorus occurs in soils indicate that the proportions occurring in different modern soils are characteristic of these soils and reflect their history and genesis. The relative proportions of primary, residual and organic phosphorus compounds were employed by Leamy and Burke (1973) to identify palaeosols in Central Otago, New Zealand. These authors conclude that the field identification of palaeosols can be confirmed by identifying and measuring the forms of phosphorus present. Also, the interpretation of the relative proportions of the phosphorus fractions provides a technique for assessing the relative degrees of weathering and possibly the length of time of soil formation. Goh (1972) identified palaeosols by using the level of amino-acid nitrogen as an indication of biological activity, Childs (1973) measured the vertical variation in total amounts of specific elements to detect the redistribution caused by soil processes, and Birrell and Pullar (1973) determined the amounts of elements such as aluminium and iron present in an extractable form as a measure of soil development. Infrared spectra of humic acids in buried Ah horizons have also been used (Dormaar 1967). In addition, various biological indicators such as pollen (Dimbleby 1952), mollusca (Kerney 1963), beetles and opal phytoliths (Dormaar & Lutwick 1969) aid the identification of palaeosols.

Problems of environmental reconstruction

Features which may be useful in recognising palaeosols may be meaningless for an accurate palaeoenvironmental reconstruction. The identification of palaeosols is very important in indicating changes in geomorphological systems, but it is even more important to be able to come to some conclusion concerning the climatic and vegetational environment represented by the palaeosol. But this step is fraught with many problems. It was stressed in Chapter 1 that detailed quantitative relationships between climate and soils have still to be established. It is generally assumed that soils which formed under similar climatic, biotic and drainage conditions during similar time intervals are similar. It is also assumed that the development of soils is a function of time in an absolute sense, such that weakly developed soils must be young and well developed soils must be old. But these are assumptions that might not always be true. There is also a great danger in using simple modern analogues to explain features of palaeosols. Colour is one of these. There is a temptation to equate palaeosols possessing deep reddish horizons with modern analogues that are developing in warm, humid climates. Pawluk (1978) has argued that the presence or absence of characteristics which reflect a high degree of weathering, may not result from the kinds of processes but rather from the length of time during which the processes have been active. Greater significance should be attached to those processes in which a threshold level of activation energy must be achieved for a reaction to take place. Identification of those processes in palaeosols may reveal much more about the environment of formation. This dilemma can be illustrated in the work of Rutter *et al.* (1978) in the Central Yukon, North America. Evidence for differences in climate between two interglacials was obtained from the type of clay minerals and their depths in two palaeosols. Montmorillonite–kaolinite mixed clay minerals were found at depths of 190 cm in one whereas vermiculite–chlorite intergrades were found at depths up to 93 cm in another. Using a formula developed by Birkeland (1974), it is possible to estimate the amount of water needed to reach the two depths mentioned. This indicated that the climate in which the first palaeosol developed was probably considerably more humid than for the second palaeosol. But the differences in depths of water penetration may also be a function of time. The nature of the clay minerals may be more indicative of climate, the inference being that the climate was warm and dry to produce montmorillonite.

The identification of biological components may be more useful in suggesting specific environments. Organic matter type and content and carbon : nitrogen ratios have been used. If the assumption can be made that the initial composition of the plants and organisms making up the bulk of the raw organic matter is relatively similar, then an evaluation of the persistence of organic fractions with different stabilities could provide a useful measure of the environmental conditions under which organic matter decomposition took place (Pawluk 1978). This procedure is complicated by further degradation after burial. The more readily decomposable fractions, such as loosely bound proteins and carbohydrates, are removed whereas the more resistant constituents, such as ligno-proteins, may be enriched. The work of Bal (1973) in this respect is extremely exciting. It is suggested that the decomposition and distribution of organic matter are related and can be regarded as an individual entity for which the name 'humon' is suggested. Humon is a fingerprint for the soil body. It is defined as a collection of macroscopically and microscopically observable organic bodies characterised by a specific morphology and spatial arrangement. Original plant components may be recognised by the identification of cellular structures and their decomposition products. The recognition of resistant organic bodies also allows original populations of plants and animals and their associated environments to be discerned.

As mentioned earlier, infrared absorption spectra of humic acids can be used to recognise palaeosols. The method may also allow the type of environment to be specified. Thus, Dormaar and his associates were able to differentiate forested soils from grassland soils by this method (Dormaar & Lutwick 1969, Reeves & Dormaar 1972). Pawluk (1978) employed the same technique in a comparison of a buried black chernozemic palaeosol in Edmonton, Canada with modern soils. The slopes on the infrared spectra for both soils confirmed the presence of grassland vegetation but a more pronounced slope for the humic acid extracted from the buried soil was believed to reflect the removal of low molecular weight constituents through post-burial degradation. A major problem with this type of analysis is that A horizons of buried soils which contain the majority of the organic matter have been removed, nevertheless it has been used successfully on the B horizon of truncated palaeosols (Dormaar 1973).

Biological indicators such as faecal pellets and pedotubules may allow specific faunal species to be identified. Similarly sclerotia and spores indicate the presence of fungi; phytoliths, pollen grains and plant macrofossils indicate vegetation characteristics; diatoms may suggest wet conditions and the resistant chitinous exoskeletons of beetles allow species identification and a picture of palaeoenvironments to emerge. A variety of techniques is available and should be used in combination, but each possesses particular problems. Some of the more important of these techniques are now discussed.

Table 10.1 The more commonly used chemical weathering indices.

$\frac{SiO_2}{Al_2O_3}$	silica : alumina ratio
$\frac{SiO_2}{Fe_2O_3}$	silica : ferric oxide ratio
$\frac{SiO_2}{Al_2O_3 + Fe_2O_3}$ or $\frac{SiO_2}{R_2O_3}$	silica : sesquioxide ratio
$\frac{K_2O + Na_2O}{Al_2O_3}$	alkali : alumina ratio
$\frac{CaO + MgO}{Al_2O_3}$	alkali earth : alumina ratio
$\frac{CaO}{MgO}$	calcic : magnesia ratio
$\frac{K_2O}{Na_2O}$	potassic : sodic ratio
$\frac{K_2O}{SiO_2}$	potassic : silica ratio

Weathering indices

The intensity of chemical weathering that soils have undergone can be assessed by constructing ratios of chemical compounds (chemical weathering indices) or minerals (mineral weathering indices). Many of the chemical weathering indices employ the amount of silica (SiO_2) or alumina (Al_2O_3) or both in soils. Many alkaline earths are removed more readily than alumina, and silica is particularly resistant to chemical decomposition. The more commonly used indices are listed in Table 10.1. The molar ratio CaO : ZrO_2 can also be used because the calcium-bearing mineral hornblende is more susceptible to weathering than the more resistant zircon. As an example, silica : sesquioxide ratios and potassic : silica ratios were used by Rutter *et al.* (1978) to differentiate three palaeosols in the Central Yukon. The potassic : silica ratios are shown in Table 10.2.

Table 10.2 Potassic : silica ratios of Yukon palaeosols (from Rutter *et al.* 1978).

Pre-Reid (early Pleistocene)		*Reid (Illinoian or early Wisconsinian)*		*McConnell (Wisconsinian)*	
Horizon	*K_2O/SiO_2 $\times 10^{-2}$*	*Horizon*	*K_2O/SiO_2 $\times 10^{-2}$*	*Horizon*	*K_2O/SiO_2 $\times 10^{-2}$*
II Bt1	2.5	II Bm1	4.2		
II B2	1.7	II Bm2	4.3	II Bm	4.1
II BC	2.0	II BC	4.3	II C	5.0
II C	2.0	II Ck	5.0	III C	5.1

The same principles underlie the use of mineral weathering indices. Goldich (1938), after studying the persistence of minerals in soils following weathering, proposed a stability series for the commonest minerals. It is generally the reverse of the crystallisation series and there have been many attempts to find reasons for this. Bond energies for cation–oxygen bonds and energies of formation for silicate minerals, calculated by Keller (1954), increase in the expected order (see Fig. 10.5) but do not correlate so well if the cation linkages are included (Brunsden 1979b). Also, energy indices (Gruner 1950), and degree of packing (Fairbairn 1943), do not agree with the series. Curtis (1976), however, has shown that Gibbs free energy values for weathering reactions and free energy changes (the sum of the free energies of formation of all the reaction products minus the sum of the free energies of the reactions, in standard states) which accompany weathering, agree well with the stability series (Fig. 10.5).

This information is utilised in constructing mineral weathering indices. One of the most widely used is the ratio of quartz to feldspar; the higher the ratio the greater the amount of chemical weathering. Some indices

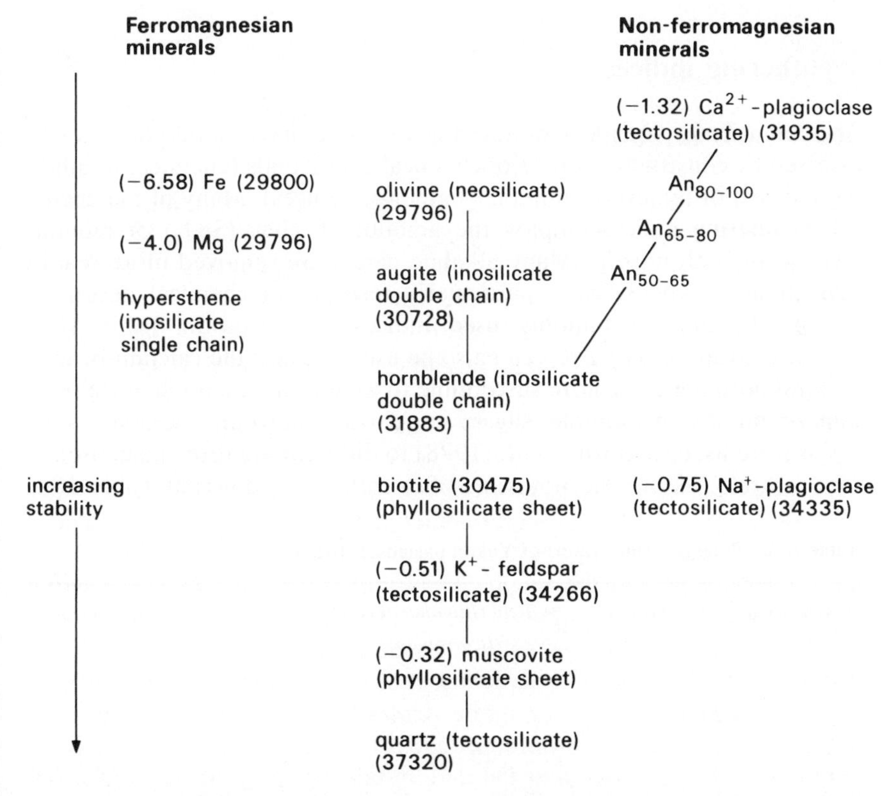

Figure 10.5 Stability series of the more common minerals, together with Gibbs free energy values and bonding energies (from Brunsden 1979b).

employ heavy minerals and rely on the stability series developed by many workers (e.g. Pettijohn 1941, Dryden & Dryden 1946). Olivine, amphiboles and pyroxenes are least stable; zircon and tourmaline are most stable. Thus, the ratio of zircon and tourmaline to the amphiboles and pyroxenes provides a useful indication of the stage reached by chemical weathering. Ruhe (1956) employed both these indices to good effect in the comparison of soils in Iowa (see Ch. 6).

This work emphasises that the state of weathering will vary within soils depending on the horizon sampled and, therefore, great care must be taken when comparing palaeosols where horizons may be difficult to identify. Also, more than one particle size fraction must be examined because mineral species content varies with particle size. These indices may be reinforced by considering the stability series of weathering of clay and clay-sized minerals. The most susceptible to weathering are gypsum, calcite, olivine and biotite and the least susceptible are anatase, haematite, gibbsite, kaolinite and montmorillonite (Jackson *et al.* 1948). These techniques rely on accurate information concerning soil formation and the sequence of weathering changes. The efforts by Evans (1978) and McKeague *et al.* (1978), to quantify the changes that take place during pedogenesis, are invaluable in this respect.

Radiocarbon dating

The radiocarbon method is the major dating method applicable to soil and superficial sediments but can only date material up to about 40 000 years old. Materials suitable for radiocarbon dating include peat, wood, charcoal, organic mud, soil humus and calcium carbonate in molluscs and bones; inorganic carbonates can also be dated. Cosmic rays produce radioactive ^{14}C by bombarding ^{14}N atoms in the atmosphere. The ^{14}C combines with oxygen, producing carbon dioxide, which is taken up by plants in photosynthesis. Animals become radioactive by eating plants. When the organism dies, radioactive decay begins and half the specific radioactivity is lost after a period of time known as the half-life. Libby (1955) calculated this as 5570 ± 30 years. Subsequently the half-life was recalculated as 5730 ± 40 years, but to avoid confusion radiocarbon dates are still published with respect to the originally calculated half-life. Thus, the sample can be dated by determining its specific activity.

The dating of palaeosols can be attempted for both the organic and inorganic carbon in the soils. The dating of soil organic matter is complicated by the fact that the different humus fractions, namely humin, humic acid and fulvic acid, will have different ages. Thus, the true age of the soil is impossible to determine and the date obtained represents the mean residence time of the various organic fractions, plus, for palaeosols, the time since burial (Campbell *et al.* 1967). Organic fractions dated for modern soils in Saskatchewan, Canada, showed humic acids as 1308 ± 64 years, fulvic acids as 630 ± 60 years and humin as 240 ± 60 years old (Pawluk 1978). Minor environmental changes, such as topography and drainage, can produce considerable differences in dates by controlling the addition of small amounts of fresh organic matter. Contamination, producing erroneous dates, is possible by further carbon exchange with the atmosphere or with groundwater and through the mixing of materials of different ages. Also, more recent carbon may be added to buried soils by the filtration of humic acids and, perhaps, by deep root penetration. As Shotton (1967) and Olsson (1974) show, only a small amount of contamination is necessary to affect considerably the date obtained.

The variability of dates within palaeosols may be large and the question of some contamination must always be considered. Ruhe (1975) has described a palaeosol from Australia where hand-separated carbonized specks were 33 700 $\pm {}^{2200}_{1730}$ years old, a fine-earth fraction containing organic carbon was 19 980 ± 370 years old with its NaOH soluble fraction 24 960 ± 580 years old and its NaOH insoluble fraction 25 360 ± 580 years old.

The dating of inorganic carbonates also poses problems (Bowler & Polach 1971). In dry environments inorganic carbonate dates are often older than they should be, whereas in moist climates, post-pedogenic exchange of modern ^{14}C gives younger dates. Nevertheless, if the technique is applied carefully realistic dates for palaeosols can be obtained.

Other techniques are now being used to supplement and extend the radiocarbon dates. Soviet workers studying loess in Tajikistan have been reasonably successful in extending dates back to 2.5 million years by thermoluminescence and palaeomagnetic methods.

Pollen analysis

The use and interpretation of pollen diagrams is standard practice in the environmental sciences and the methodology has become well established (Faegri & Iversen 1974). Pollen may be preserved in acid soils for long periods and the distribution of the various pollen types will give a general picture of past vegetational changes. But analysis of pollen from soils should not be viewed as pollen analysis of bog or peat sites. Similarly, pollen diagrams from buried peat deposits should be interpreted differently from those of buried soils. Most pollen in peat samples is transported from nearby trees; little comes from vegetation growing on the site and little has been transported in from elsewhere. Pollen analysis of soils provides a site or local picture of the regional pollen rain (Dimbleby 1961a).

All pollen, not only tree pollen, is counted and represented in soils. Thus, the predominance of non-tree pollen is a sure indication of the absence of trees. Also, the flowering of plants under trees is reduced to an extent that they represent only a small proportion of the total pollen. A mixture of non-tree and tree species suggests a mosaic of vegetation types as the trees must be near enough to contribute to the pollen rain.

Pollen analysis of buried palaeosols permits statements to be made of the vegetation at the time of soil formation. Analysis of surface, apparently modern, soils has also provided extremely useful information about surface processes. Investigations on many soils by Dimbleby (1961b) have shown that about one-third of the soils sampled contained old soil levels, more or less disturbed, buried beneath deposits of soil and gravel. Pollen is normally abundant at the soil surface and the amount decreases rapidly with depth. Old surfaces show in pollen analysis as sharp breaks in the curve due to the differences in pollen content. They may also be represented by a change in pollen composition. In many cases the boundary between transported soil and *in situ* material cannot be seen in the soil profile and it is only the pollen that indicates the change. These have been called buried levels by Dimbleby (1961b) rather than buried surfaces or buried soils. Soil creep is the most likely process involved in the movement of the transported material and it clearly leads to unusually thick A2 horizons. This thickness has been created either by a new A2 horizon developing on the transported material or the original A2 horizon extending in depth as new material is added. The rate of transportation is, therefore, of prime importance. This evidence also implies that simple statements about landscape and soil stability should be avoided and that pollen analysis deserves a wider application in both contemporary and fossil soil investigations.

Tephrochronology

In many volcanic areas such as New Zealand, Iceland, South and Central America, periodic ash or tephra falls mantle the surface. Tephra has been defined as all the clastic volcanic materials which, during an eruption, are transported from the crater through the air (Thorarinsson 1954). The colour and petrology of the tephra are often characteristic of a particular volcano and can be dated with reasonable accuracy. Thus, many of the tephra layers mantling the surface of Iceland have been dated (Thorarinsson 1944, Larsen & Thorarinsson 1978). Rhyolitic tephra eruptions tend to be paroxysmal with long periods of time separating bursts of volcanic activity. This may allow soils to form between each eruption which will be buried by the next tephra fall. But, many tephra falls are not sufficient to kill surface vegetation and are incorporated in the developing soil. Much will depend on the intensity of the eruption, the distance from the volcano and the wind strength and direction at the time of the eruption.

Typical deposits in these volcanic areas show a succession of ashes, mineral and organic layers. Some of the intervening layers may be palaeosols. The ash stratigraphy is, therefore, a great help in elucidating the sequence of palaeosols. Geomorphologically, the ash layers allow interpretation of the erosion and deposition that occurred between falls. The ash layers represent isochronous surfaces and the relative thickness of material between similar ashes at different localities enables tentative conclusions to be reached concerning landscape history. Also, as the ash layers mantle the pre-existing surface, former erosional features may be preserved. Thus, modern gullies in parts of southern Iceland show evidence of former infilled gullies in the ash stratigraphy exposed in their sides. At least two periods of gulley formation with an intervening period of gulley infill can be deduced. Tephra layers can therefore provide valuable palaeoenvironmental information.

Opal phytoliths as environmental indicators

Some of the silica absorbed by plants is precipitated in plant cells to form opaline substances known as opal phytoliths. These possess characteristic shapes and sizes and, when the plant decays, they remain in the soil. Grasses are the highest producers and yield phytoliths that can be distinguished from most other plants, although grass phytoliths are very similar to those produced by rushes and sedges. Modern forest and grassland soils differ in their phytolith contents and this difference can be used to infer gross vegetational changes (Jones & Beavers 1964). In effect, they can be used to detect relict palaeosols.

Phytoliths also persist for long periods of time and, therefore, will be present in buried palaeosols (Wilding 1967). Thus, they can provide important information on vegetational changes. In this way, counts of opal phytoliths have helped explain the origin of palaeosols in several river valleys in southern Alberta (Dormaar & Ludwick 1969). However, data on the rates of production and destruction of opal are required for really meaningful interpretations, since some silica may be easily available from the weathering of volcanic glass. The influence of climate and soil conditions on the weathering of opal is also largely unknown.

The application of soil stratigraphic principles

Studies of buried palaeosols provide strong evidence of repeated phases of slope instability in many parts of the world. Some of these phases are related to fluctuations in climate during the Pleistocene but they are also related to local environmental changes of which stripping of the vegetation and overgrazing are possible causes. The combination of the techniques and stratigraphic principles outlined in this chapter provides a powerful research tool with which to elucidate some of these changes. In this respect the methodology developed by Butler (1959) has given a great impetus to such studies. He proposed the concept of the groundsurface to represent the development of a soil mantle. The chronologic order of groundsurfaces, set by their stratigraphic order, is designated K_1, K_2, K_3, K_4, etc. from the most recent (uppermost) to lower and older ones. A succession of buried soils indicates a recurrent cycle of stable and unstable phases of landscape evolution which Butler called a K-cycle. Each cycle will have an unstable phase (Ku) of erosion and deposition followed by a stable phase (Ks), accompanied by soil development. It is necessary to establish that each proposed groundsurface is an independent layer and that it has soil profile development in it. The status of the upper layer as a groundsurface must be shown by the development of a soil profile in it but, in some places, the layer may be too thin to contain a full A/B/C soil profile and must be traced laterally to a point where it is thick enough to recognise a full profile. The underlying deposits may have several horizon remnants of truncated soil profiles but no recognisable soil profile and, therefore, do not qualify as groundsurfaces. However, by tracing the deposit laterally, a complete soil profile might be discovered. This is just the problem of composite palaeosols stressed earlier and tests of independence must be continually applied.

Detailed traverses usually indicate that each groundsurface has a restricted range of soils in it. This relationship needs to be established before firm conclusions are reached; but once it is, the task of differentiating and delineating groundsurfaces is made very much easier. The difference between soils in groundsurfaces may not be great, but some feature is often different, and Butler argues that this feature should be given a high order of significance.

Hillslopes often show three zones of mantle activity: there is a sloughing zone on the steepest part where the soil mantle is completely stripped away at each erosive phase; below this and at slightly gentler angles is an alternating zone, where erosion has been less effective and the soils have not been completely truncated; the third zone, on the gentlest, lower slopes, is the accreting zone, where erosion between depositional phases has been nil and conformably superimposed groundsurfaces occur. These relationships are well illustrated in the situation described by Butler (1967) near Canberra, Australia (Fig. 10.6). On the sloughing zones of the hillsides, K_2 groundsurface alone occurs. In the alternating zone, truncated remnants of K_3 and K_4 surfaces are found. The record of groundsurfaces is more complete on the toeslopes. The soil on K_1 surface is a dark prairie soil, soft and friable. Soils on groundsurface K_2 vary from red earths in well drained sites to yellow earths and grey earths in poorly drained sites. The red earth in the sloughing zones is often stoney. This is clearly a detailed palaeocatena and again demonstrates that studies of palaeosols should be based on transects rather than individual sites. The catena of soils, in the K_3 groundsurface, has a red podzolic soil in well drained sites and yellow podzolic soils, or solodic soils, in less well drained areas. The soils possess a strongly

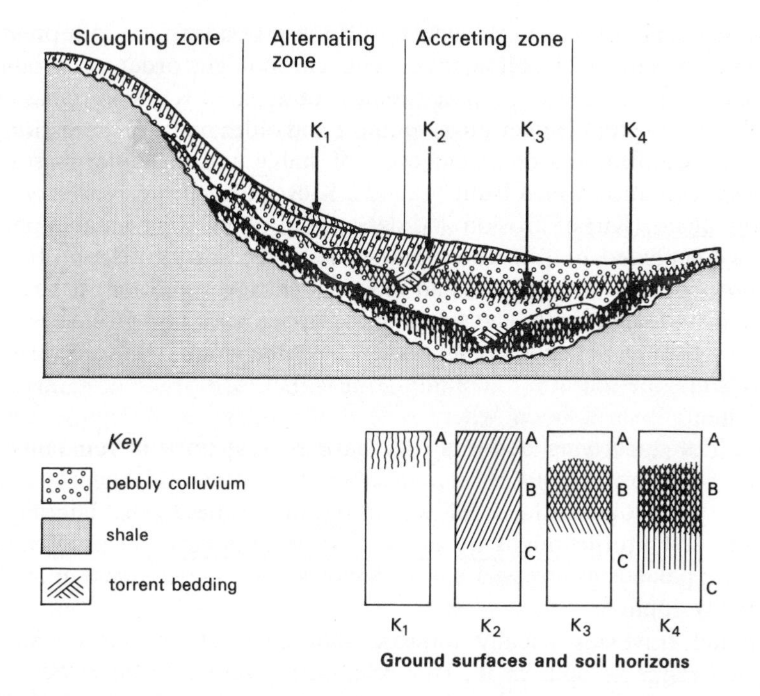

Figure 10.6 Sequence of groundsurfaces at Canberra, Australia (from Butler 1967).

contrasting pedal clay B horizon. The K_4 surface mostly occurs as a variably truncated buried layer. The catena is similar to K_3, but the B horizons are thicker with dense clay, and may include a calcareous gilgai in badly drained sites.

This sequence shows a complex sequence of buried, exhumed and relict palaeosols and requires very detailed and elaborate sampling and the application of precise stratigraphic principles to enable the correlations to be established. K_1 occurs as terraces, as small alluvial sheets and as segments in alluvial cones. K_2 occurs as hillside mantles on the lower two-thirds of slopes and as stoney shallower soils higher up. K_3 occurs generally on the more extensive, gentler parts of the landscape. K_4 is usually buried. This arrangement, and the nature of the groundsurfaces, enable geomorphological conclusions to be made. The continuity, from hillslopes to terraces, indicated that terrace aggradation and erosion and deposition on hillsides were concurrent. It also seems that erosion and deposition were widespread over the whole landscape on several occasions. Initiation of each cycle was on the hillslopes and it is suggested that periods of instability were associated with more arid phases and the soils developed in intervening more humid phases.

The problems of establishing the relationships between relict and buried palaeosols and between distinct buried palaeosols were encountered by Walker (1962a) in New South Wales, Australia. Four soil layers can be identified. Soil layer M is a dark, loam to clay loam, seldom greater than 30 cm (12 in) thick and always associated with the steepest slopes. Soil layer N is a crumbly silt loam with a weak blocky structure. The profile is a grey-brown soil, characterised by slight A/B horizon differentiation and occurs also on steep slopes. Layer Wa is a dark grey-brown apedal clay loam and occurs on undulating terrain. Layer Wb is a red plastic clay and generally occurs on gently sloping terrain. Where layers M, N and Wb occur in association there is no pedogenetic relationship between them, only an ordered stratigraphy. An upper pedogenetic horizon may be removed by erosion but it will not occur without the lower horizons. This dependence was shown to exist between Wa and Wb and they are, therefore, the A and B horizons of one soil profile. Layer N is overlain by layer M but overlies Wb.

These soils represent a sequence of groundsurfaces in the manner suggested by Butler (1959). The uppermost stratigraphically and, therefore, the youngest is layer M and is designated K_1. Layer N represents the K_2 surface and the Wa/Wb layer is the oldest or K_3 groundsurface (Fig. 10.7). On some gentle slopes K_3 (Wa/Wb) soils have persisted intact, through K_2 and K_1 cycles, and are relict palaeosols. K_2 soils are relict on some slopes also. K_1 soils alone represent simple soils developed under the present environment. Because relict K_3 soils have not been affected by soil forma-

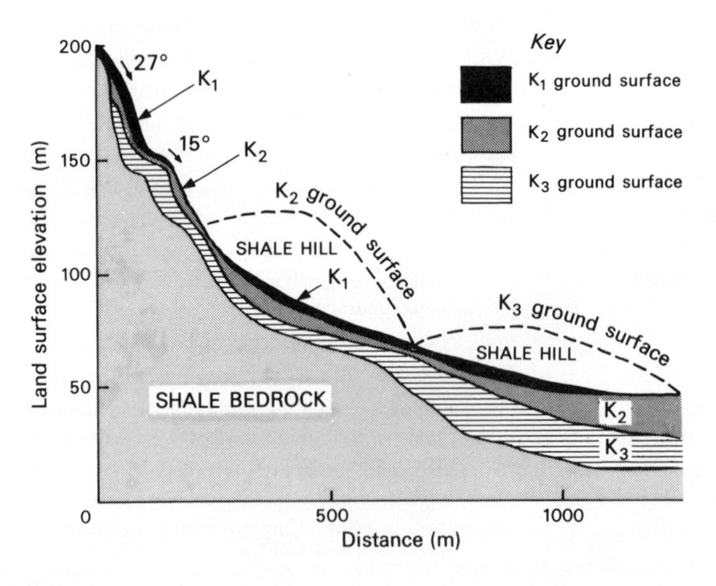

Figure 10.7 K-cycle soil layering on slopes in New South Wales, Australia (from Walker 1962a).

tion during K_2 and K_1 cycles and K_2 soils have not been altered by soil formation during the K_1 cycle, it appears that pedogenesis was stronger and/or lengthier in the K_3 cycle than in the K_2, and greater in the K_2 than in the K_1 cycle. This emphasises the vexing questions discussed in a general way earlier in this chapter.

The soil layers just described are continuous with the stream deposits and are integral members of the geomorphological systems. There are also localities where the deposits are separated as terraces in a step-like succession. This implies that each layer is the result of a separate period of erosion and deposition. This relationship and the stratigraphical information allow a sequence of events to be established. Each unstable phase in the cycle involved the truncation and removal of soil material, with subsequent deposition on the lower slopes, as unstable phases waned. Erosional phases were accompanied by incision along the stream channels. A sum-

Table 10.3 Sequence of groundsurfaces and associated processes in eastern Australia (from Walker 1962a).

Cycle	*Phase*	*Processes*
K_0	contemporary erosion and deposition	Slight channelling in the K_1 and K_2 deposits and deposition of stratified gravels, sands, and clays. No soil formation
K_1s		Soil development on depositional and eroded surfaces; minimal prairie soils formed with an A/C profile
K_1		Restricted deposition of a thin mantle over truncated slopes and in upper stream channels of weakly sorted and non-bedded sediment
K_1u		Minor truncation of K_2 soils; slight stream channelling
K_2s		Soil development on depositional and eroded surfaces; grey-brown soils formed with gradational A/B/C profiles
K_2		Deposition of an even mantle over eroded hillsides and thick deposits in upper stream channels; sediments are poorly sorted and non-bedded
K_2u		Truncating of some K_3 soils to bedrock: considerable stream channelling
K_3s		Soil development on depositional and eroded surfaces; red podzolic and yellow podzolic soils formed with strongly differentiated profiles
K_3		Deposition of a thick mantle over eroded hillsides and very thick deposits in upper stream channels; sediments poorly sorted and non-bedded
K_3u		Complete truncation of pre-K_3 soils to bedrock; very deep stream channelling

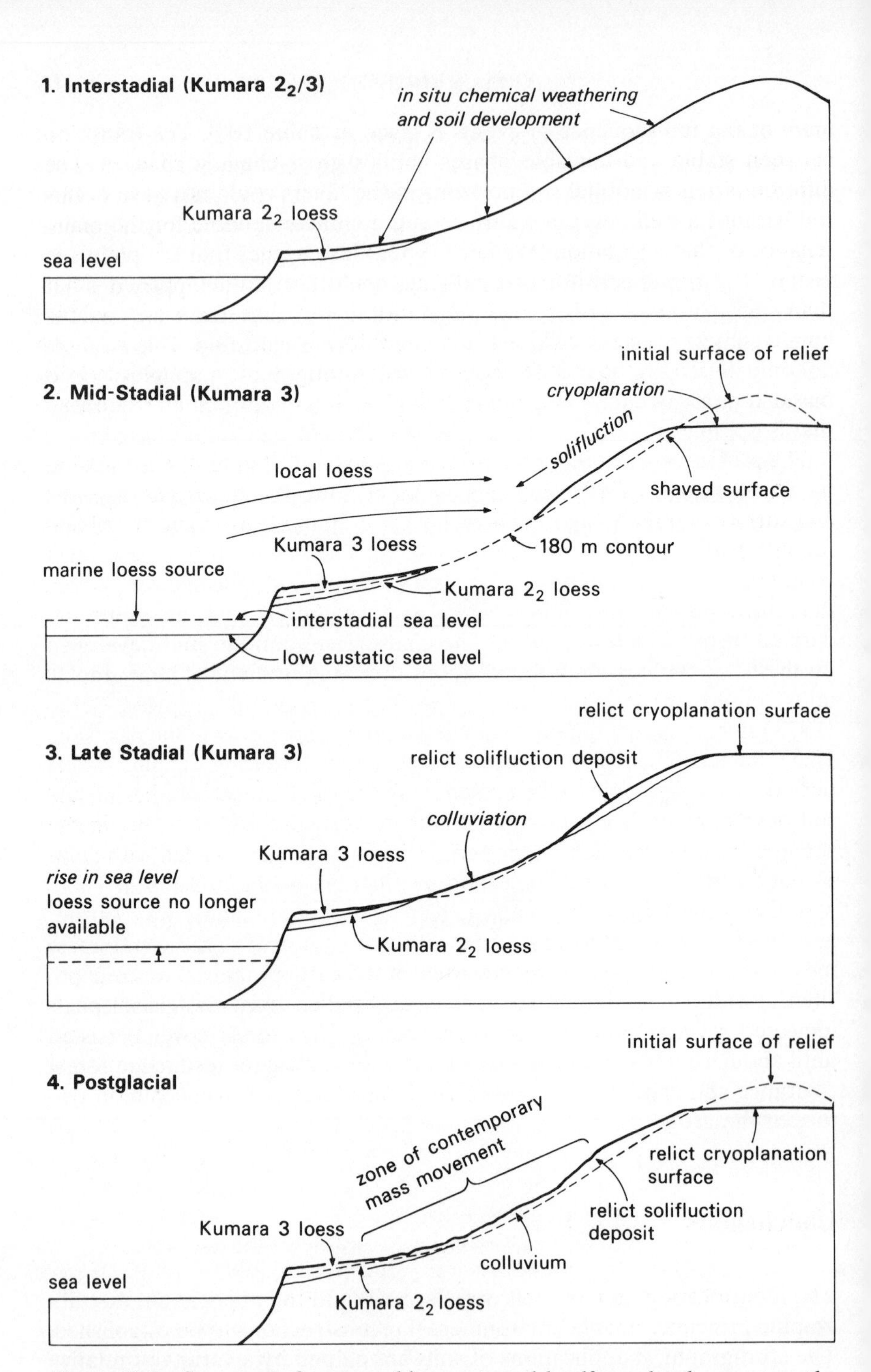

Figure 10.8 Sequence of geomorphic events and landform development on the Otago Peninsula, New Zealand (from Leslie 1973, reproduced from *New Zealand Journal of Geology and Geophysics*).

mary of the full sequence of events is given in Table 10.3. The transition between stable and unstable phases implies gross climatic changes. The differentiation of normal soil horizons in the layers could not have occurred without a well vegetated surface and a climate suitable for the maintenance of that vegetation. Walker (1962a) also argues that the phases in instability, with sheetwash and gullying, could not have happened other than in a situation with sparse vegetation. A change from an equable humid climate to one of relatively dry conditions is indicated. This example not only illustrates the precise application of stratigraphic principles to soils but also demonstrates the geomorphological and environmental synthesis that is possible.

The precise application of the principles of soil stratigraphy was found to be necessary by Leslie (1973) in his detailed study of Quaternary deposits and surfaces on the Otago Peninsula, New Zealand. Five types of soil and regolith had to be differentiated (Fig. 10.8). These were *in situ* loess, loess colluvium, colluvial mixtures of loess and weathered volcanic rocks, solifluction deposits consisting of loess and weathered rock and saprolite derived from the volcanic rocks. The landsurfaces and the soils developed on them are not contemporaneous, but the establishment of stratigraphic units, based on the lithologies in the layered regolith, allowed Leslie (1973) to reconstruct the processes and climates operating in the past (Fig. 10.8). Palaeosol morphology indicated that climate during the interstadial period was comparable to the present with *in situ* chemical weathering and soil development. The Mid-Stadial climate was cold and wet only in the summer months. Erosion under periglacial conditions prevailed with cryoplanation on the summit slopes and solifluction on the midslopes. There was also some loess accumulation. The Late Stadial climate was warmer and moist. Loess deposition and solifluction ceased, creep and mass movement became significant and much of the earlier material was redeposited as colluvium. Radiocarbon dates and pollen from postglacial peats indicated a warm climate with forest species. This forest cover persisted until about 1850 when the phase of European settlement resulted in forest clearance and caused mass movement. Landsliding is now a common feature of the area.

Conclusions

The identification and analysis of palaeosols and the application of stratigraphic principles enable environmental reconstructions to be established. The stratigraphical applications of soils are helped by a variety of relative and absolute dating techniques. But many of the techniques used are far from straightforward and considerable care has to be exercised. Also, the variability of the materials involved, including palaeosols, necessitates elaborate field sampling and the construction of detailed transects. It is clear that in many studies this has not been achieved. But, there are notable exceptions to this; the idea of K-cycles and the concept of the groundsurface provide a powerful research tool in studies of this nature. Many examples could have been chosen to illustrate the principles but all that has been attempted here has been a fairly detailed analysis of three specific studies that embody the majority of principles involved.

11 Soil survey and landforms in environmental management

Soils form one of the more important natural resources available to man. Efficient soil surveys are therefore vital to a nation's economic prosperity. But detailed soil mapping is a costly and laborious procedure especially in the large unmapped areas of less developed countries. Therefore, in reconnaissance surveys over large areas, the use of aerial photographs has proved invaluable (Goosen 1966, 1967). The mapping of river floodplains from aerial photographs gives a good indication of the soil types and characteristics likely to be encountered. It was also seen in Chapter 9 how aerial photographs and maps enabled the relationships between soils and glacial moraines to be established.

This relationship between soils and landforms has been used as the basis for a number of integrated surveys, combining elements of soil, vegetation and geomorphology. Many of these, such as land systems mapping, resource surveys and land capability studies, are examined in this chapter. The accurate assessment and mapping of surface form is also a valuable adjunct to problems of environmental management. Several schemes of landform mapping have been proposed. But, the assumption underlying all these techniques is the relationship between soils and landforms. All the procedures rely on the detailed on-site relationships between soils, vegetation, landforms and geomorphological processes that have been reviewed in this book. The success or failure of any management scheme relying on any of the mapping and surveying schemes outlined in this chapter depends on the correct interpretation of those relationships. The aim of this chapter is not to provide a comprehensive account of all the ways soils and landforms can be of use to environmental management but to indicate some of the schemes that rely on the close relationship between the two. More detailed accounts of soil surveys, land evaluation and land-use planning, are provided by Young (1976) and Davidson (1980).

Morphological mapping

A technique of landform mapping has been developed by geomorphologists that can be consistently applied in all areas (Savigear 1965). It is a scheme that allows a considerable amount of information to be mapped and is based on the recognition of breaks and changes of slope. Breaks of slope are shown by continuous lines and changes of slope by broken lines. Convex and concave boundaries are differentiated by adding a V-symbol to the lines, pointing downhill and lying on the side of the steeper slope. More detailed information can be provided by the addition of slope steepness values. If necessary, slope steepness can be highlighted by a system of colours and shading. The choice of slope categories to adopt may well be governed by local relief conditions although the IGU Manual of Detailed Geomorphological Mapping (Demek 1972) suggests categories of 0–2°, 2–5°, 5–15°, 15–35°, 35–55° and 55° and above.

The complete morphological map gives a good indication of the form and steepness of the landscape. This information is of considerable importance to soil studies, land capability assessments and land management in general. Earlier chapters have shown how the movement of soil and water on slopes is largely governed by slope form. Both Horton overland flow and saturated overland flow are governed by slope steepness and slope length. A morphological map is also invaluable in floodplain areas in explaining soil distributions and assessing agricultural potential. The information provided concerning slope steepness is useful in land management because of limiting gradients for transport and agriculture. Soil loss becomes a problem on slopes greater than 3° and 6° slopes are the maximum for heavy agricultural machinery. The standard tractor and combine harvesting equipment become dangerous to use on slopes over about 11°.

Geomorphological mapping

The mapping of surface form is often the first stage in the construction of a geomorphological map. A variety of schemes of geomorphological mapping has been proposed. The two most commonly used, and referred to, are the ITC system (Verstappen & Van Zuidam 1968) and the IGU scheme (Demek 1972). An excellent review of these schemes has been provided by Cooke and Doornkamp (1974).

Geomorphological maps provide information about the location of features formed by fluvial, glacial, fluvioglacial and aeolian processes. The amount of information provided will depend on the scale of the map and it may also be possible to show the nature of the materials. This may include consideration of geotechnical characteristics such as slope stability, unconfined compressive strength and plasticity indices.

The variety of mapping systems adopted by different countries makes strict comparison difficult. Some of these differences are a result of the characteristics of the areas mapped and some are a function of the state of geomorphological knowledge in the countries concerned. This is reflected in the study by Gilewska (1967) who applied the French, Hungarian, Russian and Polish systems to the same area in Siberia. The map produced under the Polish system was comparatively lacking in information concerning slope and river processes. Both the French and Hungarian methods emphasised structural and lithological features, while the Soviet system added information concerning tectonics.

It is interesting that geomorphological mapping was first developed in Poland as an aid to economic planning. Since then, geomorphological maps have been used extensively in various land-use and land management schemes. In Venezuela, a geomorphological map was used to define areas of limited value to agriculture thus saving time and money on more detailed surveying (Tricart 1966). A list of applications of geomorphological mapping in planning and economic development, compiled by Demek (1972), includes soil erosion control, soil conservation and reclamation and conservation of the natural landscape. Standard geomorphological maps contain much information not directly relevant to particular problems but they can be easily converted to provide information suitable for management needs.

Land systems mapping

Land systems mapping is based on the assumption that patterns of topography, soils and vegetation are so related that one can be used to predict the others. Thus, a land system is an area or group of areas, throughout which there is a recurring pattern of topography, soil and vegetation (Christian & Stewart 1952). The topography and soils are assumed to be dependent on the nature of the underlying rocks, the erosional and depositional processes that have occurred and the climate under which the processes have operated. A 'land system is a scientific classification of country based on topography, soils and vegetation correlated with geology, geomorphology and climate' (Stewart & Perry 1953, p. 55).

Land systems mapping was developed by the Commonwealth Scientific and Industrial Research Organisation (CSIRO) in Australia as a means of rapid reconnaissance survey of unmapped areas. The aim was to classify land for agricultural purposes. The method has also been adopted by the Land Resources Division of the Overseas Development Administration, Foreign and Commonwealth Office. Studies involving land systems mapping and analysis have been carried out in a variety of countries such as Lesotho (Bawden & Carroll 1968), north-east Nigeria (Bawden *et al.* 1972), Zambia (Mansfield *et al.* 1975–76) and Ethiopia (King & Birchall 1975).

Land systems are identified by analysing relief from aerial photographs and boundaries are drawn between areas having distinct photographic images. These images will be a function of geomorphological, geological, soil and vegetation characteristics. The land systems are then shown on a general map covering the whole of the survey area, together with a series of block diagrams to illustrate the character of each land system. Separate components of the land system, known as land units, are identified on the block diagrams. Land units are simple in form, usually occur on single rock types and possess soils which vary in a consistent manner across the unit. Units may themselves be composed of separate elements. More recently block diagrams have been dispensed with and stereoscopic pairs of aerial photographs of each land system are provided instead.

A somewhat similar scheme of terrain classification was devised by Webster and Beckett (1970) for the Military Engineering Experimental Establishment (MEXE), now the Military Vehicles Experimental Establishment. The scheme used aerial photographs to map land facets at scales ranging from 1 : 10 000 to 1 : 50 000. Facets were landscape elements, on a particular rock or deposit, with a uniform soil and water regime. The similarity between the MEXE system and the CSIRO schemes is striking. The applicability of the scheme devised by Webster and Beckett (1970) has been amply illustrated in Malaysia in a project undertaken by the Overseas Unit of the Transport and Road Research Laboratory (Lawrance 1972, 1978).

Although widely used with a fair measure of success, the land systems approach has been the subject of heavy criticism (Moss 1969, Thomas 1969), based on conceptual and practical considerations. Moss (1969) argues that, for agricultural purposes, soil genesis and denudation chronology are of little importance. Land systems emphasise static relationships in the landscape and not the dynamic interplay between soils, climate and vegetation. Moss (1969) prefers a biocenological approach in which agriculture is seen as part of the biological system within which it takes place since the operation of the ecological system is often independent of the information used to define land systems. The approach advocated by Moss would require not just a modification of the land system methodology but a completely new system based on a distinctly ecological view of soils, slope and climate.

There is no doubt that many of the points made by Moss are valid but it is difficult to see how these ideas could be incorporated into a scheme designed for a rapid reconnaissance of unknown areas. The advantage of land systems mapping is in its simplicity and ease of operation. The method of classification and the manner of data presentation can be easily understood by those who need the information for planning and decision-making purposes (Cooke & Doornkamp 1974).

Numerical land systems mapping

There is great scope in the future for the application of numerical landform description to land systems. Maps of single elements of landforms have

Table 11.1 Landform characteristics used in factor analysis of four land systems (from Gardiner 1976).

number of river junctions
number of intersections between contours and grid square diagonals
number of independent river networks
number of stream links
number of stream sources
number of intersections between the river network and the grid square edges
number of closed summit contours

their uses but, for most practical applications, multivariate techniques are required. An interesting comparison between areas defined by land systems mapping and numerical techniques has been provided by Gardiner (1976). He applied a factor analysis to seven landform characteristics (Table 11.1) of four land systems. Three main factors were identified. Factor 1 was heavily loaded by the number of river junctions, the number of stream links and the number of stream–grid square edge intersections and was interpreted as indicating the amount of stream length present in the grid square. Factor 2 was identified as an inverse index of the size of the basic land unit and factor 3 had high negative loadings by the relief variables and was identified as a relief–slope factor. Comparison with the land systems showed that each tended to occupy different parts of the factor plots. All three of the landform indices produced by the factor analysis showed greater variability between than within land systems. This can be seen as a justification of the criteria used to define land systems.

Multivariate analysis can also be used to produce landform regions as well as to test regions produced by other methods. Gardiner (1976) applied an automated grouping technique to an area of Uganda in which six land systems had been identified (Table 11.2). The variables used were

Table 11.2 Character of land systems from a part of Uganda (after Ollier *et al.* 1969).

	Landscape	*Altitude*	*Relief*	*Soil*
Kawanda	much dissected, no surface remnants, wide aggraded valleys	1100–1250 m	30–120 m	deep clay loams
Buwekula	rolling to rugged tor landscape	1300 m	120 m	clay loams
Nsala	quartzite ridges, steep slopes	up to 1600 m	200 m	stoney, skeletal
Buta	flat-topped hills	1500 m	200 m	skeletal soils
Lukaya	gentle ridges and hills, some flat-topped	1300 m (peaks to 1500 m)	30 m	gravelly loams
Ngoma	dissected plain, wide interfluves, broad valley bottoms	1150 m	less than 30 m	clay loams or sandy clays; laterite

number of junctions, number of contour intersections and number of stream sources. The clustering of seven regions so produced matched the six mapped land systems reasonably well. Type 2 land was restricted to one occurrence, which was almost entirely within the Ngoma land system, and although the Buwekula land system had part of five of the seven types within it, the major land type was type 3. There is, therefore, some degree of one-to-one correspondence between land systems and land types. Gardiner (1976) concluded that, although certain methodological and technological problems remain to be solved, landform analysis based upon easily derived numerical data may be used as a basis for land system description and derivation. King (1975) also established a number of correlations between geomorphic, soil and land system data in Zambia.

Classificatory procedures of this type can also be used to group soils. Cluster analysis produces a linkage diagram (dendrogram) showing the level at which fusion between sites occurs to produce larger groupings. Theoretically, a separate map would be needed to show the soil site groupings at every level of fusion but usually a particular similarity coefficient is chosen to represent the grouping. The advantage of the method is that it combines several soil properties in an objective fashion to produce one map. However, it is governed by the choice of these properties and there is also the problem of deciding which similarity coefficient to use. Nevertheless, there is great scope for this type of classificatory mapping procedure.

Land capability mapping

The land capability classifications of the United States Soil Conservation Service resemble the land systems method (Klingebiel & Montgomery 1961). The system identifies a hierarchy of groupings of capability units, capability subclasses and capability classes. Soils within each capability unit are expected to be sufficiently similar so that similar crops can be produced with similar management practices. They are also assumed to have similar potential productivities and require similar conservation treatment and management. Relief and drainage characteristics are more important at the subclass and class levels, subclasses being defined on the basis of hazards to agricultural use. The main hazards recognised are erosion, wetness, climate and rooting-zone limitations.

Eight capability classes are employed ranging from I to VIII indicating an increasing scale of limitations. Classes I to IV are potentially arable and V to VII non-arable. Soils in class VIII do not produce good crops, grasses or trees without major reclamation. In the United States an estimated 2% of land falls in class I, classes II, III, VI and VII occupy 20% each and class IV 12%. Class V only occupies 3% and class VIII 2% of the land area.

The land capability scheme operated by the Soil Survey of England and Wales uses seven classes (Bibby & Mackney 1969). Class I land possesses no or very minor physical limitations to use. Class II land possesses minor limitations that reduce crop choice. Classes III and IV land possess moderate or moderately severe limitations respectively which restrict the choice of crops and require careful management. Class V land has severe limitations restricting its use to pasture, forestry and recreation. Class VI land has very severe limitations and class VII land limitations so severe that they cannot be rectified.

The scheme adopted in Canada is based on the American method, though there are important differences. Separate land capability classifications exist for agriculture, forestry, recreation and wildlife, based on seven classes.

Many other countries are now actively constructing land capability maps. The Portuguese scheme of soil classification is very similar to the American system but is also influenced by the French School of Pedology. A land capability map, at a scale of 1 : 50 000 is also being produced, as well as the basic soils map. Capability classes are based on the degree and number of limitations for land-use, risks of soil damage if mismanaged, needs for soil management and risks of crop failure (Cardoso 1968). Five classes are used: A, B and C are suitable for cultivation whilst D and E are generally unsuitable. The principal factors limiting agricultural use are: nature of the soil, effective depth, erosion, water in or on the soil, stoniness, rock outcrops and toxic salts. A land capability index, *I*, has been established based on these limitations:

$$I = \frac{N \times E \times R_e \times H \times P \times R \times S}{100^6}$$

where

N = nature of the soil
E = effective depth
R_e = risks of erosion
H = water in or on the soil
P = stoniness
R = rock outcrops
S = toxic salts

Values ranging from 10 to 100 are estimated for each of the seven factors and the five capability classes are defined on the basis of the index value.

Land capability assessment must be adapted to meet the needs of individual countries and specific regions. This is especially so in parts of the Middle East and Africa and to illustrate the types of problems and the value of land capability assessment, two specific case studies are described.

Case study 1: the Trucial States

The aim of the land capability survey was to separate potential arable land from non-arable land (Stevens 1968). The land capability classification employed was that defined by the United States Department of the Interior, Bureau of Reclamation (1951). Until recently agricultural development was on an individual basis and of limited agricultural value. Most of the landscape is composed of sand and gravel outwash from the Oman Hills. Three major soil types have been mapped: sierozems, non-saline alkali and saline alkali soils. The sierozems are mostly developed on the finer deposits with a higher carbonate content. They include a thin silty horizon with platey structure overlying a sandy loam horizon with weak subangular blocky structure. A caliche horizon sometimes occurs below 100 cm. Calcium is the dominant exchangeable cation and high calcium values render phosphate unavailable. The non-saline alkali soils are frequently dominated by magnesium at depth. Low organic matter content reflects the absence of vegetation. Saline alkali soils have a low permeability but where cultivated they take on the characteristics of non-saline alkali soils.

Water is the major limitation to development, but soil limitations are also considerable. Gravel areas are agriculturally limited because of small boulders and cobbles and a low water-holding capacity. Alkalinity and salinity are important characteristics when determining land capability. Where pH values exceed 9 simple leaching will reduce the value to workable limits. Salinity is more of a problem. Traditional farming techniques are not affected because the cultivated areas are simply planted out to dates which are able to tolerate high salinities.

Soil limitations have been combined with physical limitations in producing a map of land capability. The gravel phases of the soil series have a minimal potential for commercial agriculture being normally assigned to class VI. Only the heavy-textured sierozems, with a calcium carbonate content of 25–50%, are always of class II or III, and therefore suitable for arable cultivation. The light-textured sierozem has both arable (classes II, III and IV) and non-arable (class VI) capability. Non-saline alkali soils usually belong to capability class VI.

Case study 2: Ghana

The soils of Ghana have been grouped under seven capability classes and four subclasses based on their degree of limitation for mechanised and hand cultivation of crops, for pasture grazing and for forestry purposes (Obeng 1968). The degree of limitation of soils becomes progressively greater from class I to class VIII. Soils in classes I to IV are suitable for both mechanised and hand cultivation of arable crops. Soils in classes V and VI are unsuitable for mechanised cultivation but suited to hand cultivation, pasture grazing and tree crops. Classes VII and VIII are only suitable for forestry. Limitations within classes are based on erosion (*e*), wetness (*w*) and soil properties (*s*). Thus, class II*s* indicates that class II land has some limitations because of soil properties.

Class I land possesses good soils with few limitations to mechanised agriculture. The soils are deep, well drained and exist on level or very gentle topography. They have a high water-holding capacity and are only subject to very slight erosion. Class II land possesses good soils with a few physical limitations. These limitations restrict the selection of crops and govern the amount of water and frequency of irrigation. Management techniques desirable are mulching and manuring, terracing, strip cropping and contour ploughing. The soils in class III are moderately good but have more limitations to mechanised cultivation. Conservation practices are more difficult to apply and the choice of crops is more restricted. More elaborate water control measures and close strip cropping are required.

The soils in class IV land are best suited for perennial vegetation. They have some major limitations but can, with care, be cultivated mechanically. The management practices for class IV land recommend that rotations should include long periods of forage or tree crop production. This class of land is very extensive in Ghana and is mainly cultivated for food crops and tree cash crops. Class V land consists of soils which are unsuitable for mechanised cultivation because of severe limitations. They are best suited to grazing and the hand cultivation of perennial crops. These soils commonly occur on steep slopes and are subjected to moderate or severe erosion. Deep, heavy soils with poor drainage on level topography also fall within this class. But with suitable drainage, they can be raised to class III or IV levels.

Class VI land possesses shallow soils on steep slopes and are only suited to tree crops such as cacao, oil palm, coffee and citrus. Soils in class VII and VIII have limited use. They are too shallow, steep or wet for any type of cultivation. Soils in class VII are underlain by loose gravel or soft weathered rock and soils in class VIII are shallow or possess solid iron pans or impermeable clay pans.

In order to make the systems understandable and workable by indigenous farmers, the land capability classes are grouped into A, B and C categories depending upon the degree of limitation of 50% or more of soils within a broad land area. Group A refers to a land area where the majority of soils fall within class I to IV. Group B refers to areas where the majority of soils fall within classes V and VI and are only suitable for hand cultivation. Group C land consists of classes VII and VIII and must be devoted to forestry.

Land resource studies

Many countries have published land resource studies but the most comprehensive output has been from the Land Resource Division of the Ministry of Overseas Development in the United Kingdom. Since 1966, 27 *Land resource studies* have been published as well as two *Technical bulletins*.

These have been reviewed thoroughly by Young (1978). The emphasis in most studies is on identifying realistic development options and then on the collection of information necessary to an appraisal of such objectives.

The general-purpose surveys make use of the land systems approach but many of them also involve a quantitative assessment of the physical landscape. There is also a series of resource inventories at intermediate scale which include detailed soil mapping and a series of special-purpose feasibility surveys. The last group of studies has been called comprehensive development feasibility surveys by Young (1978). They are surveys which cover all aspects of land resource development, from mapping of the physical resources to the technology of their use and the economics and social aspects of their development. By integrating surveys of physical resources with an assessment of the means of their development, they are a new and distinctive contribution to the methodology of land resource survey (Young 1978).

Land evaluation frameworks

The land capability studies that were examined in greater depth emphasised that assessment was in terms of a capability for arable cultivation. There was some recognition in the Ghanaian example that other land-uses and farming practices should be included. Recognising this necessity, the *Framework for land evaluation* (FAO 1976) was produced. It was the work of an international team coordinated by the Soil Resources Management and Conservation Service of the FAO. It offers a set of principles and concepts as well as a terminology which can be used as the basis for national systems of land evaluation. It stresses that a multi-disciplinary approach is required and that evaluation involves a comparison of at least two kinds of land-use. Evaluation must be in terms relevant to the local conditions and requires an assessment of the benefits to be obtained from a certain level of input.

The classification proposed is extremely simple and straightforward containing only two orders: suitable or not suitable. The suitable category is qualified by using the terms highly, moderately and marginally. The not suitable category contains only two classes: permanently or currently not suitable. Four levels of decreasing generalisation are defined. Land suitability orders reflect the kinds of suitability. Land suitability classes reflect the degrees of suitability within orders and land suitability subclasses reflect the kinds of limitations and the improvement measures required within classes. Finally, land suitability units represent the minor differences required in management within subclasses. This scheme has been tested in Malawi and found to be extremely successful (Young & Goldsmith 1977).

This is very similar to the specific interpretive soil map proposed by Wohletz (1968). Interpretive maps may include agricultural land capability, soil limitations for various recreational uses, soil erosion hazards, soil shrink–swell behaviour, pipe corrosivity and many more. Interpretive maps such as these and other visual aids are helping to convey land-use objectives to planning officials and the public in California.

Conclusions

This chapter has attempted to outline the practical application of the theoretical ideas and empirical information presented in the previous chapters. These applications range from simple soil and landform maps to more complicated resource surveys involving the interaction and interrelationships of many factors. But the success or failure of any scheme depends, ultimately, on the correct understanding of the soil–landform process–response system.

12 A pedogeomorphic synthesis

The rationale behind the specific examples considered in this book is that soils and landforms are very closely related. Thus, soil patterns and landscape elements often coincide and a knowledge of one allows predictions to be made of the other. This was seen vividly in the case of alluvial and glacial landforms. This coincidence of spatial distribution can occur at any scale. The major landform units of the 130 000 km^2 of the Llanos Orientales, the eastern tropical savanna plains of Colombia, are a case in point (Goosen 1972). Three major units occur: the alluvial overflow plains, the aeolian plains and the high plains; each with their characteristic assemblage of soils. Each of these major landscape units is composed of individual landforms which, because of varying morphology and surface materials, subtly affect the soils. Thus, the aeolian plains possess five soil associations occupying areas with distinct physiographic features. One association comprises excessively to moderately well drained, coarse-textured soils related to sand dunes. Another association is related to widely spaced, very shallow and often broad drainage channels called esteros. The esteros are permanently wet and the surface horizon is characterised by a high organic matter content. A further soil association is developing as a consequence of the rejuvenating drainage system in the aeolian plain. The slightly convex relief and rather open grass vegetation, which leaves bare about 50% of the surface, results in moderate but locally severe sheet erosion.

This last point emphasises that the spatial coincidence of soils and landforms reflects the interaction between pedological and geomorphological processes. Indeed, the distinction between the two is blurred and in many cases highly artificial. As was stressed in the introduction, for many years the two disciplines paid scant attention to each other. They are now more integrated, each providing valuable information for the other.

Pedological boost to geomorphology

The soil acts as the buffer zone between atmospheric and surface processes and the underlying rock. Therefore, the soil profile should reflect the history of the landscape if only the signals can be deciphered. It is not surprising then that Tricart and Cailleux (1972) state that the most important law of pedologic geomorphology is that chemical erosion is approximately proportional to the intensity of the soil-forming process and that the normal evolution of soils is all the more advanced as mechanical erosion is restricted. The existence of a typical, complete soil with defined horizons shows that mechanical erosion is slower than soil-forming processes. This has been embodied in the concept of the denudational balance of slopes and weathering versus transport-limited situations, as was stressed in Chapter 1. Thus, models developed to explain and predict slope evolution must include soil as a major factor.

Many slope processes, such as overland flow and rill development, show extreme spatial and temporal variability, making detailed process measurements extremely difficult. This is why many such processes are measured by their responses. These responses are often visible in soils and some have been described by Conacher and Dalrymple (1978). Responses to the movement of materials by overland flow in the Kimberley region of Western Australia included the formation of cohesionless lenses, specific microroughness and near-surface cohesion of soil materials (Pilgrim 1972). On granite slopes, cohesionless lenses up to 1 cm thick were created by the movement of material by overland flow. Mapping of these lenses on different parts of the slope enabled generalisations to be made about surface processes. Areas subject to the removal of material had lenses covering less than 10% of the landsurface, whereas areas where redeposition was more significant had a 40–90% cover of lenses. The results also showed that the mean microroughness of mobilisation/translocation surfaces was greater than that of redeposition zones. Penetration resistance was also greater on zones of translocation.

Subsurface soil water movement can also be inferred from soil properties (Conacher & Dalrymple 1977). In podzols, these properties include repetitive variations in the numbers, size, shape, colour and pattern of mottling in the Ea horizon. Three-dimensional variations in the thickness of the Ea horizon and associated features of the illuvial B horizon are also significant. Responses on adjacent non-podzol soils were different. In gleyed-lessive soils, grey mottles elongated downslope were an indication of throughflow.

These are merely two examples of the information on currently acting processes that can be obtained from detailed soil analysis. Pedological features also provide valuable information concerning long-term landscape evolution; this was seen in Chapter 10 in the discussions of buried soils. Buried soils allow palaeoenvironmental reconstructions to be made. But more important in conceptual terms, are the data provided concerning alternating phases of stability and instability (e.g. Butler 1967, Mabbutt & Scott 1966). Some of these phases can be related to gross climatic changes but many can only be explained by subtle changes in the erosion : deposition ratio on slopes. This work dovetails nicely with modern geomorphological thought concerning dynamic equilibrium and thresholds. The synthesis that now seems to be emerging is that landscape evolution is characterised by short, but relatively intense, periods of change followed by relatively lengthy periods of stability. Pedological information is a vital part of this synthesis.

The role of geomorphology in pedology

The identification and accurate dating of geomorphic surfaces and landforms gives some indication of the length of time soils have been forming. Sand dunes and glacial moraines have been used in this way. In many parts of the world intermittently falling sea levels and/or rising landmasses have created suites of coastal plains of varying age and elevation. The sediments on which the soils have developed are, in many instances, very similar and it is mainly local drainage differences coupled with the age of the surface that has created the soil differences. If the ages of the surfaces can be identified by independent means then soil differences may be equated with the length of the soil-forming interval.

The Swan Coastal Plain of Western Australia is an area where these relationships have been examined in detail (McArthur & Bettenay 1960). The coastal plain is formed almost entirely of fluviatile and aeolian depositional material and consists of a series of geomorphic entities subparallel to the present coastline. The Pinjarra Plain is the main geomorphic unit and is bounded on the west by a series of coastal sand dunes. The pattern of the plain is a series of coalescing piedmonts which can be subdivided into distinct depositional systems with their age relationships established stratigraphically. The names given to the systems–Coolup, Wellesley, Boyanup, Blythewood, Belhus, Dardanup, Vasse and Pyrton – are those of the major soil series and they range in age from approximately 400 000 years BP (Coolup) to the presently forming Pyrton system. As a summary the following are some of the temporal soil trends that have been identified:

(a) colour changes from dark brown through brown, red and yellow to grey with yellow-brown mottles because of iron segregation;
(b) differentiation in texture and colour becomes more marked;
(c) less stable primary minerals break down and the ratio of clay to silt increases;
(d) proportion of kaolinite to illite increases and gibbsite forms in the final stages;
(e) the percentage of saturation of the exchange complex decreases;
(f) the ratio of calcium to magnesium in the exchange complex decreases; calcium dominates in the younger soils and magnesium in the older.

The separation between the various elements of this sequence is not always clear cut altitudinally which is far from the case in many elevated coastal plains such as those of the south-east United States. The age sequences are also different in that the unconsolidated fluvial, marine and aeolian deposits range in age from Pleistocene to Cretaceous. The surfaces form a prominent stepped sequence with well marked intervening scarps and in a series of articles, Daniels, Gamble and their associates have established the soil differences between them (e.g. Daniels *et al*. 1970, Daniels *et al*. 1971, Daniels and Gamble 1978). The middle and upper surfaces are composed essentially of fluvial materials although there is a small marine component, whereas the lower surfaces are mainly marine in origin. Because of the extreme age of some of these surfaces and the similar material composition the same soils or group of soils can occur on more than one surface. But, nevertheless, distinct decreasing trends in features such as solum thickness, depth to water table, depth to and thickness of plinthite and percentage gibbsite content, can be identified from older to younger surfaces.

The need to identify landsurface pedons and polypedons in a variety of situations has led to fundamental research on soil modality (Conacher & Dalrymple 1977). It has also initiated research into more efficient means of clustering soil pedons. Thus, principal components analysis and principal coordinates analysis are now being used to define clusters of soils. In addition, spatial autocorrelation techniques are enabling the more efficient location of soil boundaries.

Detailed measurements of process, such as throughflow, require more detailed observations and descriptions of the morphological properties of soils such as structural peds, mottles, cutans, and intra- and interped pores. In this respect the work of Sleeman (1963) and Lafeber (1965, 1966) is important. This has been taken up and extended by Conacher and Dalrymple (1977) and their many associates and includes the use of close-up stereophotography and field sieving techniques to soil B horizons. Most developments have been concerned with the measurement of volume shapes and surface shapes of soil aggregates. Thus, 'what is now very much a pedological study of a morphological property of soils . . . has evolved from the need to quantify catenary relationships of soil structures' (Conacher & Dalrymple 1977, p. 136).

The integration between pedology and geomorphology, or pedogeomorphic research, is the basis of the nine-unit landsurface model that has been examined in Chapters 1 and 5. It is probably the most important statement of the integration of the two disciplines since the formulation of the catena concept by Milne. Conacher and Dalrymple (1977) argue that four elements of pedogeomorphic research are involved: the conceptualisation, classification, modelling and explanation of soil–slope relationships. The nine-unit landsurface model focusses attention at one or more of four distinct levels; these are the landsurface pedon and polypedon, landsurface unit, landsurface catena and the drainage basin. Examples of all four situations have been examined in this book to illustrate the integration of pedology and geomorphology.

Conclusions

Pedogeomorphology is emerging as a new synthesis to aid our understanding of the physical environment; it is a major focus and director of research; it can also have a pedogogic function. A present challenge for geography, geomorphology and pedology lies in the re-awakening interest in the workings of the environment and the exploration of man–environment relations. A potential new focus has been suggested in a report by an Association of American Geographers Commission on College Geography (Carter *et al*. 1972). This report defines physical geography as a study of the workings of the environment at the interface at the bottom of the atmosphere. The interface is chosen not so much as an object of study but as a convenience for reviewing the processes of the environment and their timing. This interface is effectively the soil and vegetation and is the only place where most major natural systems impinge on one another. It serves as the 'accountant's bench' for natural systems. It is also the prime consideration for many applied environmental problems. Thus, knowledge of the relationships between soils and geomorphology is essential for many reasons.

Glossary

aggregate An amalgam of primary soil particles bound together by clay, humus, etc.
aggregate stability The resistance of aggregates to dispersal into their primary particles.
Atterberg limits The boundary values of a soil between the liquid, plastic or solid states (see also **liquid** and **plastic limits**).
caliche A surface or near-surface layer cemented by secondary calcium or magnesium carbonate.
cation exchange The exchange between cations in solution and cations held on the surface of soil colloids.
cation exchange capacity The total amount of exchangeable cations that a soil can absorb.
clay ratio The ratio between sand and silt–clay.
Devensian The name given to the most recent Glacial period in the British Isles.
dispersion ratio The ratio of the amount of silt–clay in an undispersed soil sample with that in a sample treated with a dispersing agent.
eluviation The removal of soil material from a layer of a soil.
erosion ratio A ratio of the dispersion ratio to the colloid content/moisture equivalent ratio.
gibbsite An aluminium oxide; usually a weathering product.
gleyed soil A soil developed under poor drainage conditions, characterised by the reduction of iron, grey colour and mottling.
head A term used in the British Isles for solifluction deposits.
hydraulic conductivity The rate at which water can move through a soil.
Illinoian The name given to the penultimate Glacial period in North America.
illite A hydrous mica.
illuviation The process of deposition of soil material that has been removed from another, usually upper horizon.
Kansan The name given to the antepenultimate Glacial period in North America.
kaolinite An aluminosilicate clay mineral with a 1:1 crystal lattice form.
leaching The removal of soil materials in solution.
liquid limit The moisture content at which a soil changes from a plastic to a liquid state.
montmorillonite An aluminosilicate clay mineral with a 2 : 1 expanding crystal lattice structure.
ped A comparatively permanent aggregate separated by planes of weakness.
pedon The smallest three-dimensional unit of soil that can be analysed.
permeability The ease with which gases or liquids pass through the soil.
plastic limit The moisture content at which a soil changes from a solid to a plastic state.
Riss The name given to the penultimate Glacial period in Europe.
Sangamon The name given to the last Interglacial period in North America.
sierozem A term, now largely obsolete, to describe a soil type found in arid and semi-arid areas, characterised by a low organic content, a lack of leaching and an accumulation of calcium carbonate in the lower horizons.
smectite A group of swelling three-layer clay minerals including montmorillonite.
soil association A group of taxonomic soil units occurring together over a region.
soil series A grouping of soil profiles characterised by a similar sequence of horizons developed on uniform parent materials.
soil structure The size, shape and development of the structural units called peds.
solonchak A light-coloured soil with high concentrations of soluble salts such as sodium sulphate and sodium chloride.
solonetz A dark-coloured soil formed from a solonchak by leaching of some of the sodium. The soil is highly alkaline and develops a columnar structure when dry.

takyr A clay–silt playa or enclosed desert drainage basin.
Wisconsin The name given to the most recent Glacial period in North America.
Würm The name given to the most recent Glacial period in Europe.
Yarmouth The name given to the penultimate Interglacial period in North America.

Bibliography

Acton, D. F. 1965. The relationship of pattern and gradient of slopes to soil type. *Can. J. Soil Sci.* **45**, 96–101.

Acton, D. F., and J. B. Fehrenbacher 1976. Mineralogy and topography of glacial tills and their effect on soil formation in Saskatchewan. In *Glacial till: an inter-disciplinary study*, R. T. Legget (ed.), R. Soc. Can. Spec. Pubn no. 12.

Adams, G. F. (ed.) 1975. *Planation surfaces: peneplains, pediplains and etchplains*. Stroudsburg, Pennsylvania: Dowden, Hutchinson & Ross.

Agarwal, R. R., C. L. Mehrotra and R. N. Gupta 1957. Development and morphology of Vindhyan soils: I. Catenary relationship existing among the soils of the upper Vindhyan plateau, Uttar Pradesh. *Ind. J. Agric. Sci.* **27**, 395–411.

Ahn, P. M. 1970. *West African agriculture 3rd edn. Vol. 1: West African Soils*. Oxford: Oxford University Press.

American Commission on Stratigraphic Nomenclature 1961. Code of stratigraphic nomenclature. *Bull. Am. Assoc. Petrolm Geol.* **45**, 645–65.

Anderson, E. W., and B. Finlayson 1975. *Instruments for measuring soil creep*. Br. Geomorph. Res. Group Tech. Bull. no. 16.

Anderson, H. W. 1954. Suspended sediment discharge as related to streamflow, topography, soil and land-use. *Trans Am. Geophys. Union* **35**, 268–81.

Anderson, M. G., and T. P. Burt 1978. Experimental investigations concerning the topographic control of soil water movement on hillslopes. *Z. Geomorph., N.F. Suppl. Band* **29**, 52–63.

Arnett, R. R. 1971. *Slope form and geomorphological process: an Australian example*. Inst. Br. Geogs Spec. Pubn no. 3, 81–92.

Arnett, R. R., and A. J. Conacher 1973. Drainage basin expansion and the nine unit landsurface model. *Australian Geog.* **12**, 237–49.

Askew, G. P., D. J. Moffatt, R. E. Montgomery and P. L. Searl 1970. Soil landscapes in north eastern Mato Grosso. *Geog. J.* **136**, 211–27.

Augustinius, P. G. E. F., and S. Slager 1971. Soil formation in swamp soils of the coastal fringe of Surinam. *Geoderma* **6**, 203–11.

Avery, B. W. 1958. A sequence of beechwood soils on the Chiltern Hills, England. *J. Soil Sci.* **9**, 210–24.

Bagnold, R. A. 1941. *The physics of blown sand and desert dunes*. London: Methuen.

Bal, L. 1973. *Micromorphological analysis of soils*. Wageningen, The Netherlands: Soil Survey Institute.

Balme, O. E. 1953. Edaphic and vegetational zoning on the Carboniferous Limestone of the Derbyshire dales. *J. Ecol.* **41**, 331–44.

Barr, D. J., and D. N. Swanston 1970. Measurement of creep in a shallow slide-prone till soil. *Am. J. Sci.* **269**, 467–80.

Barratt, B. C. 1962. Soil organic regime of coastal sand dunes. *Nature* **196**, 835–7.

Baver, L. D. 1937. Soil characteristics influencing the movement and balance of soil moisture. *Proc. Soil Sci. Soc. Am.* **1**, 431–7.

Bawden, M. G., and D. M. Carroll 1968. *The land resources of Lesotho*. Land Resource Study, no. 7. Land Resources Development Centre, Ministry of Overseas Development, Surbiton, England.

Bawden, M. G., D. M. Carroll and P. Tuley 1972. *The land resources of North East Nigeria*. Vol. 3: *The land systems*. Land Resource Study no. 9, Land Resources Development Centre, Ministry of Overseas Development, Surbiton, England.

Beckett, P. 1968. Soil formation and slope development: I. A review of W. Penck's aufbereitung concept. *Z. Geomorph.* **12**, 1–24.

Bennema, J. 1953. De outkalking tijdens de opslibbing bij Nederlandse alluviale gronden. *Boor en Spade* **6**, 30–40.

Bibby, J. S., and D. Mackney 1969. *Land use capability classification*. Tech. Monogr. no. 1, Soil Survey, Harpenden.

Birkeland, P. W. 1974. *Pedology, weathering and geomorphological research*. New York: Oxford Unversity Press.

Birot, P. 1960. *Le cycle d'érosion sous les differents climats.* Universidade do Brasil.

Birrell, K. S., and W. A. Pullar 1973. Weathering of paleosols in Holocene and late Pleistocene tephras in central North Island, New Zealand. *N. Z. J. Geol. Geophys.* **16**, 687–702.

Bisal, F. 1960. The effect of raindrop size and impact velocity on sand splash. *Can. J. Soil Sci.* **40**, 242–5.

Biswas, T. D., and S. P. Gawande 1962. Studies in genesis of catenary soils on sedimentary formation in Chhatishgarh basin of Madhya Pradesh. I. Morphology and mechanical composition. *J. Ind. Soc. Soil Sci.* **10**, 223–34.

Black, C. 1969. Slopes in SW Wisconsin, USA, periglacial or temperate. *Biuletyn Peryglacjalny* **18**, 69–82.

Blake, D. H., and C. D. Ollier 1971. Alluvial plains of the Fly River, Papua. *Z. Geomorph.* **12**, 1–17.

Boast, C. W. 1973. Modelling the movement of chemicals in soils by water. *Soil Sci.* **115**, 224–9.

Bodman, G. B., and C. A. Coleman 1943. Moisture and energy conditions during downward entry of water into soils. *Proc. Soil Sci. Soc. Am.* **8**, 116–22.

Bogucki, D. 1976. Debris slides in the Mt. LeComte Area, Great Smoky Mtns. National Park, USA. *Geografiska Annaler* **58A**, 179–92.

Bolline, A. 1976. Étude de l'importance du splash et du reissellement sous culture dans les sols limoneaux de Hesbaye. Consequences géomorphologiques de la mise en culture de cette region. Paper presented to *1st Benelux Colloq. on Geomorphological Processes, Leuven*.

Bouwer, H. 1962. Analysing groundwater mounds by resistance networks. *ASCE Proc. Irrigation and Drainage Division* **88**, 15–93.

Bouyoucos, G. J. 1935. The clay ratio as a criterion of susceptibility of soils to erosion. *J. Am. Soc. Agron.* **27**, 738–41.

Bowler, J. M., and H. A. Polach 1971. Radiocarbon analyses of soil carbonates: an evaluation from paleosols in southeastern Australia. In *Paleoledology*, D. H. Yaalon (ed.). International Society of Soil Science and Israel Universities Press.

Brammer, H. 1964. An outline of the geology and geomorphology of East Pakistan in relation to soil development. *Pakistan J. Soil Sci.* **1**, 14–19.

Brammer, H. 1966. FAO/UNSF soil survey project of Pakistan: progress of work in East Pakistan, 1961–1965. *Pakistan J. Soil Sci.* **2**, 39–40.

Brammer, H. 1971. Coatings in seasonally-flooded soils. *Geoderma* **5**, 5–16.

Brewer, R., and J. R. Sleeman 1960. Soil structure and fabric: their definition and description. *J. Soil Sci.* **11**, 172–85.

Bricheteau, J. 1954. An example of sequence in red Mediterranean soil. *Bull. Ass. fr. Étude Sol* **56**, 139–48.

Brown, I. C., and J. Thorp 1942. *Morphology and composition of some soils of the Miami family and the Miami catena.* US Dept Agric. Tech. Bull. no. 834.

Brown, W. M. III, and J. R. Ritter 1971. *Sediment transport and turbidity in the Eel River Basin, California*. US Geol. Surv. Water Supply Paper no. 1968.

Bruce, J. G. 1973. Loessial deposits in southern South Island, with a definition of Stewarts Claim Formation. *N. Z. J. Geol. Geophys.* **16**, 533–48.

Bruin, P., and J. Ten Have 1935. Hat bepalen van magnesium carbonaat naast calcium carbonat in grond. *Chem. Weekblad* **32**, 375–8.

Brunsden, D. 1979a. Mass movements. In *Process in geomorphology*, C. Embleton and J. Thornes (eds). London: Edward Arnold.

Brunsden, D. 1979b. Weathering. In *Process in geomorphology*, C. Embleton and J. Thornes (eds). London: Edward Arnold.

Brunsden, D., and D. K. C. Jones 1974. The evolution of landslide slopes in Dorset. *Phil. Trans R. Soc.* A, **283**, 605–31.

Bryan, K. 1922. *Erosion and sedimentation in the Papago County, Arizona*. US Geol. Surv. Bull. no. 730.

Bryan, R. B. 1969. The relative erodibility of soils developed in the Peak District of Derbyshire. *Geografiska Annaler* **51**, 149–59.

Bryan, R. B. 1977. Assessment of soil erodibility: new approaches and directions. In *Erosion: research techniques, erodibility and sediment delivery*, T. J. Toy (ed.). Norwich: Geo Abstracts.

Bryan, R. B. 1979. The influence of slope angle on soil entrainment by sheetwash and rainsplash. *Earth Surface Processes* **4**, 43–58.

Budel, J. 1957. Double surfaces of levelling in the humid tropics. *Z. Geomorph.* **1**, 223–5.

Bullock, P. 1971. The soils of the Malham Tarn area. *Field Studies* **3**, 381–408.

Bunting, B. T. 1961. The role of seepage moisture in soil formation, slope development and stream initiation. *Am. J. Sci.* **259**, 503–18.

Bunting, B. T. 1965. *The geography of soil*. London: Hutchinson.

Buringh, P., and C. H. Edelman 1955. Some remarks about the soils of the alluvial plain of Iraq, south of Baghdad. *Neth. J. Agric. Sci.* **3**, 40–9.

Bushnell, T. M. 1943. Some aspects of the soil catena concept. *Proc. Soil Sci. Soc. Am.* **7**, 466–76.

Bushnell, T. M. 1945. The 'catena-drainage profile' key-form as a frame of reference in soil classification. *Proc. Soil Sci. Soc. Am.* **9**, 219–22.

Butler, B. E. 1958. *Depositional systems of the Riverine Plain in relation to soils*. CSIRO Aust. Soil Publ. no. 10, Canberra.

Butler, B. E. 1959. *Periodic phenomena in landscapes as a basis for soil studies*. CSIRO Aust. Soil Publ. no. 14, Canberra.

Butler, B. E. 1967. Soil periodicity in relation to landform development in south-eastern Australia. In *Landform studies from Australia and New Guinea,* J. Jennings & J. A. Mabbutt (eds), 231–55. Cambridge: Cambridge University Press.

Cailleux, A. 1959. Études sur l'érosion et la sedimentation en Guyana. *Mem. Serv. Carte Geol. Fr.,* 1959, 49–73.

Callow, W. J., M. J. Baker and D. H. Pritchard 1964. National Physical Laboratory radiocarbon measurements: II. *Radiocarbon* **6**, 25–30.

Campbell, C. A., E. A. Paul, D. A. Rennie and K. J. McCallum 1967. Applicability of the carbon-dating method of analysis to soil humus studies. *Soil Sci.* **2**, 217–24.

Cardoso, J. C. 1968. Soil survey and land use planning in Portugal. *Trans 9th Int. Congr. of Soil Science, Adelaide*.Vol. 4, 261–9. London: International Society of Soil Science.

Carson, M. A. 1967. *The evolution of straight debris mantled hillslopes*. Ph.D. Thesis. University of Cambridge.

Carson, M. A., and M. J. Kirkby 1972. *Hillslope form and process*. Cambridge: Cambridge University Press.

Carter, D. B., T. H. Schmudde and D. M. Sharpe 1972. *The interface as a working environment: A purpose for physical geography*. Commission on College Geography Tech. Rep. no. 7, Association of American Geographers.

Catt, J. A., and L. F. Penny 1966. The Pleistocene deposits of Holderness, East Yorkshire. *Proc. Yorks. Geol. Soc.* **35**, 375–420.

Chandler, R. J. 1971. Landsliding on the Jurassic escarpment near Rockingham, Northamptonshire. In *Slopes, form and process*, D. Brunsden (ed.) Inst. Br. Geogs Spec. Pubn no. 3, 111–28.

Charter, C. F. 1949. The detailed reconnaissance soils survey of the cocoa country of the Gold Coast. *Proc. Cocoa Conf. London 1949.*

Charter, C. F. 1958. *Report on the environmental conditions prevailing in Block A Southern Province, Tanganyika*. Ghana Dept Agric. Occasional Paper no. 1.

Chartres, C. J. 1980. A Quaternary soil sequence in the Kennet Valley, Central Southern England. *Geoderma* **23**, 125–46.

Chepil, W. S. 1945. Dynamics of wind erosion: II. Initiation of soil movement. *Soil Sci.* **60**, 397–411.

Chepil, W. S. 1951. Properties of soil which influence wind erosion: V. Mechanical stability of structure. *Soil Sci.* **72**, 465–78.

Chepil, W. S. 1955. Factors that influence clod structure and erodibility of soil by wind: IV. Sand, silt and clay. *Soil Sci.* **80**, 155–62.

Chepil, W. S., and R. A. Milne 1941. Wind erosion of soil in relation to roughness of surface. *Soil Sci.* **52**, 417–31.

Chepil, W. S., and N. P. Woodruff 1963. The physics of wind erosion and its control. *Adv. Agron.* **15**, 211–302.

Childs, C. W. 1973. Patterns of total element concentrations in Quaternary loess columns. *Proc. INQUA Congr. IX Abstract*, 61–2. International Union for Quaternary Research.

Childs, E. C. 1969. *An introduction to the physical basis of soil water phenomena*. Chichester: Wiley.

Chorley, R. J. 1978. The hillslope hydrological cycle. In *Hillslope hydrology*, M. J. Kirkby (ed.). Chichester: Wiley.

Chorley, R. J., and B. A. Kennedy 1971. *Physical geography: a systems approach*. London: Prentice-Hall.

Chow, V. T. (ed.) 1964. *Handbook of applied hydrology: a compendium of water-resources technology*. New York: McGraw-Hill.

Christian, C. S., and G. A. Stewart 1952. *Summary of general report on Survey of Katherine-Darwin Region*, 1946 (CSIRO Australia). Land Res. Ser. no. 1.

Clarke, G. R. 1954. *Soils in the Oxford region*, A. F. Martin & R. W. Steel (eds). Oxford: Oxford University Press.

Clarke, G. R. 1957. *The study of the soil in the field*, 4th edn. Oxford: Oxford University Press.

Clayden, B. 1964. *The soils of the Middle Teign Valley district of Devon*. Bull. Soil Surv. GB. Harpenden: Soil Survey.

Clayden, B. 1971. *Soils of the Exeter District*. Mem. Soil Surv. GB. Harpenden: Soil Survey.

Coleman, J. D., D. M. Farrar and A. D. Marsh 1964. The moisture characteristics, composition, and structural analysis of a red clay soil from Kenya. *Geotechnique* **14**, 262–76.

Conacher, A. J. and J. B. Dalrymple 1977. The nine unit landsurface model: An approach to pedogeomorphic research. *Geoderma* **18**, 1–154.

Conacher, A. J., and J. B. Dalrymple 1978. Identification, measurement and interpretation of some pedogeomorphic processes. *Z. Geomorph., NF Suppl. Band,* **29**, 1–9.

Conaway, A. W., and E. Strickling 1962. A comparison of selected methods for expressing soil aggregate stability. *Proc. Soil Sci. Soc. Am.* **24**, 426–30.

Cook, H. L. 1946. The infiltration approach to the calculation of surface runoff. *Trans Am. Geophys. Union* **27**, 726–43.

Cooke, R. U., and J. C. Doornkamp 1974. *Geomorphology in environmental management*. Oxford: Oxford University Press.

Cooke, R. U., and A. Warren 1973. *Geomorphology in deserts*. London: Batsford.

Corless, J. F., and R. V. Ruhe 1955. The Iowan terrace and terrace soils of the Nishnabotna Valley in western Iowa. *Proc. Iowa Acad. Sci.* **62**, 345–60.

Cotton, G. A. 1961. The theory of savanna planation. *Geography* **46**, 89–101.

Coutts, J. R. H., M. F. Kandil, J. L. Nowland and J. Tinsley 1968. Use of radioactive ^{59}Fe for tracing soil particle movement: I. Field studies of splash erosion. *J. Soil Sci.* **19**, 311–24.
Crampton, C. B., and J. A. Taylor 1967. Solifluction terraces in South Wales. *Biuletyn Peryglacjalny* **16**, 15–36.
Crickmay, C. H. 1933. The later stages in the cycle of erosion. *Geol Mag.* **70**, 337–47.
Crocker, R. L. 1952. Soil genesis and the pedogenic factors. *Biol Rev.* **27**, 139–68.
Crocker, R. L., and B. A. Dickson 1957. Soil development on the recessional moraines of the Herbert and Mendenhall glaciers, south-eastern Alaska. *J. Ecol.* **45**, 169–85.
Crocker, R. L., and J. Major 1955. Soil development in relation to vegetation and surface age at Glacier Bay, Alaska. *J. Ecol.* **43**, 427–48.
Crompton, E. 1966. *The soils of the Preston District of Lancashire*. Mem. Soil Surv. GB. Harpenden: Soil Survey.
Culling, W. E. H. 1963. Soil creep and the development of hillside slopes. *J. Geol.* **72**, 127–61.
Currey, D. T. 1977. The role of applied geomorphology in irrigation and groundwater studies. In *Applied geomorphology*, J. R. Hails (ed.). Amsterdam: Elsevier.
Curtis, C. D. 1976. Stability of minerals in surface weathering reactions. *Earth Surf. Proc.* **1**, 63–70.
Curtis, L. F. 1971. *Soils of Exmoor Forest.* Special Surv., Soil Surv. GB, no 5. Harpenden: Soil Survey.

Dalrymple, J. B., R. J. Blong and A. J. Conacher 1968. A hypothetical nine unit landsurface model. *Z. Geomorph.* **12**, 60–76.
Dan, J., and D. H. Yaalon 1968. Pedomorphic forms and pedomorphic surfaces. *Trans 9th Int. Congr. Soil Science, Adelaide*. Vol. 3, 577–84. London: International Society of Soil Science.
Daniels, R. B., and E. E. Gamble 1978. Relations between stratigraphy geomorphology and soils in Coastal Plain areas of southeastern USA. *Geoderma* **21**, 41–65.
Daniels, R. B., E. E. Gamble and J. G. Cady 1970. Some relations among Coastal Plain soils and geomorphic surfaces in North Carolina. *Proc. Soil Sci. Soc. Am.* **34**, 648–53.
Daniels, R. B., E. E. Gamble and L. A. Nelson 1971. Relations between soil morphology and water-table levels on a dissected North Carolina Coastal Plain surface. *Proc. Soil Sci. Soc. Am.* **35**, 781–4.
Davidson, D. A. 1980. *Soils and land use planning*. London: Longman.
Davis, W. M. 1899. The geographical cycle. *Geog. J.* **14A**, 481–503.
Davison, C. 1889. On the creeping of the soil cap through the action of frost. *Geol Mag.* **6**, 255.
Delvigne, J. 1965. *Pedogenese en zone tropicale. La formation des mineraux sécondaires en milieu ferrallitique*. Mem. ORSTOM no. 13.
Demek, J. (ed.) 1972. *Manual of detailed geomorphological mapping*. Prague: Academica.
De Smet, L. A. H. 1954. Enkele opmerkingen over kalkarme zeekleiafzettingen. *Boor en Spade* **7**, 169–73.
De Swardt, A. M. J. 1964. Lateritisation and landscape development in parts of Equatorial Africa. *Z. Geomorph.*, NS **8**, 313–33.
Diephuis, J. G. H. R. 1966. The Guiana Coast. *Tijdschr. koninkl. Ned. Aardrijkskundig Genoot.* **83**, 145–52.
Dijkerman, J. C. 1974. Pedology as a science: the role of data, models and theories in the study of natural soil systems. *Geoderma* **11**, 73–93.
Dimbleby, G. W. 1952. The historical status of moorland in northeast Yorkshire. *New Phytol.* **56**, 12–28.
Dimbleby, G. W. 1961a. Soil pollen analysis. *J. Soil Sci.* **12**, 1–11.
Dimbleby, G. W. 1961b. Transported material in the soil profile. *J. Soil Sci.* **12**, 12–22.
Doeglas, D. J. 1950. Die interpretatie van karrelgrootte–analysen II: karrelgrootte–ouderzoek van Nederlandse strandzanden. *Verh. koninkl. Ned. Geol. Mijmbouwk. Genoot., Geol. Ser.* **15**, 257–75.

Dormaar, J. F. 1967. Infrared spectra of humic acids from soils formed under grass or trees. *Geoderma* **1**, 37–45.

Dormaar, J. F. 1973. A diagnostic technique to differentiate between buried Gleysolic and Chernozemic B horizons. *Boreas* **2**, 13–15.

Dormaar, J. F., and L. E. Lutwick 1969. Infrared spectra of humic acids and opal phytoliths as indicators of paleosols. *Can. J. Soil Sci.* **49**, 29–37.

Dryden, L., and C. Dryden 1946. Comparative rates of weathering of some common heavy minerals. *J. Sed. Petrol.* **16**, 91–6.

D'Souza, V. P. C., and R. P. C. Morgan 1976. A laboratory study of the effect of slope steepness and curvature on soil erosion. *J. Agric. Engng Res.* **21**, 21–31.

Dunne, T. 1978. Field studies of hillslope flow processes. In *Hillslope hydrology*, M. J. Kirkby (ed.). Chichester: Wiley.

Dunne, T., and R. D. Black 1970. An experimental investigation of runoff production in permeable soils. *Water Resources Res.* **6**, 1296–311.

Edelman, C. H. 1950. *Soils of the Netherlands*. Amsterdam: North-Holland.

Edelman, C. H., and Pk. J. Van der Voorde 1963. Important characteristics of alluvial soils in the tropics. *Soil Sci.* **95**, 258–63.

Ellis, J. H. 1938. *The soils of Manitoba*. Winnipeg: Manitoba Economic Survey Board.

Ellison, W. D. 1944. Two devices for measuring soil erosion. *Agric. Engng* **25**, 53–5.

Ellison, W. D. 1945. Some effects of raindrops and surface-flow on soil erosion and infiltration. *Trans Am. Geophys. Union* **26**, 415–29.

Emmett, W. W. 1970. *The hydraulics of overland flow on hillslopes*. US Geol. Surv. Prof. Paper no. 662-A.

Emmett, W. W. 1978. Overland flow. In *Hillslope hydrology*, M. J. Kirkby (ed.). Chichester: Wiley.

England, C. B., and H. N. Holtan 1969. Geomorphic grouping of soils in watershed engineering. *J. Hydrol.* **7**, 217–25.

England, H. N. 1964. Problems of irrigated areas. In *Water resource use and management*, E. S. Hills (ed.). Melbourne: University Press.

English, C. 1977. *An investigation into regolith thickness and its possible relationships with slope angle and slope position on the Upper Chalk of the South Downs, Sussex*. B.Sc. Diss., Department of Geography, University of Birmingham.

Evans, C. J. 1978. Quantification and pedological processes. In *Quaternary soils*, W. C. Mahaney (ed.). Norwich: Geo Abstracts.

Eyles, R. J., and R. Ho 1970. Soil creep on a humid tropical slope. *J. Trop. Geog.* **31**, 40–2.

Faegri, K., and J. Iversen 1974. *Textbook of pollen analysis*, Oxford: Blackwell Scientific.

Fairbairn, H. W. 1943. Packing in ionic minerals. *Bull. Geol Soc. Am.* **54**, 1305–74.

FAO 1976. *A framework for land evaluation*. Rome FAO Soils Bull. no. 32.

Findlay, D. C. 1965. *Soils of the Mendip District of Somerset*. Mem. Soil Surv. GB. Harpenden: Soil Survey.

Firman, J. B. 1968. Soil distribution—a stratigraphic approach. *Trans 9th Int. Congr. of Soil Science, Adelaide*. Vol. 4, 569–76. London: International Society of Soil Science.

Fleming, R. W., and A. M. Johnson 1975. Rates of seasonal creep of silty clay soil. *Q. J. Engng Geol.* **10**, 83–93.

Follmer, L. R. 1978. The Sangamon Soil in its type area—a review. In *Quaternary soils*, W. C. Mahaney (ed.). Norwich: Geo Abstracts.

Foss, J. E., and R. H. Rust 1962. Soil development in relation to loessial deposition in southeastern Minnesota. *Proc. Soil Sci. Soc. Am.* **26**, 270–4.

Foster, G. R., and W. H. Wischmeier 1974. Evaluating irregular slopes for soil loss prediction. *Trans Am. Soc. Agric. Engrs* **17**, 305–9.

Foster, W. D. A. 1950. Comparison of 9 indices of raintall intensity. *Trans Am. Geophys. Union* **31**, 894–900.

Franzmeier, D. P., and E. P. Whiteside 1963. A chronosequence of podzols in Northern Michigan: I Physical and chemical properties. *Michigan State Univ. Agric. Exptl Stn Q. Bull.* **46**, 21–36.

Free, G. R. 1960. Erosion characteristics of rainfall. *Agric. Engng* **41**, 447–9.

Free, G. R., M. Browning and G. W. Musgrave 1940. *Relative infiltration and related physical characteristics of certain soils.* US Dept Agric. Tech. Bull., no. 729.

French, H. M. 1971. Slope asymmetry of the Beaufort Plain, northwest Banks Island, N.W.T., Canada. *Can. J. Earth Sci.* **8**, 717–31.

French, H. M. 1976. *The periglacial environment*. London: Longman.

Fridland, V. M. 1974. Structure of the soil mantle. *Geoderma* **12**, 35–41.

Frye, J. C., H. B. Willman and H. D. Glass 1960. *Gumbotil, accretion-gley and the weathering profile*. Ill. St. Geol. Surv. Circ., no. 295.

Furley, P. A. 1968. Soil formation and slope development: 2 The relationship between soil formation and gradient angle in the Oxford area. *Z. Geomorph.*, NF **12**, 25–42.

Furley, P. A. 1971. Relationships between slope form and soil properties developed over chalk parent materials. In *Slopes, form and process*, D. Brunsden (ed.). Inst. Br. Geographers Special Publ., no. 3, 141–64.

Gardiner, V. 1976. Land evaluation and the numerical delimitation of natural regions. *Geogr. Pol.* **34**, 17–30.

Gardner, W., and J. A. Widstoe 1921. The movement of soil moisture. *Soil Sci.* **11**, 215–32.

Gerrard, A. J. W. 1978. Hillslope profile analysis. *Area* **10**, 129–30.

Gerrard, A. J. W. 1980. Large-scale forms of hillslope failure in the Severn and Wye drainage basins. In *Palaeohydrology of the temperate zone, subproject A: fluvial environments, Severn Basin*, K. J. Gregory (ed.). Unpublished Preliminary Report.

Gerrard, A. J. W., and L. Morris 1981. *Mass movement forms and processes on Bredon Hill, Worcestershire.* Dept Geog., Univ. of Birmingham Working Paper, no. 10.

Gerrard, A. J. W., and D. A. Robinson 1971. Variability in slope measurements. *Trans Inst. Br. Geog* **54**, 45–54.

Gerrard, A. J. W., and M. Webster 1979. *Terracettes in Wolfescotedale, Derbyshire: a deductive approach*. Dept Geog., Univ. of Birmingham Occasional Publ., no. 7.

Gerson, R. 1972. *Geomorphic processes of Mount Sdom (Dead Sea area)*. Ph.D. Thesis, The Hebrew University of Jerusalem.

Gilbert, C. J. 1933. The evolution of Romney Marsh. *Arch. Cant.* **45**, 246–72.

Gile, L. H. 1967. Soils of an ancient basin floor near Las Cruces, New Mexico, Mexico. *Proc. Soil Sci. Soc. Am.* **34**, 465–72.

Gile, L. H., and J. W. Hawley 1966. Periodic sedimentation and soil formation on an alluvial fan piedmont in southern New Mexico. *Proc. Soil Sci. Soc. Am.* **30**, 261–8.

Gilewska, S. 1967. Different methods of showing the relief on the detailed geomorphological maps. *Z. Geomorph.* **11**, 481–90.

Gillham, M. E. 1957. Coastal vegetation of Mull and Iona in relation to salinity and soil reaction. *J. Ecol.* **45**, 157–75.

Gilman, K., and M. D. Newson 1980. *Soil pipes and pipeflow*. Br. Geomorph. Res. Group Res. Monogr. 1. Norwich: Geo Abstracts.

Ginsburg, R. N., L. B. Isham, S. J. Bein and J. Kuperberg 1954. *Laminated algal sediments of south Florida and their recognition in the fossil record*. Rep 54-21, Marine Laboratory, University of Miami, Coral Gables, Florida.

Glazovskaya, M. A. 1968. Geochemical landscapes and types of geochemical soil sequences. *Trans 9th Int. Congr. Soil Science, Adelaide.* Vol. 4, 303–12. London: International Society of Soil Science.

Glentworth, R. 1954. *The soils of the country round Banff, Huntly and Turriff.* Mem. Soil Surv. GB (Scotland). Harpenden: Soil Survey.

Glentworth, R., and H. G. Dion 1949. The association or hydrologic sequence in certain soils of the podzolic zone of north-east Scotland. *J. Soil Sci.* **1**, 35–49.

Goh, K. M. 1972. Amino acid levels as indicators of paleosols in New Zealand soil profiles. *Geoderma* 7, 33–47.

Goldich, S. S. 1938. A study of rock weathering. *J. Geol.* **46**, 17–58.

Goosen, D. 1966. The classification of landscapes as the basis for soil surveys. *Trans 2nd Int. Symp. Photo-Interpretation, Paris.* Vol. 4, 1.45–50.

Goosen, D. 1967. *Aerial photo interpretation in soil survey*, FAO Soils Bull. no. 6.

Goosen, D. 1972. *Physiography and soils of the Llanos Orientales of Colombia*. Enschede: ITC.

Goss, D. W., and B. L. Allen 1968. A genetic study of two soils developed on granite in Llanos County, Texas. *Proc. Soil Sci. Soc. Am.* **32**, 409–13.

Gray, A. J., and R. G. H. Bunce 1972. The ecology of Morecambe Bay, VI Soils and vegetation of the salt marshes: a multivariate approach. *J. Appl. Ecol.* **9**, 221–34.

Green, P. 1974. Recognition of sedimentary characteristics in soils by size-shape analysis. *Geoderma* **11**, 181–93.

Green, R. D. 1968. *Soils of Romney Marsh*. Bull. Soil Surv. GB, no. 4. Harpenden: Soil Survey.

Green, R. D., and G. P. Askew 1965. Observations on the biological development of macropores in soils of Romney Marsh. *J. Soil Sci.* **16**, 342–9.

Green, W. H., and G. A. Ampt 1911. Studies in soil physics I. The flow of air and water through soils. *J. Agric. Sci.* **4**, 1–24.

Greene, H. 1947. Soil formation and water movement in the tropics. *Soils and Fertilizer* **10**, 253–6.

Gregory, K. J., and D. Walling, 1973. *Drainage basin form and process*. London: Edward Arnold.

Grisak, G. E., J. A. Cherry, J. A. Vonhof and J. P. Blumele 1976. Hydrogeologic and hydrochemical properties of fractured till in the interior plains region. In *Glacial till: an interdisciplinary study*, R. F. Legget (ed.). R. Soc. Can. Special Publ., no. 12.

Gruner, J. W. 1950. An attempt to arrange silicates in the order of reaction series at relatively low temperatures. *Am. Mineral.* **35**, 137–8.

Gupta, R. N. 1958. Development and morphology of Vindhyan soils. II. Nature of exchangeable bases in the soil sequence of the upper Vindhyan plateau, in Uttar Pradesh. *Ind. J. Agric. Sci.* **28**, 491–8.

Gwynne, C. S. 1942. Swell and swale pattern of the Wisconsin Drift Plain of Iowa. *J. Geol.* **50**, 200–8.

Gwynne, C. S., and R. W. Simonson 1942. Influence of low recessional moraines on soil type pattern of the Mankato Drift Plain in Iowa. *Soil Sci.* **53**, 461–6.

Hack, J. T., and J. G. Goodlett 1960. *Geomorphology and forest ecology of a mountain region in the Central Appalachians*. US Geol. Surv. Professional Paper, no. 347.

Hall, B. R., and C. J. Folland 1970. *Soils of Lancashire*. Bull. Soil Surv. GB, no. 5. Harpenden: Soil Survey.

Hamdi, H. 1959. Alteration in the clay fraction of Egyptian soils. *Z. Pflanzenernahr. Dung. Bodenkd.* **84**, 204–11.

Hamdi, H. 1967. The mineralogy of the fine fraction of the alluvial soils of Egypt. *J. Soil Sci., UAR* **7**, 15–21.

Hamdi, H., and Y. Barrada 1960. Transformation of the clay fraction of the alluvial soils of Egypt. *Ann. Agric. Sci., Cairo* **2**, 135–9.

Hamdi, H., and R. Iberg 1954. Information on the alluvial clay of the Nile. *Z. Pflanzenernahr. Dung. Bodenkd.* **67**, 193–7.

Hanna, F. S., and H. Beckmann 1975. Clay minerals of some soils of the Nile Valley in Egypt. *Geoderma* **14**, 159–70.

Harradine, F., and H. Jenny 1958. Influence of parent material and climate on texture and nitrogen and carbon contents of virgin California soils. *Soil. Sci.* **85**, 235–43.

Harris, S. A. 1958. The gilgaied and bad-structured soils of Central Iraq. *J. Soil Sci.* **9**, 169–85.

Harrison, S. C. 1975. Tidal-flat complex, Delmarva Peninsula, Virginia. In *Tidal deposits: a casebook of recent examples and fossil counterparts*, R. N. Ginsburg (ed.). New York: Springer Verlag.

Heede, B. H. 1971. *Characteristics and processes of soil piping in gullies*. US Dept Agric. Forest Serv. Res. Paper RM-68.

Heine, K. 1972. Die Bedeuting pedolgischer Untersuchungen bei der Trennung von Reliefgenerationen. *Z. Geomorph.* **14**, 113–37.

Henkel, J. S., A. W. Bayer and J. R. H. Coutts 1938. Subsurface erosion on a Natal Midlands farm. *S.A. J. Sci.* **35**, 236–43.

Herath, J. W., and R. W. Grimshaw 1971. A general evaluation of the frequency distribution of clay and associated minerals in the alluvial soils of Ceylon. *Geoderma* **5**, 119–30.

Hewlett, J. D., and W. L. Nutter 1970. The varying source area of streamflow from upland basins. Paper presented at *Symp. on Interdisciplinary Aspects of Watershed Management, Montana State University, Bozeman*. New York: Am. Soc. Civ. Engrs.

Hoek, E. 1973. Methods for the rapid assessment of the stability of three-dimensional rock slopes. *Q. J. Engng Geol.* **6**, 243–56.

Hole, F. D. 1976. *The soils of Wisconsin*. Wisconsin: University of Wisconsin Press.

Holmes, C. D. 1955. Geomorphic development in humid and arid regions: a synthesis. *Am. J. Sci.* **253**, 377–90.

Holmes, D. A., and S. Western 1969. Soil-texture patterns in the alluvium of the lower Indus Plains. *J. Soil Sci.* **20**, 23–37.

Hoover, M. D., and C. R. Hursh 1943. Influence of topography and soil depth on runoff from forest land. *Trans Am. Geophys. Union* **24**, 693–7.

Horton, J. H., and R. H. Hawkins 1965. Flow path of rain from the soil surface to the water table. *Soil Sci.* **100**, 377–83.

Horton, R. E. 1933. The role of infiltration in the hydrological cycle. *Trans Am. Geophys. Union* **14**, 446–60.

Horton, R. E. 1935. *Surface runoff phenomena: Part I analysis of the hydrograph.* Horton Hydrological Lab., Publ., no. 101, Vorheesville, New York.

Horton, R. E. 1945. Erosional development of streams and their drainage basins: hydrophysical approach to quantitative morphology. *Bull. Geol Soc. Am.* **56**, 275–370.

Horvath, V., and B. Erodi 1962. Determination of natural slope category limits by functional identity of erosion intensity. *Bull. Int. Assoc. Sci. Hydrol.* **59**, 131.

Huddleston, J. H., and F. F. Riecken 1973. Local soil–landscape relationships in Western Iowa, I. Distribution of selected chemical and physical properties. *Proc. Soil Sci. Soc. Am.* **37**, 264–70.

Hudson, N. W., and D. C. Jackson 1962. *Results achieved in the measurement of erosion and runoff in southern Rhodesia.* Fed. Dept Conservation and Extension, Rhodesia and Nyasaland Tech. Mem., no. 4.

Huggett, R. J. 1973. *The theoretical behaviour of materials within soil landscape systems.* University College London, Dept Geog. Occasional Paper 19.

Huggett, R. J. 1975. Soil landscape systems: a model of soil genesis. *Geoderma* **13**, 1–22.

Hughes, P. J. 1972. Slope, aspect and tunnel erosion in the loess of Banks Peninsula, New Zealand. *J. Hydrol. (NZ)* **11**, 94–8.

Hutcheson, T. B., R. J. Lewis and W. A. Seay 1959. Chemical and clay mineralogical properties of certain Memphis catena soils of western Kentucky. *Proc. Soil Sci. Soc. Am.* **23**, 474–8.

Hutchinson, J. N. 1967. The free degradation of London Clay cliffs. *Proc. Geotech. Conf., Oslo*. Vol. 1, 113–18.

Hutchinson, J. N. 1971. Field and laboratory studies of a fall in Upper Chalk cliffs at Jess Bay, Isle of Thanet. *Roscoe Memorial Symp., University of Cambridge, 29–31 March 1971.*

Hutchinson, J. N. 1974. Discussion to engineering problems caused by fossil permafrost features in the English Midlands, by A. V. Morgan. *Q. J. Engng Geol.* **7**, 100.

Hutchinson, J. N., and R. K. Bhandari 1971. Undrained loading, a fundamental mechanism of mudflows and other mass movements. *Geotechnique* **21**, 353–8.

Imeson, A. C., and P. D. Jungerius 1976. Aggregate stability and colluviation in the Luxembourg Ardennes: An experimental and micromorphological study. *Earth Surface Processes* **1**, 259–71.

Inbar, M. 1972. *A geomorphic analysis of a catastrophic flood in a Mediterranean, basaltic, watershed.* Paper submitted to 22nd Int. Geogr. Congr., Montreal.

Ismail, F. T. 1970. Biotite weathering and clay formation in arid and humid regions, California. *Soil Sci.* **109**, 257–61.

Jackson, M. L., S. A. Tyler, G. A. Bourbeau and R. P. Penningtor 1948. Weathering sequence of clay-size minerals in soils and sediments. I. Fundamental generalisations. *J. Phys. & Colloid Chem.* **52**, 1237–60.

Jacobsen, T., and R. M. Adams 1958. Salt and silt in ancient Mesopotamian agriculture. *Science* **128**, 1251–8.

Jahn, A. 1963. Importance of soil erosion for the evolution of slopes in Poland. *Nach. Akad. Wiss. Gottingen, Math-Phys. Kl.* **15**, 229–37.

Jahn, A. 1968. Denudational balance of slopes. *Geog. Pol.* **13**, 9–29.

Jelgersma, S. 1961. Holocene sea level changes in the Netherlands. *Meded. Geol. Sticht, Ser C VI* **7**, 1–100.

Jenny, H. 1941. *Factors of soil formation. A system of quantitative pedology*. New York: McGraw-Hill.

Jenny, H. 1961a. Derivation of state factor equations of soils and ecosystems. *Proc. Soil Sci. Soc. Am.* **25**, 385–8.

Jenny, H. 1961b. *E. W. Hilgard and the birth of modern soil science. Agrochimica* (Pisa, Italy) and Berkeley, California: Forallon Publishers.

Jones, J. A. A. 1971. Soil piping and stream channel initiation. *Water Resources Res.* **7**, 602–10.

Jones, R. L., and A. H. Beavers 1964. Variation of opal phytolith content among some great soil groups of Illinois. *Proc. Soil Sci. Soc. Am.* **28**, 711–12.

Jordan, S. 1974. *The variability of soil in a Cotswold Valley*. B.Sc. diss., Department of Geography, University of Birmingham.

Joseph, K. T. 1968. A toposequence of limestone parent material in north Kedah, Malaya. *J. Trop. Geog.* **27**, 19–22.

Kamps, L. F. 1962. Mud distribution and land reclamation in the eastern Wadden shallows. *Rijkswat St. Commun. No.* 4, 1–73.

Kay, G.F. 1916. Gumbotil, a new term in Pleistocene geology. *Science* **44**, 637–8.

Keller, W. D. 1954. Bonding energies of some silicate minerals. *Am. Mineralogist* **39**, 783–93.

Kerney, M. P. 1963. Late-glacial deposits on the Chalk of southeast England. *Phil Trans R. Soc.*, B **246**, 203–54.

Kilinc, M., and E. V. Richardson 1973. *Mechanics of soil erosion from overland flow generated by simulated rainfall. Colorado St. Univ. Hydrol. Papers*, no. 63.

King, L. C. 1953. Canons of landscape evolution. *Bull. Geol Soc. Am.* **64**, 721–51.

King, R. B. 1975. Geomorphic and soil correlation analysis of land systems in Northern and Luapula Provinces of Zambia. *Trans Inst. Br. Geogs* **64**, 67–76.

King, R. B., and C. J. Birchall 1975. *Land systems and soils of the Southern Rift Valley, Ethiopia*. Land Resource Rep., no. 5. Land Resources Development Centre, Ministry of Overseas Development, Surbiton, England.

Kirkby, M. J. 1963. *A study of rates of erosion and mass movement on slopes with special reference to Galloway*. Ph.D. Thesis, University of Cambridge.

Kirkby, M. J. 1967. Measurement and theory of soil creep. *J. Geol.* **75**, 359–78.

Kirkby, M. J. 1969. Erosion by water on hillslopes. In *Water, Earth and Man*, R. J. Chorley (ed.). London: Methuen.

Kirkby, M. J. (ed.) 1978. *Hillslope hydrology*. Chichester: Wiley.

Kirkby, M. J., and R. J. Chorley 1967. Throughflow, overland flow and erosion. *Bull. Int. Assoc. Sci. Hydrol.* **12**, 5–21.

Kirkham, D. 1947. Studies of hillside seepage in the Iowan drift area. *Proc. Soil Sci. Soc. Am.* **12**, 73–80.

Kirkham, D. 1965. Seepage of leaching water into drainage ditches of unequal water level heights. *J. Hydrol.* **3**, 207–24.

Kline, J. R. 1973. Mathematical simulation of soil–plant relationships and soil genesis. *Soil Sci.* **115**, 240–9.

Klingebiel, A. A., and P. H. Montgomery 1961. *Land capability classification*. US Dept Agric. Handb., no. 210.

Klohn, E. J. 1961. General discussions on tills. *Proc. 14th Can. Soil Mech. Conf., NRC Tech. Memo*. 69, 93–4.

Knapp, B. J. 1978. Infiltration and storage of soil water. In *Hillslope hydrology*, M. J. Kirkby (ed.). London: Methuen.

Kobayashi, K. 1965. Late Quaternary chronology of Japan. *Earth Sci., Japan* **79**, 1–17.

Kojan, E. 1968. Mechanics and rates of natural soil creep. *Proc. 5th A. Symp. on Engng Geol. Soils Engng, Bocatello, Idaho*, 233–53.

Kostiakov, A. N. 1932. On the dynamics of the coefficient of water-percolation in soils and on the necessity for studying it from a dynamic point of view for purposes of amelioration. *Trans 6th Comm. Int. Soc. Soil Sci. (Russ.) Part* A, 17–21.

Krusekopf, H. H. 1948. Gumbotil – its formation and relation to overlying soils with clay pan subsoils. *Proc. Soil Sci. Soc. Am.* **12**, 413–4.

Kubiena, W. L. 1938. *Micropedology*. Ames, Iowa: Collegiate Press.

Kurtz, L. T., and S. W. Melsted 1973. Movements of chemicals in soils by water. *Soil Sci.* **115**, 231–9.

Lafeber, D. 1965. The graphical representation of planar pore patterns in soils. *Aust. J. Soil Res.* **3**, 143–64.

Lafeber, D. 1966. Soil structural concepts. *Engng Geol.* **4**, 261–90.

Lai, S.-H., and J. J. Jurinak 1972. The transport of cations in soil columns at different pore velocities. *Proc. Soil Sci. Soc. Am.* **36**, 730–2.

Larsen, G., and S. Thorarinsson 1978. H4 and other acid Hekla tephra layers. *Jokull* **27**, 28–46.

Lawrance, C. J. 1972. *Terrain evaluation in West Malaysia: Part 1, Terrain classification and survey methods*. Transport and Road Res. Lab., Rep., LR 506.

Lawrance, C. J. 1978. *Terrain evaluation in West Malaysia: Part 2, Land Systems of South West Malaysia*. Transport and Road Res. Lab., Suppl. Rep., no. 378.

Leamy, M. L., and A. S. Burke 1973. Identification and significance of paleosols in cover deposits in Central Otago. *N.Z. J. Geol. Geophys.* **16**, 623–35.

Leighton, M. M., and P. MacClintock 1962. The weathered mantle of glacial tills beneath original surfaces in north-central United States. *J. Geol.* **70**, 267–93.

Leopold, L. B., W. W. Emmett and R. M. Myrick 1966. *Channel and hillslope processes in a semiarid area, New Mexico*. U.S. Geol Surv., Prof. Pap., 352G.

Leopold, L. B., and W. W. Emmett 1972. Some rates of geomorphological processes. *Geogr. Pol.* **23**, 5–9.

Leopold, L. B., and M. G. Wolman 1957. *River channel patterns—braided, meandering and straight.* U.S. Geol Surv. Prof. Pap., 282D, 39–85.

Leopold, L. B., M. G. Wolman and J. P. Miller 1964. *Fluvial processes in geomorphology*. San Francisco: W. H. Freeman.

Leslie, D. M. 1973. Quaternary deposits and surfaces in a volcanic landscape on Otago peninsula. *N.Z. J. Geol. Geophys.* **16**, 557–66.

Lewin, J. 1978. Floodplain geomorphology. *Prog. Phys. Geog.* **2**, no. 3, 408–37.

Lewis, W. V. 1932. The formation of Dungeness foreland. *Geog. J.* **80**, 309–24.

Lewis, W. V., and W. G. V. Balchin 1940. Past sea-levels at Dungeness. *Geog. J.* **96**, 258–85.

Libby, W. F. 1955. *Radiocarbon dating*, 2nd edn. Chicago: Chicago University Press.

Lobova, E. V. 1967. *Soils of the desert zone of the U.S.S.R.* (translated). Jerusalem: Israel Programme for Scientific Translations.

Lotspeich, F. B., and H. W. Smith 1953. Soils of the Palouse loess: I. The Palouse catena. *Soil Sci.* **76**, 467–80.

Louis, H. 1964. Uber Rumpfflachen-und Talbilding in den wechselfenchten Tropen besonders nach Studien in Tanganyika. *Z. Geomorph.* **8**, 43–70.

Mabbutt, J. A., and R. M. Scott 1966. Periodicity of morphogenesis and soil formation in a Savannah landscape near Port Moresby, Papua. *Z. Geomorph.* **10**, 69–89.

McArthur, W. M., and E. Bettenay 1960. *The development and distribution of the soils of the Swan coastal plain Western Australia*. CSIRO Soil Publ., no. 16.

MacClaren, M. 1906. On the origin of certain laterites. *Geol Mag.* **43**, 536–47.

McConnell, R. G., and R. W. Brock 1904. *The great landslide at Frank, Alberta*. Rep. Dept of the Interior, 1902–3, Paper 25, 4–17.

MacFarlane, M. J. 1971. Laterization and landscape development in Kyagive, Uganda. *Q. J. Geol Soc. Lond.* **126**, 501–39.

MacFarlane, M. J. 1973. Laterite and topography in Buganda. *Uganda J.* **36** (for 1972), 9–22.

MacFarlane, M. J. 1976. *Laterite and landscape*. London: Academic Press.

McGee, W. J. 1891. *The Pleistocene history of northeastern Iowa.* U.S. Geol Surv., A. Rep., 11 Pt, 189–577.

McGown, A., A. Saldivar-sali and Amv. A. Radwan 1974. Fissure patterns and slope failures in till at Hurlford, Ayrshire. *Q. J. Engng Geol.* **7**, 1–26.

McKeague, J. A., G. J. Ross and D. S. Gamble 1978. Properties, criteria of classification and concepts of genesis of podzolic soils in Canada. In *Quaternary soils*, W. C. Mahaney (ed.). Norwich: Geo Abstracts.

McIntyre, D. S. 1958. Soil splash and the formation of surface crusts by raindrop impact. *Soil Sci.* **85**, 261–6.

McLellan, A. G. 1971. Some economic implications of research methods used in glacial geomorphology. *Research methods in geomorphology, Proc. 1st Guelph Symp.*, 57–72.

Macumber, P. G. 1969. Interrelationship between physiography, hydrology sedimentation and salinization of the Loddon River Plains, Australia. *J. Hydrol.* **7**, 39–57.

Mahaney, W. C. 1978. *Quaternary soils.* Norwich: Geo Abstracts.

Mansfield, J. E. *et al.* 1975–76. *Land resources of the Northern and Luapula Provinces, Zambia—a reconnaissance assessment* (6 Vols). Land Resource Study no. 19. Land Resource Development Centre, Ministry of Overseas Development, Surbiton, England.

Martel, Y. A., and E. A. Paul 1974. The use of radiocarbon dating of organic matter in the study of soil genesis. *Proc. Soil Sci. Soc. Am.* **38**, 501–6.

Matthews, B. 1971. Soils in Yorkshire I: Sheet SE65 (York East). *Soil Surv. Rec.*, no. 6. Harpenden: Soil Survey.

Mein, R. G., and C. L. Larson 1973. Modelling infiltration during a steady rain. *Water Resources Res.* **9**, 384–94.

Meyer, L. D., and L. A. Kramer 1969. Erosion equations predict land slope development. *Agric. Engng* **50**, 522–3.

Middleton, H. E. 1930. *Properties of soils which influence soil erosion*. U.S. Dept Agric. Tech. Bull., no. 178, 1–16.

Milne, G. 1935a. Some suggested units of classification and mapping particularly for East African soils. *Soil Res.* **4**, no. 3.

Milne, G. 1935b. Composite units for the mapping of complex soil associations. *Trans 3rd Int. Congr. Soil Sci.* **1**, 345–7.

Milne, G. 1936a. Normal erosion as a factor in soil profile development. *Nature, Lond.* **138**, 548–9.

Milne, G. 1936b. *A provisional soil map of East Africa.* East Afr. Agric. Res. Stn, Amani Mem., no. 34.

Milne, G. 1947. A soil reconnaissance journey through parts of Tanganyika Territory, Dec. 1935, to Feb. 1936. *J. Ecol.* **35**, 192–265.

Mohr, E. C., and F. A. Van Baren 1954. *Tropical soils.* N.V. Vitgeverij W. van Hoeve.

Morel-Seytoux, H. J., and J. Khanji 1974. Derivation of an equation of infiltration. *Water Resources Res.* **10**, 795–800.

Morgan, R. P. C. 1977. *Soil erosion in the United Kingdom: field studies in the Silsoe area, 1973–75.* Occasional Paper no. 4, National College of Agricultural Engineering, Silsoe.

Morgan, R. P. C. 1978. Field studies of rainsplash erosion. *Earth Surface Processes* **3**, 295–9.

Morris, L. 1974. The geomorphology of Bredon Hill. In *Worcester and its region, field studies in the former county of Worcestershire*, B. H. Adlam (ed.). Worcester Geographical Association.

Morrison, R. B. 1967. Principles of Quaternary soil stratigraphy. In *Quaternary soils*, R. B. Morrison and H. E. Wright Jr (eds). *Int. Assoc. for Quaternary Res. (INQUA) 7th Congr., 1965, Proc. no. 9, University of Nevada.*

Morrison, R. B. 1978. Quaternary soil stratigraphy–concepts, methods and problems. In *Quaternary soils*, W. C. Mahaney (ed.). Norwich: Geo Abstracts.

Morrison, R. B., and H. E. Wright Jr (eds) 1967. *Quaternary soils. Int. Assoc. for Quaternary Res. (INQUA) 7th Cong., 1965, Proc. no. 9, University of Nevada.*

Moss, A. J. 1962. The physical nature of common sandy and pebbly deposits. *Am. J. Sci.* **260**, 337–73.

Moss, A. J. 1963. The physical nature of common sandy and pebbly deposits, II. *Am. J. Sci.* **261**, 297–343.

Moss, A. J. 1972. Bed-load sediments. *Sedimentology* **18**, 159–219.

Moss, R. P. 1963. Soils, slopes and land use in a part of south-west Nigeria: some implications for the planning of agricultural development in inter-tropical Africa. Trans Inst. Br. Geogs **32**, 143–68.

Moss, R. P. 1965. Slope development and soil morphology in a part of south-west Nigeria. *J. Soil Sci.* **16**, 192–209.

Moss, R. P. 1968. Soils, slopes and surfaces in tropical Africa. In *The soil resources of tropical Africa*, 29–60. Cambridge: Cambridge University Press.

Moss, R. P. 1969. The appraisal of land resources in tropical Africa. *Pacific Viewpoint* **10**, 18–27.

Muckenhirn, R. J., E. P. Whiteside, E. H. Templin, R. F. Chandler Jr and L. T. Alexander 1949. Soil classification and the genetic factors of soil formation. *Soil Sci.* **67**, 93–105.

Mulcahy, M. J. 1960. Laterites and lateritic soils in south-western Australia. *J. Soil Sci.* **11**, 206–26.

Mulcahy, M. J. 1961. Soil distribution in relation to landscape development. *Z. Geomorph., Suppl. bd.*, **5**, 211–25.

Musgrave, G. W. 1947. Quantitative evaluation of factors in water erosion—a first approximation. *J. Soil Water Conserv.* **2**, 133–8.

Nabhan, H. M., C. Sys and G. Stoops 1969. Mineralogical study on the suspended matter in the Nile water. *Pedologie* **29**, 34–48.

Neal, J. H. 1938. *The effect of the degree of slope and rainfall characteristics on runoff and soil erosion.* Missouri Agric. Exptl Stn Res. Bull., no. 280.

Newill, D. 1961. A laboratory investigation of two red clays from Kenya. *Geotechnique* **11**, 302–18.

Nikiforoff, C. C. 1949. Weathering and soil evolution. *Soil Sci.* **67**, 219–30.

Norton, E. A., and R. S. Smith 1930. Influence of topography on soil profile character. *J. Am. Soc. Agron.* **22**, 251–62.

Nye, P. H. 1954–5. Some soil forming processes in the humid tropics. I–IV. *J. Soil Sci.* **5**, 7–21 and 51–83.

Obeng, H. B. 1968. Land capability classification of the soils of Ghana under practices of mechanised and hand cultivation for crop and livestock production. *Trans 9th Int. Congr. of Soil Science, Adelaide*. Vol. 4, 215–23.

Odum, H. 1922. On the nature of so-called sheep tracks, *Meddr Dansk. Geol Forem.* **6**, 1–29.

Oertel, A. C., and J. B. Giles 1966. Quantitative study of a layered soil. *Aust. J. Soil Res.* **4**, 19–28.

Ollier, C. D. 1959. A two-cycle theory of tropical pedology. *J. Soil Sci.* **10**, 137–48.

Ollier, C. D. 1976. Catenas in different climates. In *Geomorphology and climate*, E. Derbyshire (ed.). Chichester: Wiley.

Ollier, C. D., and A. J. Thomasson 1957. Asymmetrical valleys of the Chiltern Hills. *Geog. J.* **123**, 71–80.

Ollier, C. D., *et al*. 1969. *Terrain classification and data storage: Land systems of Uganda*. MEXE Rep., no. 959.

Olsson, I. V. 1974. Some problems in connection with the evaluation of C^{14} dates. *Geol. Foren. i Stockh. Forh.* **96**, 311–20.

Ongley, E. D. 1970. Determination of rectilinear profile segments by automatic data processing. *Z. Geomorph., Suppl.* **14**, 383–91.

Oschwald, W. R., *et al*. 1965. *Principal soils of Iowa*, Iowa St. Univ. Ext. Service Special Rep., no. 42.

Pallister, J. W. 1951. *Occurrence of laterite in south Buganda.* Rep. Geol Surv. Uganda, JWP/7.

Palmer, R. S. 1963. The influence of a thin water layer on waterdrop impact forces. *Bull. Int. Assoc. Sci. Hydrol.* **65**, 141–8.

Panabokke, C. R. 1959. A study of some soils in the dry zone of Ceylon. *Soil Sci.* **87**, 67–74.

Parizek, E. J., and J. Woodruff 1957. Description and origin of stone layers in soils of the southeastern States. *J. Geol.* **65**, 24–34.

Parker, G. G. 1964. *Piping, a geomorphic agent in landform development of the drylands*. Int. Assoc. Sci. Hydrol., Assembly of Berkeley, Publ., no. 65.

Parsons, R. B., C. A. Balster and A. O. Ness 1970. Soil development and geomorphic surfaces, Willamette Valley, Oregon. *Proc. Soil Sci. Soc. Am.* **34**, 485–91.

Pawluk, S. 1978. The pedogenic profile in the stratigraphic section. In *Quaternary soils*, W. C. Mahaney (ed.). Norwich: Geo Abstracts.

Peck, A. J. 1978. Salinization of non-irrigated soils and associated streams: a review. *Aust. J. Soil Res.* **16**, 157–68.

Penck, W. 1924. *Die Morphologische Analyse* (translated by H. Czech & K. C. Boswell 1953). London: Macmillan.

Pettijohn, F. J. 1941. Persistence of heavy minerals and geological age. *J. Geol.* **49**, 610–25.

Philip, J. R. 1957–8. The theory of infiltration. *Soil Sci.* **83**, 345–57, 435–48; **84**, 163–77, 257–64, 329–39; **85**, 278–86, 333–7.

Pilgrim, A. T. 1972. The identification of geomorphological and pedological criteria for the recognition and delimitation of landsurface units 5 and 6 in a semi-arid environment, Western Australia. Paper presented to *1972 Conf. of Australian Geographers, Canberra*.

Pollard, E., and A. Millar 1968. Wind erosion in the East Anglian Fens. *Weather* **23**, 415–17.

Pons, L. J., and I. S. Zonneveld 1965. *Soil ripening and soil classification; initial soil formation of alluvial deposits with a classification of the resulting soils.* Wageningen: Int. Inst. for Land Reclamation and Improvement.

Powell, J. W. 1876. *Geology of the Uinta Mountains*. Washington.

Prest, V. K. 1968. *Nomenclature of moraines and ice-flow features as applied to the glacial map of Canada.* Geol. Surv. Can. Paper, no. 67.

Price, R. J. 1973. *Glacial and fluvioglacial landforms*. Edinburgh: Oliver and Boyd.
Pullan, R. A., and P. N. De Leeuw 1964. *The land capability survey prepared for the Niger Dams Resettlement Authority*. Samaru, Zaria, Northern Nigeria: Inst. Agric. Res., Ahmadu Bello Univ., Soil Surv. Bull.

Quigley, R. M., and T. A. Ogunbadejo 1976. Till geology, mineralogy and geotechnical behaviour. In *Glacial till: an interdisciplinary study*, R. F. Legget (ed.). R. Soc. Can., Spec. Pubn no. 12.

Raad, A. T., and R. Protz 1971. A new method for the identification of sediment stratification in soils of the Blue Springs Basin, Ontario. *Geoderma* **6**, 23–41.
Radley, J., and C. Sims 1967. Wind erosion in East Yorkshire. *Nature* **216**, 20–2.
Radwanski, S. A., and C. D. Ollier 1959. A study of an East African catena. *J. Soil Sci.* **10**, 149–68.
Raeside, J. D. 1964. Loess deposits of the South Island, New Zealand and the soils formed on them. *N.Z. J. Geol. Geophys.* **7**, 811–38.
Rapp, A., and L. Stromquist 1976. Slope erosion due to extreme rainfall in the Scandinavian Mountains. *Geografiska Annaler* **58A**, 193–200.
Rathjens, C. 1973. Subterrane Abtragung (piping). *Z. Geomorph., Suppl.* **17**, 168–76.
Rawitz, E., E. T. Engman and G. D. Cline 1970. Use of the mass balance method for examining the role of soils in controlling watershed performance. *Water Resources Res.* **6**, 1115–23.
Reeves, B. O. K., and J. F. Dormaar 1972. A partial Holocene pedological and archaeological record from the southern Alberta Rocky Mountains. *Arctic & Alpine Res.* **4**, 325–36.
Reijne, A. 1961. On the contribution of the Amazon River to accretion of the coast of the Guianas. *Geol. Mijnbouw* NS **23**, 219–26.
Rice, R. M., and G. T. Foggin 1971. Effects of high intensity storms on soil slippage on mountainous watersheds in Southern California. *Water Resources Res.* **7**, 1485–96.
Richmond, G. M. 1962. *Quaternary stratigraphy of the La Sol Mountains, Utah*. U.S. Geol. Surv. Prof. Pap., no. 324.
Richmond, G. M. 1970. Comparison of the Quaternary stratigraphy of the Alps and Rocky Mountains. *Quaternary Res.* **1**, 3–28.
Robinson, D. N. 1969. Soil erosion by wind in Lincolnshire, March 1968. *East Midland Geographer* **4**, 351–62.
Robinson, S. W. 1949. *Soils, their origin, constitution and classification*, 3rd edn. London: George Allen & Unwin (Murby).
Roose, E. J. 1972. *Contribution a l'etude de la résistance a l'érosion de quelques sols tropicaux*. Office de la Recherche Scientifique et Technique Outre-Mer, Centre D'Adiopodoune, Abidjan. Rep.
Rougerie, G. 1960. Le façonnement actuel des modeles en Cote d'Ivorie forestière. *Mem. Inst. Francais d'Afrique Noire*, no. 58.
Rubin, J. 1966. Theory of rainfall uptake by soils initially drier than their field capacity and its application. *Water Resources Res.* **2**, 739–94.
Ruellan, A. 1971. The history of soils: some problems of definition and interpretation. In *Paleopedology*, D. H. Yaalon (ed.). Jerusalem: International Society of Soil Science and Israel Universities Press.
Ruhe, R. V. 1950. Graphic analysis of drift topographies. *Am. J. Sci.* **248**, 435–43.
Ruhe, R. V. 1956. Geomorphic surfaces and the nature of soils. *Soil Sci.* **82**, 441–55.
Ruhe, R. V. 1959. Stone lines in soils. *Soil Sci.* **87**, 223–31.
Ruhe, R. V. 1969. *Quaternary landscapes in Iowa*. Ames, Iowa: Iowa State University Press.
Ruhe, R. V. 1975. *Geomorphology*. Boston: Houghton Mifflin.
Runge, E. C. A. 1973. Soil development sequences and energy models. *Soil Sci.* **115**, 183–93.
Russell, R. J. 1967. *River plains and sea coast*. Los Angeles.

Rutter, N. W., A. E. Foscolos and O. L. Hughes 1978. Climatic trends during the Quaternary in Central Yukon based upon pedological and geomorphological evidence. In *Quaternary soils*, W. C. Mahaney (ed.). Norwich: Geo Abstracts.

Ruxton, B. P., and L. Berry 1961. Weathering profiles and geomorphic position on granite in two tropical regions. *Rev. Geomorph. Dynamique* **12**, 16–31.

Salisbury, W. 1925. Notes on the edaphic succession in some dune soils with respect to time. *J. Ecol.* **13**, 322–8.

Savigear, R. A. G. 1965. A technique of morphological mapping. *Ann. Assoc. Am. Geogs* **53**, 514–38.

Scharpenseel, H. W., and W. Kerpen 1967. Studies on tagged clay migration due to water movement. *Proc. IAEA Atomic Energy Agency Symp., Istanbul*, 287–90. Vienna: IAEA.

Schumm, S. A. 1956a. Evolution of drainage systems and slopes in badlands at Perth Amboy, New Jersey. *Bull. Geol Soc. Am.* **67**, 597–646.

Schumm, S. A. 1956b. The role of creep and rainwash on the retreat of badland slopes. *Am. J. Sci.* **254**, 693–706.

Schumm, S. A. 1964. Seasonal variations of erosion rates and processes on hillslopes in western Colorado. *Z. Geomorph. Suppl. Bd.* **5**, 215–38.

Scott, G. A., and J. M. Street 1976. Chemical weathering in the formation of Hawaiian amphitheatre-headed valleys. *Z. Geomorph.* **20**, 171–89.

Scott, J. S. 1976. Geology of Canadian tills. In *Glacial till: an interdisciplinary study*, R. F. Legget (ed.). R. Soc. Can. Special Publ., no. 12.

Scott, R. M. 1962. Exchangeable bases of mature well-drained soils in relation to rainfall in East Africa. *J. Soil Sci.* **13**, 1–9.

Scrivner, C. L., J. C. Baker and D. R. Brees 1973. Combined daily climatic data and dilute solution chemistry in studies of soil profile formation. *Soil Sci.* **115**, 213–23.

Sharpe, C. F. S. 1938. *Landslides and related phenomenon*. New York: Columbia University Press.

Shaw, C. F. 1930. Potent factors in soil formation. *Ecology* **11**, 239–45.

Shotton, F. W. 1967. The problems and contributions of methods of absolute dating within the Pleistocene period. *Q. J. Geol Soc. Lond.* **122**, 357–83.

Shreve, R. L. 1966. Statistical law of stream numbers. *J. Geol.* **74**, 17–37.

Simonett, D. S., and D. L. Rogers 1970. *The contribution of landslides to regional denudation in New Guinea*. Tech. Rep. no. 6, Off. Naval Res., Geog. Branch, Contract no. 583 (II) Task no. 389–133.

Simonson, R. W. 1954. Identification and interpretation of buried soils. *Am. J. Sci.* **252**, 705–32.

Simonson, R. W. 1968. Concept of soil. *Adv. Agron.* **20**, 1–47.

Skempton, A. W. 1953. Soil mechanics in relation to geology. *Proc. Yorkshire Geol. Soc.* **29**, 33–62.

Slaymaker, H. O. 1972. Patterns of present sub-aerial erosion and landforms in Mid-Wales. *Trans Inst. Br. Geogr* **55**, 47–68.

Sleeman, J. R. 1963. Cracks, peds and surfaces in some soils of the Riverine Plain, New South Wales. *Aust. J. Soil Res.* **1**, 91–102.

Sleeman, J. R. 1964. Structure variations within two red-brown earth profiles. *Aust. J. Soil Res.* **2**, 146–61.

Smalley, I. J. 1970. Cohesion of soil particles and the intrinsic resistance of simple soil systems to wind erosion. *J. Soil Sci.* **21**, 154–61.

Smeck, N. E., and E. C. A. Runge 1971a. Phosphorus availability and redistribution in relation to profile development in an Illinois landscape segment. *Proc. Soil Sci. Soc. Am.* **35**, 952–9.

Smeck, N. E., and E. C. A. Runge 1971b. Factors influencing profile development exhibited by some hydromorphic soils in Illinois. In *Pseudo-gleys and gleys–development and use of hydromorphic soils*. Stuttgart: Transactions of International Society of Soil Sciences, Commission V and VI.

Smith, D. D., and W. H. Wischmeier 1957. Factors affecting sheet and rill erosion. *Trans Am. Geophys. Union* **38**, 889–96.

Smith, R. 1957. The relations between water quality and drainage characteristics of some Iraq soils. *Proc. 3rd Congr. of the Int. Comm. Irrigation and Drainage, San Francisco*, Question 10, RI, 1–26.

Smith, R., and V. C. Robertson 1956. A classification of the saline soils of the old irrigation lands of the Middle Tigris Valley. *Proc. 6th Congr., Int. Soc. Soil Sci., Paris.* Vol. 6, 693–8.

Smith, R., and V. C. Robertson 1962. Soil and irrigation classification of shallow soils overlying gypsum beds, Northern Iraq. *J. Soil Sci.* **13**, 106–15.

Soons, J. M. 1971. Factors involved in soil erosion in the Southern Alps, New Zealand. *Z. Geomorph.* **15**, 460–70.

Sparrow, G. W. A. 1966. Some environmental factors in the formation of slopes. *Geog. J.* **132**, 390–5.

Starkel, L. 1970. Cause and effects of a heavy rainfall in Darjeeling and the Sikkim Himalayas. *J. Bombay Nat. Hist. Soc.* **67**, 45–50.

Starkel, L. 1972. The role of catastrophic rainfall in the shaping of the relief of the lower Himalaya (Darjeeling Hills). *Geog. Pol.* **21**, 103–47.

Stearns, L. A., and D. MacCreary 1957. The case of the vanishing brick dust. *Mosquito News* **17**, 303–4.

Stevens, J. H. 1968. The soils of the trucial states: classification and capability. *Trans 9th Int. Congr. of Soil Science, Adelaide*. Vol. 4, 253–69.

Stewart, G. A., and R. A. Perry 1953. Survey of Townsville-Bowen Region (1950). *CSIRO Aust. Land Res. Ser.* Vol. 2.

Strahler, A. N. 1952. Hypsometric (area-altitude) analysis of erosional topography. *Bull. Geol Soc. Am.* **63**, 1117–42.

Strahler, A. N. 1954. Statistical analysis in geomorphic research. *J. Geol.* **62**, 1–25.

Strahler, A. N. 1964. Quantitative geomorphology of drainage basins and channel networks. In *Handbook of applied hydrology*, V. T. Chow (ed.). New York: McGraw-Hill.

Strahler, A. N., and A. H. Strahler 1973. *Environmental geoscience*. Santa Barbara, California: Hamilton.

Sugden, D. E., and B. J. John 1976. *Glaciers and landscape: a geomorphological approach*. London: Edward Arnold.

Swartzendruber, D., and M. R. Huberty 1958. Use of infiltration equation parameters to evaluate infiltration differences in the field. *Trans Am. Geophys. Union* **39**, 84–93.

Talsma, T. 1963. The control of saline groundwater. *Meded. Landb. Wegeningen* **63**, 1–68.

Tanaka, M. 1976. Rate of erosion in the Tanzawa Mountains, Central Japan. *Geografiska Ann.* **58A**, 155–63.

Tedrow, J. C. F. 1966. Polar desert soils. *Proc. Soil Sci. Soc. Am.* **30**, 381–7.

Tedrow, J. C. F. 1968. Pedogenic gradients of the Polar Regions. *J. Soil Sci.* **19**, 197–204.

Tedrow, J. C. F. 1974. Soils of the high Arctic landscapes. In *Polar deserts and modern man*, T. L. Smiley and J. H. Zumberge (eds). Tucson: University of Arizona Press.

Temple, P. H., and A. Rapp 1972. Landslides in the Mgeta area, Western Uluguru Mountains, Tanzania. *Geograf. Ann.* **54A**, 157–93.

Ter-Stephanian, G. 1965. *In-situ* determination of the rheological characteristics of soil on slopes. *Proc. 6th Int. Conf. on Soil Mechanics and Foundation Engineering.* Vol. 2, 375–7.

Terzaghi, K. 1950. Mechanisms of landslides. *Bull. Geol Soc. Am., Berkeley Vol.,* 83–122.

Thomas, M. F. 1969. Geomorphology and land classification in tropical Africa. In *Environment and land use in Africa*, M. F. Thomas & G. T. Whittington (eds). London: Methuen.

Thorarinsson, S. 1944. *Tefrokronologiska studier pa Island*. Copenhagen: Ejnar Munksgaard.

Thorarinsson, S. 1954. The tephra-fall from Hekla on March 29th, 1947. Pt. 2. In *The eruption of Hekla, 1947–1948*. T. Erinarsson, G. Kjartansson & S. Thorarinsson (eds). Reykjavik: Ejnar Munksgaard.

Thorarinsson, S. 1962. L'érosion éolienne en Islande. *Rev. Geomorph. Dynamique* **13**, 107–24.

Thornthwaite, C. W. 1931. Climates of North America according to a new classification. *Geog. Rev.* **21**, 633–55.

Tischendorf, W. G. 1969. *Tracing stormflow to varying source area in small forested watersheds in the Southeastern Piedmont.* Ph.D. Thesis, University of Georgia, Athens, Georgia.

Trendall, A. F. 1962. The formation of apparent peneplains by a process of combined lateritisation and surface wash. *Z. Geomorph.* NS **6**, 183–97.

Tricart, J. 1966. Geomorphologie et amenagement rural (example du Venezuela). *Cooperation Technique* 44–5, 69–81.

Tricart, J. 1972. *Landforms of the humid tropics, forests and savannas.* London: Longman.

Tricart, J., and A. Cailleux 1972. *Climatic geomorphology*. London: Longman.

Trudgill, S. T. 1977. *Soil and vegetation systems.* Oxford: Oxford University Press.

Twidale, C. R. 1962. Steepened margins of inselbergs from north-western Eyre Peninsula, South Australia. *Z. Geomorph.,* NF **6**, 51–69.

United States Department of Agriculture 1970. *Weros: a FORTRAN IV program to solve the wind erosion equation.* Agric. Res. Serv., ARS-174.

United States Department of the Interior 1951. *Bureau of reclamation manual.* Vol. V: *Irrigated land use*. Washington D.C.: US Department of the Interior.

Valentine, K. W. G., and J. B. Dalrymple 1976. Quaternary buried paleosols: a critical review. *Quaternary Res.* **6**, 209–22.

Van der Sluijs, P. 1970. Decalcification of marine clay soils connected with decalcification during silting. *Geoderma* **4**, 209–27.

Vanoni, V. A. 1971. Sediment transportation mechanics question: genetic classification of valley sediment deposits. *J. Hydraulics Div., Am. Soc. Civil Engrs*, **95**, HY 1, 43–53.

Van Straaten, L. M. J. U. 1954. Composition and structure of recent marine sediments in the Netherlands. *Leidse Geol. Mededel.* **19**, 1–110.

Varnes, D. J. 1958. Landslide types and processes. In *Landslides and engineering practice*, E. B. Eckel (ed.). Special Report of the Highways Research Board.

Verhoeven, B. 1962. On the calcium carbonate content of young marine sediments. *Neth. J. Agric. Sci.* **10**, 58–71.

Verstappen, H. Th., and R. A. Van Zuidam 1968. I.T.C. system of geomorphological survey. *I.T.C. textbook for photo-interpretation*. Delft: I.T.C.

Vine, H. 1941. A soil catena in the Nigerian Cocoa Belt. *Farm & Forest* **2**, 139–41.

Vine, H. *et al*. 1954. Progress of soils surveys in south-west Nigeria. *Proc. 2nd inter-African soils Conf.* 211–36.

Walker, P. H. 1962a. Soil layers on hillslopes: a study at Nowra, New South Wales, Australia. *J. Soil Sci.* **13**, 167–77.

Walker, P. H. 1962b. Terrace chronology and soil formation on the south coast of New South Wales. *J. Soil Sci.* **13**, 178–86.

Walker, P. H. 1966. *Postglacial environments in relation to landscape and soils on the Cary Drift, Iowa.* Iowa St. Univ. Agric. Home Econ. Exptl Stn, Res. Bull., no. 549, 835–75.

Walker, P. H., and R. V. Ruhe 1968. Hillslope models and soil formation: II. Closed systems. *Trans 9th Congr. Int. Soil Sci. Soc., Adelaide*. Vol. 4, 561–8.

Watson, J. P. 1964–5. A soil catena on granite in southern Rhodesia. *J. Soil Sci.* **15**, 238–57; **16**, 158–69.

Watson, J. P. 1965. Soil catenas. *Soils & Fertiliser* **28**, 307–10.

Wayland, E. J. 1921. *A general account of the geology of Uganda by the geologist*. Rep. Geol Dept Uganda (1921) 8–20.

Wayland, E. J. 1931. *Summary of progress of the Geological Survey of Uganda, 1919–29*.

Wayland, E. J. 1933. The peneplains of East Africa. *Geog. J.* **82**, 95.

Wayland, E. J. 1934. The peneplains of East Africa. *Geog. J.* **83**, 79.

Webster, R. 1965. A catena of soils on the Northern Rhodesia plateau. *J. Soil Sci.* **16**, 31–43.

Webster, R., and P. H. T. Beckett 1970. Terrain classification and evaluation using air photography: a review of recent work at Oxford. *Photogrammetria* **26**, 51–75.

Weyman, D. R. 1970. Throughflow on hillslopes and its relation to the stream hydrograph. *Bull. Int. Assoc. Sci. Hydrol.* **15**, 25–33.

Whipkey, R. Z. 1965. Subsurface stormflow from forested slopes. *Bull. Int. Assoc. Sci. Hydrol.* **10**, 74–85.

Whipkey, R. Z. 1969. Storm runoff from forested catchments by subsurface routes. *Int. Assoc. Sci. Hydrol., Leningrad Symp.*, Publ. 85, 773–9.

Whitfield, W. A. D., and P. A. Furley 1971. The relationship between soil patterns and slope form in the Ettrick Association, south-east Scotland. In *Slopes, form and process*, D. Brunsden (ed.). Inst. of Br. Geographers, Special Publ., no. 3, 165–75.

Wiklander, L. 1964. Leaching of plant nutrients in soils. *Acta Agric. Scand.* **24**, 349–56.

Wilding, L. P. 1967. Radiocarbon dating of biogenic opal. *Science* **156**, 66–7.

Williams, M. A. J. 1968. A dune catena on the clay plains of the West Central Gezira, Republic of the Sudan. *J. Soil Sci.* **19**, 367–78.

Wischmeier, W. H. 1974. New developments in estimating water erosion. In *Land use: persuasion or regulation*, 179–86. Soil Conservation Society of America.

Wischmeier, W. H. 1975. Cropland erosion and sedimentation. In *Control of water pollution from cropland.* Vol. II *An overview*. Agricultural Research Service and Environmental Protection Agency.

Wohletz, L. R. 1968. Interpretive soil maps for land use planning. *Trans 9th Int. Congr. Soil Sci., Adelaide*. Vol. 4, 225–33.

Wolman, M. G., and R. Gerson 1978. Relative scales of time and effectiveness of climate in watershed geomorphology. *Earth Surface Processes* **3**, 189–208.

Woolnough, W. G. 1918. The physiographic significance of laterite in Western Australia. *Geol Mag.* **5**, 385–93.

Working Group on the Origin and Nature of Paleosols 1971. In *Paleopedology*, D. H. Yaalon (ed.). Jerusalem: International Society of Soil Science and Israel Universities Press.

Yaalon, D. H. 1971. Soil-forming processes in time and space. In *Paleopedology*, D. H. Yaalon (ed.). Jerusalem: International Society of Soil Science and Israel Universities Press.

Yaalon, D. H. 1975. Conceptual models in pedogenesis: can soil forming factors be solved? *Geoderma* **14**, 189–205.

Yaalon, D. H., and E. Ganor 1966. The climatic factor of wind erodibility and dust blowing in Israel. *Israel J. Earth Sci.* **15**, 27–32.

Young, A. 1958. *Some considerations of slope form and development, regolith and denudational processes*. Ph.D. Thesis, University of Sheffield.

Young, A. 1960. Soil movement by denudation processes on slopes. *Nature* **188**, 120–2.

Young, A. 1963. Deductive models of slope evolution. *Neue Beitrage zur internationalen Hangforschung*. Gottingen: Vandenhoeck and Ruprecht.

Young, A. 1968. *Slope form and the soil catena in savanna and rainforest environments*. Occasional publ. Br. Geomorph. Res. Group, no. 5, 3–12.

Young, A. 1969. The accumulation zone on slopes. *Z. Geomorph.* NF **13**, 231–3.

Young, A. 1971. *Slope profile analysis: the system of best units.* Inst. Br. Geogs Sp. Pubn no. 3, 1–13.

Young, A. 1972a. *Slopes*, Edinburgh: Oliver and Boyd.

Young, A. 1972b. The soil catena: a systematic approach. In *International geography 1972*, W. P. Adams and F. M. Helleiner (eds) Toronto.

Young, A. 1974. *The rate of slope retreat*. Inst. Br. Geogr, Sp. Pubn no. 7, 65–78.

Young, A. 1976. *Tropical soils and soil survey*. Cambridge: Cambridge University Press.

Young, A. 1978. Recent advances in the survey and evaluation of land resources. *Prog. Phys. Geog.* **2**, 462–79.

Young, A., and P. F. Goldsmith 1977. Soil survey and land evaluation in developing countries: a case study in Malawi. *Geog. J.* **153**, 407–38.

Young, A., and I. Stephen 1965. Rock weathering and soil formation on high altitude plateaux of Malawi. *J. Soil Sci.* **16**, 323–33.

Young, R. A., and C. K. Mutchler 1969. Effect of slope shape on erosion and runoff. *Trans Am. Soc. Agric. Engrs* **12**, 231–3.

Zaslavsky, D., and A. Rogowski 1969. Hydrologic and morphologic implications of anisotropy and infiltration in soil profile development. *Proc. Soil Sci. Soc. Am.* **33**, 594–9.

Zingg, A. W. 1940. Degree and length of slope as it affects soil loss in runoff. *Agric. Engng* **21**, 59–64.

Zonneveld, I. S. 1960. De Brabantse Biesbosch: a study of soil and vegetation of a fresh water tidal delta. *Stichting voor Bodemkartering Wageningen–Bodemkundige Studies*. Vol. 4.

Zuur, A. J. 1936. *Over de bodemkundige gesteldheid van de Wieringermeer*. The Hague: Algemeene Landsdrukkeriz.

Author index

Page numbers printed in bold type refer to tables and those printed in italic type refer to figures

Subject index